The Passing of the Armies

Joshua Lawrence Chamberlain

The Passing of the Armies

An Account of the Final Campaign of the Army of the Potomac, Based upon Personal Reminiscences of the Fifth Army Corps

By

Joshua Lawrence Chamberlain
Brevet Major-General U. S. Volunteers

With Portraits and Maps

G. P. Putnam's Sons
New York and London
The Knickerbocker Press
1915

The Knickerbocker Press, New York

BIOGRAPHICAL NOTE

JOSHUA LAWRENCE CHAMBERLAIN, who won distinction both as a soldier and as a citizen, for the State of Maine, and for the whole country, was born in Brewer, Maine, September 8, 1828. His parental lineage is traced back to England, but on the mother's side he is descended from Jean Dupuis, who came, in 1685, with other Huguenots, from La Rochelle to Boston. Young Chamberlain was brought up in the country district of Brewer. As Greek was not included in the curriculum of the school where he prepared for college, with the aid of a tutor he attacked that language at home, and in six months, at the age of nineteen, had mastered the amount required for entrance to Bowdoin. In his college course, he took honors in every department. After his graduation in 1852, he entered the Theological Seminary at Bangor, and for several years gave attention to the reading of theology, and of church history in Latin and German. His work included the study of the Hebrew, Syriac, and Arabic languages. He earned an ample income for his sojourn in the seminary by teaching classes of young ladies the German language and literature, while he also served as Supervisor of

Schools in his native town of Brewer. He continued his interest in Sunday-school work, helping to maintain a flourishing school some three miles from Bangor.

In 1856, as a result of his "Master's Oration" on "Law and Liberty," he was appointed instructor in Bowdoin in Natural and Revealed Religion, a post that had been vacated by Professor Stowe. A year later, he was elected a Professor of Rhetoric and Oratory, which place he held for four years. In 1861, he was elected Professor of Modern Languages, and in July, 1862, was granted leave of absence for two years for the purpose of pursuing studies in Europe. The need at this time of the Republic for all its able-bodied citizens caused him, however, to give up the European trip and to offer his services for action in the field. In August, 1862, he went to the front as Lieutenant-Colonel of the Twentieth Regiment of Maine Volunteers. In May, he received commission as Colonel, the duty of which post he had been fulfilling for some months. His regiment was included with the Fifth Corps, and at Gettysburg on the second of July, 1863, it held the extreme left of the Union line. Colonel Chamberlain's conduct in the memorable defense of Little Round Top (a position which with admirable judgment had been seized by General Warren) was recognized by the Government in the bestowal of the Congressional Medal of Honor for "conspicuous personal gallantry and distinguished service."

After Gettysburg, Colonel Chamberlain was

placed in command of the "Light Brigade," which he handled with marked skill in the action at Rappahannock Station. The wounds received in that battle made necessary retirement for a time to the Georgetown Hospital, but during his convalescence he gave valuable service as member of a Court-Martial. He returned to the front in May, 1864, when General Warren, at that time in command of the Fifth Corps then stationed at Spottsylvania, made Colonel Chamberlain the commander of a "forlorn hope" of nine regiments which had been selected to make a night assault on the enemy's works. The position was gained, but Chamberlain found his line outflanked, and was compelled to withdraw under heavy fire. Shortly after the action at Cold Harbor, while still holding the rank of Colonel, he was placed in charge of six regiments, consolidated as a veteran brigade. With this brigade, he made a charge on the enemy's main works at Petersburg, as a result of which action he was promoted on the field by General Grant to the rank of Brigadier-General "for gallant conduct in leading his brigade against the superior force of the enemy and for meritorious service" throughout the campaign. Such promotion on the field was most exceptional, and there is possibly no other instance during the war. In this charge General Chamberlain was seriously wounded, and his death was in fact announced. His life was saved through the activity of his brother Thomas, late Colonel of the Twentieth Maine, and the skill and tireless fidelity of the regimental surgeon, Dr. Shaw.

During the last campaign of the war, General Chamberlain, with two brigades, led the advance of the infantry with Sheridan, and in the fight on the Quaker Road he was twice wounded and his horse was shot under him. For his "conspicuous gallantry" in this action, he was promoted to the brevet rank of Major-General. In the fight at White Oak Road, March 31st, although seriously disabled by wounds, General Chamberlain distinguished himself by recovering a lost field; while in the battle of Five Forks, of April 1st, his promptitude and skillful handling of troops received again official commendation. In the final action near Appomattox Court House on the ninth of April, Chamberlain was called by General Sheridan to replace the leading division of cavalry, and the first flag of truce from Longstreet came to Chamberlain's headquarters. His Corps Commander says in an official report: "In thè final action, General Chamberlain had the advance, and at the time the announcement of the surrender was made he was driving the enemy rapidly before him."

At the surrender of Lee's army, General Chamberlain was designated to command the parade, and it was characteristic of his refined nature that he received the surrendering army with a salute of honor. At the final grand review in Washington, Chamberlain's division was placed at the head of the column of the Army of the Potomac. The General was mustered out of military service on the sixteenth of January, 1866, having declined the offer of a Colonelcy in the regular army. In his service of three-and-a-half years, he had participated in twenty hard-fought battles and a long series of minor engagements, and he had been struck six times by bullet and shell.

During his campaign experience, he had shown marked ability as a commander, but he had other qualities as important, namely, foresight, prudence, and a strong sense of responsibility. On his return to Maine, he was offered the choice of several diplomatic offices abroad, but was at once elected Governor of Maine by the largest majority ever given in the State. As Governor, while rendering exceptional service to the State, he suffered criticism on various grounds, and among others through his support of the course of Senator Fessenden, of Maine, in the impeachment of President Johnson.

In 1876, General Chamberlain was elected President of Bowdoin College. In 1878, he was appointed by the President of the United States to represent the educational interests of the country as a commissioner at the World's Exposition in Paris, and for this service he received a medal of honor from the Government of France.

In 1883, he resigned the presidency of Bowdoin College, but continued for two years longer his lectures on public law. During this time, he put to one side urgent invitations to the presidency of three other colleges of high standing. In 1885, finding that the long strain of work and wounds demanded a change of occupation, he went to Florida as president of a railroad construction company. In 1900, General Chamberlain was appointed by President McKinley Surveyor of Customs at the port of Portland, and through the courtesy of the Government he was enabled to make visits to Italy and to Egypt. The General was in great request as a speaker, and on various occasions his utterances showed a power that was thrilling. Among the more noteworthy of these addresses may be mentioned the following:

"Loyalty," before the Loyal Legion in Philadelphia.

"The Sentiment and Sovereignty of the Country," at the Meade Memorial Service in Philadelphia.

"The State, the Nation, and the People," on the dedication of the Maine monument at Gettysburg.

"Maine, Her Place in History," at the Centennial Celebration in Philadelphia in 1876.

"The Ruling Powers in History," at the celebration of the beginnings of English settlement on the east shores.

Among his Memorial Addresses were:

"The Two Souls: Self and Other Self;" "The Concentric Personalities."

"The Higher Law," conditions on which it may override the actual.

"Personal and Political Responsibility."

"The Old Flag and the New Nation"; "The Expanding Power of Principles."

"The Destruction of the *Maine*"; "Salute to the New Peace Power."

The General received from Pennsylvania University in 1866, the degree of Doctor of Laws, and from Bowdoin in 1869 the same degree.

His death came on the 24th of February, 1914. His life had been well rounded out and his years were crowded with valuable service to his state and to his country.

A gallant soldier, a great citizen, and a good man; the name of Joshua L. Chamberlain will through the years to come find place in the list of distinguished Americans.

G. H. P.

New York, April, 1915.

NOTE.—The narrative here presented is substantially complete, but the author's death prevented it from receiving the advantage of a final revision. The book has been prepared for the press under the supervision of his children. It now comes into publication just half a century after the period of the stirring events described.

INTRODUCTORY

HISTORY is written for the most part from the outside. Truth often suffers distortion by reason of the point of view of the narrator, some pre-occupation of his judgment or fancy not only as to relative merits but even as to facts in their real relations. An interior view may not be without some personal coloring. But it must be of interest, especially in important transactions, to know how things appeared to those actually engaged in them. Action and passion on such a scale must bear some thoughts "that run before and after." It has been deemed a useful observance "to see ourselves as others see us," but it may sometimes be conducive to a just comprehension of the truth to let others see us as we see ourselves.

The view here presented is of things as they appeared to us who were concerned with them as subordinate commanders,—having knowledge, however, of the general plan, and a share in the responsibility for its execution. This is a chapter of experiences,—including in this term not only what was done, but what was known and said and thought and felt,—not to say, suffered; and in its darkest passages showing a steadfast purpose, patience, and spirit of obedience deserving of record even if too often without recompense, until the momentous consummation.

These memoirs are based on notes made nearly at the time of the events which they describe. They give what may be called an interior view of occurrences on the front of the Fifth Corps, Army of the Potomac, during the last essay in Grant's Virginia campaign. This was so distinctive in character, conditions, and consequences, that I have ventured to entitle it "The Last Campaign of the Armies."

I trust this narrative may not seem to arrogate too much for the merits of the Fifth Corps. No eminence is claimed for it beyond others in that campaign. But the circumstance that this Corps was assigned to an active part with Sheridan during the period chiefly in view—the envelopment and final out-flanking of Lee's army—warrants the prominence given in this review.

It may be permitted to hope that this simple recital may throw some light on a passage of the history of this Corps, the record of which has been obscured in consequence of the summary change of commanders early in the campaign.

The Fifth Corps had a certain severity of reputation quite distinctive in the comradeship of the army. Early in its history, Porter's Division—the nucleus of it—had drawn the especial praise of General McClellan for its soldierly bearing and proficiency, being unfortunately referred to in orders as a model for the rest of the army. This had the effect of creating on the part of others a feeling of jealousy towards that Division or an opposition to apparent favoritism shown its commander, which was extended to the whole Corps on its formation in the summer of 1862, when the Regulars were assigned to it as its Second Division, and the choice Pennsylvania Reserves became its Third Division. This feeling certainly was neither caused nor followed by anything like boastfulness or self-complacency on the part of the Fifth Corps; but, if anything, created a sense of responsibility and willingness to "endure hardness as good soldiers" to make good their reputation. And no doubt the discipline of the Corps was quite severe. Most of its commanding officers in the superior grades were West Pointers, and experienced officers of the old army, and prided themselves on strict observance of Army Regulations and military habitudes. The required personal relations between officers and men were quite novel and but slowly acquiesced in by volunteers who were first-class citizens at home,—many of them equal to their official "superiors." For example: my young brother, Tom, when a private in my regiment came sometimes to see me in my tent, but would not think of sitting down in my presence unless specially invited to do so. But he went home from Appomattox Lieutenant-Colonel of his regiment and Brevet-Colonel of United States Volunteers—and this on his own merits, not through any suggestion of mine.

Passages in the history of the Corps had endeared its members to each other, and brought out soldierly pride and manly character; but boastful assertion and just glorification of their Corps were remarkably less manifest among its members than with those of every one of the other splendid Corps of the Army of the Potomac.

It may not be improper to state here that there was a manifest prejudice against the Fifth Corps at Government Headquarters,—particularly at Stanton's,—on account of the supposed attachment for McClellan and Porter among its members. This was believed to be the reason why no promotion to the rank of General Officers was made in this Corps for a long time, unless secured by political influence. Brigades and even divisions were in many cases commanded by colonels of State regiments. This worked a great injustice in the fact that officers of similar commands in the different Corps were not of similar relative rank, and some were therefore unduly subordinated to those who were not in fact their superiors in service. There was also a practical injustice in the added expense of supporting headquarters above lineal rank, which, with no extra pay or allowance, quite cancelled the compliment.

It had not been the habit in the Fifth Corps to encourage detailed reports on the part of subordinates, and in the rush and pressure of this last campaign there was less opportunity or care than ever for such matters, and the impressiveness of its momentous close left little disposition to multiply words upon subordinate parts or participants. The fact also of an early and sudden change in the grand tactics of the campaign confused the significance and sometimes the identity of important movements; and the change of commanders in the crisis of its most important battle induced consequences which, even in official reports and testimony afterwards called for, affected the motive in sharply defining actions where personal concern had come to be an embarrassing factor.

Very naturally, the immediate reports of those days are meager in the extreme; and very much of what has come out since, partaking of official character, has been under the disadvantage of being elicited as *ex parte* testimony before military tribunals where the highest military officers of the Government were parties, and the attitudes of plaintiff and defendant almost inevitably biased expression.

In the strange lull after the surrender of Lee and the sudden release from intense action and responsibility, but as yet in the field and in the active habit not readily relinquished, it occurred to me, impressed with the deep-wrought visions of those tragic days, to write down, while fresh in mind and mood, some salient facts of that last campaign, within my personal knowledge and observation, to serve for fireside memories in after years, and for the satisfaction of some others who had given of their best for the great issues in which these scenes were involved.

It has been suggested to me of late that these reminiscences might be of interest to a wider circle whose hearts respond to the story of things done and suffered for truth and honor's sake, which they would have gladly shared in their own persons. In preparing for this more exacting demand I have availed myself of additional material which, in the later consolidations in the Fifth Corps, successive assignments brought into my hands: particularly the office-copy of the Corps field-orders for the last campaign, and also the invaluable original records of the Medical Inspector of the Corps for that period. Later, came the (now suppressed) volumes of the records of the Warren Court of Inquiry, and the extensive *Records of the War of the Rebellion.* In revising this personal memoir, I have diligently consulted these, but have found no occasion to correct or modify the account given from my own point of view, however limited. Qualifying or corroborative testimony from these sources, when introduced, has been clearly indicated.

I confess some embarrassments of a personal nature in giving forth certain passages of this record. These facts, however simply stated, cannot but have some bearing on points which have been drawn into controversy on the part of persons who were dear to me as commanders and companions in arms, and who have grown still dearer in the intimacies of friendship since the war. Alas! that no one of them can answer my greeting across the bar. I feel therefore under increased responsibility in recounting these things, but assure myself that I know of no demand of personality or partisanship which should make me doubtful of my ability to tell the truth as I saw and knew it, or distrust my judgment in forming an opinion.

J. L. C.

CONTENTS

		PAGE
Biographical Note		iii
Introductory		xi
CHAPTER		
I.	The Situation	1
II.	The Overture	36
III.	The White Oak Road	60
IV.	Five Forks	113
V	The Week of Flying Fights	182
VI.	Appomattox	230
VII.	The Return of the Army	273
VIII.	The Encampment	318
IX.	The Last Review	326
X.	Sherman's Army	364
XI.	The Disbandment	375

ILLUSTRATIONS

PAGE

Joshua Lawrence Chamberlain *Frontispiece*

Joshua Lawrence Chamberlain 2

General Map Showing "Operations of the Army of the Potomac" 38

Map Showing the White Oak Road and Five Forks 98

Map of Five Forks, Genfral Engagement of Cavalry and Infantry 124

The Passing of the Armies

CHAPTER I

THE SITUATION

IT was a dreamy camp along the lines investing Petersburg in the winter following the "all-summer" campaign of 1864,—that never-to-be-forgotten, most dismal of years. Although shadowed at the very beginning by melancholy tokens of futile endeavor and grievous losses,—consolidations of commands which obliterated the place and name of proud and beloved corps and divisions,—flags made sacred by heroic service and sacrifice of noble manhood now folded away with tender reverence, or perhaps by special favor permitted to be borne beside those of new assignments, bearing the commanding presence of great memories, pledge and talisman of unswerving loyalty, though striking sorrow to every heart that knew their history,—yet this seemed not to make for weakness but rather for settled strength. We started out full of faith and hope under the new dispensation, resolved at all events to be worthy of our past and place.

Now all was over. The summer had passed, and the harvest was but of death. New and closer consolidations, more dreary obliterations, brought the survivors nearer together.

For this dismal year had witnessed that ever repeated, prolific miracle,—the invisible, ethereal soul of man resisting and overcoming the material forces of nature; scorning the inductions of logic, reason, and experience, persisting in its purpose and identity; this elusive apparition between two worlds unknown, deemed by some to be but the chance product of intersecting vortices of atoms and denied to be even a force, yet outfacing the solid facts of matter and time, defying disaster and dissolution, and, by a most real metempsychosis, transmitting its imperishable purpose to other hearts with the cumulative courage of immortal energies.

Give but the regard of a glance to the baldest outline of what was offered and suffered, given and taken, lost and held, in that year of tragedy. That long-drawn, *tête baissée* (bull-headed), zig-zag race from the Rapidan to the Appomattox; that desperate, inch-worm advance along a front of fire, with writhing recoil at every touch; that reiterated dissolving view of death and resurrection: the Wilderness, Spottsylvania, the North Anna, Cold Harbor, Petersburg; unspoken, unspeakable history. Call back that roseate May morning, all the springs of life athrill, that youthful army pressing the bridges of the Rapidan, flower of Northern homes, thousands upon thousands; tested

Joshua Lawrence Chamberlain

in valor, disciplined by experience, hearts swelling with manly courage, confident trust, and supreme devotion,—to be plunged straightway into hell-like horrors; the murderous maze where desperate instinct replaced impossible tactics; men mowing each other down almost at hand-reach, invisible each to each till the flaming muzzles cut lurid windows through the matted brush and bramble walls, and underneath the darkened woods low-lying cannon and bursting shells set the earth itself on fire, and wrapped in winding sheets of flame unnumbered, thick-strewn bodies of dead and dying, never to be found or known on earth again.

Then the rushing, forced flank-movements, known and overmatched by the ever alert enemy; followed by reckless front attacks, where highest valor was deepest loss; buffetings on bloody angles; butcherings in slaughter pens,—all the way down to the fateful Chickahominy once more—a campaign under fire for twenty-seven days and nights together; morning reports at last not called for, and when we asked explanation our superiors answered,—confidentially, lest it seem disloyal: "Because the country would not stand it, if they knew."

What wonder that men who have passed through such things together,—no matter on which side arrayed,—should be wrought upon by that strange power of a common suffering which so divinely passes into the power of a common love.

A similar fate befell the new hope kindled by Grant's sudden change to a new base of operations,—a movement bold if not hazardous, being practically a change of front under fire for the whole army on a grand scale. Skillfully withdrawing from the enemy's front by secret orders and forced marches, swiftly crossing the James River on transports and pontoons, hurrying forward to strike a surprise on weakly-defended Petersburg, and thus cut Lee's main communications and turn his entire position—seemed good generalship. But the bold plan and generous following stultified by confusion of understandings and supine delays of subordinates, brought all to nought once more with terrible recoil and reckoning. Then the long slow fever of profitless minor action and wasteful inaction, with the strange anomaly of a mutual siege; crouching in trenches, skulking under bombproofs and covered ways, lining parapets where to show a head was to lure a bullet, picketing a crowded hostile front where the only tenure of life was the tacit understanding of a common humanity, perpetual harassing by spasmodic raid or futile dash, slow creepings flankward yet never nearer the main objective;—such was the wearisome, wearing experience, month after month, the new year bringing no sign nor hope that anything better could be done on that line than had been so dearly and vainly tried before.

The resultant mood of such a front was not relieved by what reached us from the rear. The long-suffering, and helpless grief of homes; the sore-tried faith and patience of the whole North almost faltering; recruiting disenchanted, supplemented by enormous bounties and finally by draft and conscription; newspapers jeering at the impotence of the army; self-seeking politicians at the Capitol plotting against the President; hosts of spoilsmen at all points seizing advantage of the country's distress, enriching themselves out of the generous, hard-earned offerings to meet her needs and repair her losses; cabal and favoritism in places of power, perpetrating a thousand injustices upon officers and soldiers in the field;—through all this, seen and known and felt, from first to last, these men of the Army of the Potomac,—godlike, if something short of sainthood,—this army, on which the heaviest brunt had fallen and was to fall, held up its heart where it could not hold up its head; with loyalty unswerving, obedience unquestioning, courage that asks not cheer, and devotion out-vying all that life holds dearest or death most terrible.

This army—but what army? Is this identity a thing of substance, or spirit, or of name only? Is this the army which bright as its colors thronged the bridges of the Rapidan on that May morning less than a year before, and vanished into the murk of the Wilderness? Or is it scarcely the half of them; stern-faced by realities, saddened and perchance also strengthened by visions of the lost, the places of these filled by fresh youth's vicarious offering, united as one by the comradeship of arms and strong with the contagion of soul?

But perhaps this vein of emotion is tiresome. Let us seek relief in figures,—which some people regard as the only reliable facts.

The number of men of all arms present for duty equipped in the Army of the Potomac at the opening of Grant's campaign, as shown by the consolidated morning reports of May 4, 1864, was 97,162. In the Annual Report of Secretary Stanton, November 22, 1865, this total is stated as 120,384. He evidently takes the number as borne upon the rolls in his office, which by no means always agrees with the field lists of those present for duty equipped, the absent on leave or detail, or otherwise, being usually at a high percentage of the total. The careful compilation of Adjutant-General Drum made from official field returns at this time gives the number present for duty equipped at 97,273—in remarkable agreement with the figures taken in the field.[1] The number of men available for battle in the Fifth Corps at the start was 25,695. The character of the fighting in this campaign may be shown, however dimly, by citing here the report of our Corps field hospital for one day only, that of the engagement at Laurel Hill, May 8, 1864: "Admitted to hospital, 3001; of whom 106 were from other corps; 27 Confederates; 107 sick. Sent to the rear, 2388; fell into the hands of the enemy, 391; died in hospital, 121; left 206, of whom 126 were able to walk in the morning."

Or take the totals treated in the field hospital alone for the first nine days of the campaign. Number admitted, 5257; sent to the rear, 4190; died in hospital, 179; fell into hands of the enemy,

[1] Compare the admirable showing of that clear-headed officer, General A. A. Humphreys, *Virginia Campaign*, Appendix, p. 409.

787. Adding to this the number killed outright, not less than 1200, and the "missing," a list we do not like to analyze, not less than 1555, makes a total loss in the Corps of more than 7000 men. And the casualties of the six weeks from the Rapidan to the James bring the total to 16,245. This is 3398 more than half the present for duty at the start.

The records of the Medical Inspector of the Fifth Corps show the number admitted to the field hospitals alone from May 5th to June 19th to have been 11,105 of the Corps, besides many from other corps and not a few Confederates. Reckoning the killed outright as 2200, and the missing as 4000,—which is quite within the fact,—makes a total of casualties for this period 17,305.

Taking another source of information, we find in the Adjutant-General's Report of losses in the Corps as given in the official returns of regiments for the same period, the killed as 1670; the wounded 10,150; the missing, 4416,—a total of 16,235. Taking the additional wounded given in the field hospital records, 955,—who would not appear on the regimental morning reports,—we reach the total of 17,190. The difference in these figures is remarkably slight considering that they come from sources so distinct.

And the restless, fruitless fighting before Petersburg during the remainder of that year brought the total loss in the Corps up to 18,000,—this being almost a thousand more than two thirds of the bright faces that crossed the Rapidan in the starlight of that May morning, now gone down to earth, or beneath it,—and yet no end!

Colonel W. H. Powell in his *History of the Fifth Corps*, published since the above was written, gives this total loss as 17,861. It does not appear whether he takes into account the losses of the Corps in the assault of June 18th on the salient covering the Norfolk Railroad and the Jerusalem Plank Road. Owing to the casualties among commanders, the action of that day has never been adequately reported. Colonel Powell had no data on which to base a just account of the overture of Forts Sedgwick and Mahone,—surnamed by the performers Fort Hell and Fort Damnation.

Glance now at the record of the whole army. Those treated in the field hospitals up to the end of October were officially reported as numbering 57,498, and to the end of December, 68,840.[1] Some of these, no doubt were cases of sickness, a no less real casualty; but taking the ratio of one fifth the wounded as indicating the number of the killed outright, we reach a total of 59,000 men killed and wounded in this campaign up to October 31, 1864. This is to take no account of the "missing," —a list governed by no law of ratios, but determined by the peculiar circumstances of each battle; always a list sad to contemplate, made up by no means of skulkers and deserters, but mostly of those who had been placed by the incompetence of commanders or thrown by the

[1] Report of Surgeon McParlin, Medical Director of the Army of the Potomac.

vicissitudes of battle into positions where they were helpless, and fell into the hands of the enemy as prisoners, or some too brave spirits that had cut their way through the enemy's lines, or others still who had been left wounded and had crawled away to die. But adding here to the 59,000 killed and wounded given above the 6000 more lost in the various operations around Petersburg up to March 28, 1865, and counting the missing at the moderate number of 10,000 for this period, we have the aggregate of 75,000 men cut down in the Army of the Potomac to mark the character of the service and the cost of the campaign thus far.

If any minds demanding exactitude are troubled at the slight discrepancies in these reports, they may find relief in a passage in the Report of Surgeon Dalton, Chief Medical Officer of Field Hospitals for this campaign. He says of his experience with the treatment of disabled men in the field:

> It is impossible to convey an accurate idea of the number of sick and wounded who have received attention in this hospital,—that following the army. Hundreds passed through under circumstances which rendered it impossible to register their names or even accurately estimate their numbers So unremitting were the calls for professional duty during the first fortnight that it was impossible to prepare morning reports, and it was not until the 10th of May that even a numerical report was attempted. From that date the daily reports show that from the 16th of May to the 31st of October, 1864, there have been received into this hospital and treated for at least forty-eight hours, 68,540 sick and wounded officers and men.[1]

[1] *Rebellion Records*, Serial 60, p 271, and Serial 67, p. 269.

I have often thought it would be profitable reading for some if a competent observer would recount the scenes at the rear of a fighting army removing from the field after a great battle. A glimpse of this was given at Fredericksburg in '62.

But to throw light on our present topic by one more comparison, let us turn to the records of the Confederates for this campaign. According to the careful investigations of General Humphreys, the number of effective men in Lee's army, including cavalry, at the opening of Grant's campaign, was not less than 62,000; and at the opening of the spring campaign of '65, not less than 57,000. The accuracy of this is undoubted.

The striking fact is thus established that we had more men killed and wounded in the first six months of Grant's campaign, than Lee had at any one period of it in his whole army. The hammering business had been hard on the hammer.

If these conclusions seem to rest too much on estimates (although in every case inductions from unquestioned fact), let me offer the solid testimony of General Grant in his official report of November 1, 1864. He gives the casualties in the Army of the Potomac from May 5th to October 30th as: killed 10,572; wounded, 53,975; missing, 23,858;—an aggregate of 88,405, a result far more striking than those adduced, and more than confirming the statement of our losses as by far exceeding the whole number of men in Lee's army at any time in this last campaign.[1]

[1] *Rebellion Records*, Serial 67, p. 193.

I offer no apology for this long survey of figures. There is abundant reason for it for the sake of fact, as well as occasion in existing sentiment. Among other interesting reflections, these facts and figures afford useful suggestions to those easily persuaded persons of the South or elsewhere, who please themselves with asserting that our Western armies "did all the fighting." Lorgnettes will get out of order—especially to the cross-eyed.

The aspect in which the men of our army have been presented has been mainly that of their elementary manhood, the antique virtues that made up valor: courage, fortitude, self-command. It is not possible to separate these from other personal activities of perhaps higher range than the physical; because, in truth, these enter largely into the exercise and administration of manhood. It seems now to be an accepted maxim of war that the "moral" forces—meaning by that term what we call the spiritual, pertaining specially to the mind or soul—far outweigh the material. Few would now claim that "victory is always with the heaviest battalions." All great contests are inspired by sentiments, such as justice, pity, faith, loyalty, love, or perhaps some stirring ideal of the rightful and possible good. Even the commoner instincts partake of this nature: self-respect, sanctity of the person, duty and affection towards others, obedience to law, the impulse to the redress of injury, vengeance for outrage. Something of this entered into our motive at first. But deeper tests brought deeper thought. In the strange succession of reverses greater reaches were disclosed; sentiments took on their highest sanction. Our place in human brotherhood, our responsibility not only in duty for Country, but as part in its very being, came impressively into view. Our volunteer soldiers felt that they were part of the very people whose honor and life they were to maintain; they recognized that they were entitled to participate so far as they were able, in the thought and conscience and will of that supreme "people" whose agents and instruments they were in the field of arms.

This recognition was emphasized by the fact that the men in the field were authorized to vote in the general election of President of the United States, and so to participate directly in the administration of the government and the determination of public policy. The result of this vote showed how much stronger was their allegiance to principle than even their attachment to McClellan, whose personal popularity in the army was something marvelous. The men voted overwhelmingly for Lincoln. They were unwilling that their long fight should be set down as a failure, even though thus far it seemed so. The fact that this war was in its reach of meaning and consequent effect so much more than what are commonly called "civil wars,"—this being a war to test and finally determine the character of the interior constitution and real organic life of this great people,—brought into the field an amount of thoughtfulness and moral reflection not usual in armies. The Roman army could make emperors of generals, but thoughtful minds and generous hearts were wanting to save Rome from the on-coming, invisible doom.

But volunteers like ours were held by a consciousness not only rooted in instinctive love and habitual reverence but also involving spiritual and moral considerations of the highest order. The motive under which they first sprung to the front was an impulse of sentiment,—the honor of the old flag and love of Country. All that the former stood for, and all that the latter held undetermined, they did not stop to question. They would settle the fact that they had a country and then consider the reasons and rights of it. There was, indeed, an instinctive apprehension of what was involved in this; but only slowly as the struggle thickened, and they found their antagonists claiming to rest their cause on principles similar to their own, they were led to think more deeply, to analyze their concrete ideals, to question, to debate, to test loyalty by thoughts of right and reason. We had opportunity to observe the relative merits of Regulars and Volunteers. Two rather divergent opinions had been common as to the professional soldiers of the rank and file. One was that they were of inferior grade as men; the other that they were vastly superior as soldiers to any volunteers. It must be allowed that the trained soldier has the merit of habitual submission to discipline, obedience to orders, a certain professional pride, and at least a temporary loyalty to the cause in which he is engaged. The superior efficiency of the regular over the volunteer is generally asserted. But this is founded more on conditions than on character. It derives its acceptance from the fact that volunteers are called out in an exigency, and take the field in haste, without experience or preparation, or even knowledge of the conditions pertaining to the art of war. They answer some call of the heart, or constraining moral obligation. But these volunteers may in due time become skilled in all these requisites: discipline, obedience, and even practical knowledge of the many technicalities of the art of war. Such veterans may become quite the equals of regulars in the scale of military merit.

So, on the other hand, the regular may be as intelligent as the citizen soldier, and animated by motives as high. As to the regular officers, there can be no question of their superior qualifications. They are educated for this profession, and specially in all that serves as basis for loyalty to country. As to the rank and file of regular troops, history sometimes refers to them as mercenaries, workers for pay, and they have been stigmatized as "hirelings." But this is abuse, even of history. The word soldier does indeed mean the man paid for his service instead of being bound to serve by feudal obligation.[1] But no one can despise such soldiers who remember the conduct of the Swiss Guard of Louis XVI. of France, cowardly forsaken by his

[1] This pay was in the form of the "soldi" (from the Latin "solidus"), the real money, the piece of solid metal, represented to-day in the French "sou."

own; but these loyal spirits, for the manhood that was in them and not for pay, stood by him to the last living man of them, whose heroism the proud citizens of their native home have fittingly commemorated in Thorwaldson's *Lion of Lucerne.*

And we certainly held our regulars dear, from long association, and could only speak their name with honor when we thought of the desperate charge down from the Round Tops of Gettysburg into the maelstrom of death swirling around the "Devil's Den," from which but half their numbers emerged, and these so wrought upon that they were soon after released from service in the field to recover strength.

These veterans of ours were the equals of regulars even if they received a nominal pay; equals in discipline, in knowledge, skill, and valor. They were superior in that they represented the homes and ideals of the country, and not only knew what they were fighting for but also held it dear.

The same tendency of thought and feeling was, no doubt, in the hearts of our adversaries, although their loyalty seems to have been held longer by the primal instincts. This appeared not merely in the fervid exhortations of commanders and officials, but in the prevailing spirit of the men in the ranks, with whom we had occasional conference across the picket lines, or in brief interviews with prisoners. The prime motive with these men was no doubt, like ours, grounded in the instincts of manhood. They sprang to arms for the vindication of what they had been accustomed to regard as their rights by nature and law. By struggling and suffering for the cause this thought was rather intensified than broadened. But in these lulls reflection began to enlarge vision. This matter of rights and duties presents itself, as it were, in concentric spheres, within which polarities are reversed as values rise. The right to property must yield to the right to life; individual happiness must be subordinated to the general well-being; duty to country must outweigh all the narrower demands of self-interest. So the sight of "the old flag," which stood for the guaranty of highest human rights, and which they were now striving to beat down in defeat and dishonor, must have affected their sober thoughts. There was no little evidence of this as the winter and the weary siege wore on. It came to our knowledge in the early months of the new year that heavy desertions were going on every day in Lee's army,—especially among the Virginians. We had reason to believe that it was the personal magnetism of their great commander that kept alive the spirit of that brave army. The chivalrous sense of personal loyalty was strong with those men.

Our acquaintance had been peculiarly intimate and deep, and we had for them a strong personal regard. The "causes" were wide apart, but the manhood was the same. We had occasion to observe their religious character. More free thought and wider range of code no doubt prevailed in our Northern army; but what we are accustomed to call simple, personal piety was more manifest in the Confederate ranks than in ours. Not presuming to estimate the influence of particular cases of higher officers, like Stonewall Jackson or General Howard, making prominent their religious principles and proclivities, but fully recognizing the general religious character of most of the officers and men from our Northern homes, it must be admitted that the expression of religious sentiment and habit was more common and more earnest in the Confederate camp than in ours.

In one thing we took "the touch of elbow." It was no uncommon incident that from close opposing bivouacs and across hushed breastworks at evening voices of prayer from over the way would stir our hearts, and floating songs of love and praise be caught up and broadened into a mighty and thrilling chorus by our men softening down in cadences like enfolding wings. Such moments were surely a "Truce of God."

I have said the men kept up heart. So they did, —exactly that. It was a certain loyalty of soul, rather than persistence of vital energies. The experiences which had hardened the spiritual nerve, had relaxed the physical fiber. The direct effects of bodily over-strain reach to the nervous centers and the boundaries of spirit. Exhausting forced marches, through choking dust, burning suns, stifling heat even in the shade, swampy bivouacs, malarious airs laden with the off-castings of rotting vegetation, or worse at times, from innumerable bodies of men and animals dead or living; strange forms of sickness, unexampled and irremediable, experiences borne only by stubborn patience or heroic pride,—such things tell at last. Then the battles, horrible scenes, shocking the senses, burrowing in memory to live again in dreams and haunting visions, all these things together work upon the inner, vital, or spiritual forces which relate us to the real persistent substance—whether ethereal or of some yet finer form not yet dreamed of in our philosophy.

But men are made of mind and soul as well as body. We deal not only with exercises of the senses, but with deeper consciousness; affections, beliefs, ideals, conceptions of causes and effects, relations and analogies, and even conjectures of a possible order and organization different from what we experience in the present world of sense. All these powers and workings have part in the make-up of manhood. Men are not machines; although it is said the discipline of army life tends to make them such, and that this is essential to their efficiency. A remark which needs to be set in larger light.

The men of the rank and file in our army of volunteers before Petersburg besides being seasoned soldiers were endowed and susceptible according to their spiritual measure. Their life was not merely in their own experiences but in larger sympathies. Their environment, which is thought to determine character so largely, consisted for them not only in material things but also much in memories and shadowings. Things were remnants and reminders. Lines stood thinner; circles ever narrowing. Corps fought down to divisions; divisions to brigades; these again broken and the shattered regiments consolidated under the token and auspices of their States,—as if reverting to their birthright, and being "gathered to their fathers." Old flags,—yes, but crowded together not by on-rush to battle, but by thinning ranks bringing the dear more near. Then the vacant places of lost comrades, seen as "an aching void" both as to fact and suggestion. And even the coming in of new, fresh faces was not without its cast of shadow. The officers, too, who had gone down were of the best known, trusted, and beloved. What has gone takes something with it, and when this is of the dear, nothing can fill the place. All the changes touched the border of sorrows.

The strength of great memories, pride of historic continuity, unfailing loyalty of purpose and resolve held these men together in unity of form and spirit. But there seemed some slackening of the old nerve and verve; and service was sustained more from the habit of obedience and instinct of duty, than with that sympathetic intuition which inspires men to exceed the literal of orders or of obligations.

Curious people often ask the question whether in battle we are not affected by fear, so that our actions are influenced by it; and some are prompt to answer, "Yes, surely we are, and anybody who denies it is a braggart or a liar." I say to such, "Speak for yourselves." A soldier has something else to think about. Most men at the first, or at some tragic moment, are aware of the present peril, and perhaps flinch a little by an instinct of nature and sometimes accept the foregoing confession,—as when I have seen men pin their names to their breasts that they may not be buried unknown. But any action following the motive of fear is rare,—for sometimes I have seen men rushing to the front in a terrific fire, "to have it over with."

But, as a rule, men stand up from one motive or another—simple manhood, force of discipline, pride, love, or bond of comradeship—"Here is Bill; I will go or stay where he does." And an officer is so absorbed by the sense of responsibility for his men, for his cause, or for the fight that the thought of personal peril has no place whatever in governing his actions. The instinct to seek safety is overcome by the instinct of honor.

There are exceptions. This is the rule and law of manhood: fearlessness in the face of all lesser issues because he has faced the greater—the commanding one.

This exposition of the state of mind and body among our officers and men in the later operations along the Petersburg lines may help to find a reason for their failure. For instance, the fiasco of the mine explosion of July 30th, where well-laid plans and costly and toilsome labors were brought to shameful disaster through lack of earnest co-operation, and strange lethargy of participants. For another instance, the unexampled reverses of our renowned Second Corps at Ream's Station, August 24th, where, after every purpose and prospect of success, these veterans were quickly driven from their entrenchments, even abandoning their guns,—conduct contrary to their habit and contradictory of their character.

But these were exceptional even if illustrative cases. Along our lines reigned a patient fortitude, a waiting expectation, unswerving loyalty, that kind of faith which is the "evidence of things unseen."

Among these men were some doubly deserving—comrades whom we thought lost, bravely returning. Many of those earlier wounded, or sickened, and sent to general hospital, proving to be not utterly disabled, and scorning the plea of the poltroon, came back to their appointed place. So others, too, with like spirit, from the starving, wasting, and wearing experience of prisons, passing though the valley of the shadow of death, came to answer again the names that honored our roll-call,—those who could stand up to do it.

Such were the remnants of that great company of heroic souls named the Army of the Potomac. Knowing full well the meaning of such words as hardship and suffering, facing unknown fields of sorrows yet to come, they stood fast by their consecration, offering all there is in manhood for the sake of what is best in man. If sometimes a shadow passes over such spirits, it needs neither confession nor apology.

Within a short time now the term of enlistment of not a few regiments had expired, and they were mustered out of service with honor. It was a time when they were sorely needed; but we can scarcely blame those who thought duty did not call them to prolong their experiences. Many, however, straightway enlisted in other regiments, new or old, and thus rendered a double service—material force and inspiring example.

In some instances whole regiments had re-enlisted, under the old name or a new one. Such were five noble Pennsylvania regiments of my own brigade of June, 1864. Remnants of regiments also, left from casualties of the field or by term of enlistment, were consolidated into one, named and numbered by its State order. Such were the 1st Maine Veterans, made up of the 5th, 6th, and 7th, of glorious record.

Others, too, had come in to replace and reinforce, with like brave spirit, and perhaps with severer test,—heavy artillery regiments, full to the maximum in numbers, from important positions in the rear, as the defenses of Washington, and not expecting to be called to the front. With the advantage of military discipline and acclimatization, their ponderous lines rolled on the astonished foe, with swift passages to glorious death and undying fame. Witness the action of the 1st Maine Heavy Artillery, losing in one fight at Spottsylvania 264 men, and again more than 600 in stern obedience to orders which should not have been given in the first futile charge on the lines of Petersburg.

New regiments of infantry also came in, necessarily assigned to duty at the front,—high hearts, brave spirits; some of them rushed into the field without instruction in arms or training in practice of endurance, the fiber of their bodies for a time not equal to the sincerity of their resolution. But with the quickening of sharp demand and compelling need, spirit soon transformed body to its likeness, and meantime cheered and braced other hearts beating their old rhythm beneath the iron breasts of veterans.

No jeering now for newness and niceness; but silent welcome, of respect and almost reverence, seeing that the young men had come willingly at such a time to such a front. The last two years had brought prismatic colors down to plain monotone. Names of things were charged with deeper definitions. War was no longer a holiday excursion; it was "hard-shelled" business; not maturing in three months, nor nine, nor twelve, nor twenty-four. And the way of it was more bitter than the end. The regiments passing to the front marched not between festoons of ladies' smiles and waving handkerchiefs, thrown kisses and banner presentations. They were looked upon sadly and in a certain awe, as those that had taken on themselves a doom. The muster rolls on which the name and oath were written were pledges of honor,—redeemable at the gates of death. And they who went up to them, knowing this, are on the lists of heroes.

It is true not all who came in now were strictly "volunteers." Some may have enlisted from shame of staying comfortably at home while manly men were at the front. Some may have preferred this to standing "draft" under terrors of the lot; for so the free will is sometimes bound. And others may have been persuaded by the large local bounties, which the stern realities adverted to above induced many loud loyalists to offer to "substitutes," to whom life, liberty, and the pursuit of happiness were not quite so dear. Glory had come to exemplify the altruistic virtues, and in such honor as "dying for your country," self-regarding men scripturally "preferred one another"!

But there were those coming last who represented the heroism of homes. For wives, who had early offered the fathers of their children, house-bonds of human well-being, as sacrifices for their country's redemption, sent now their sons, to share their father's honor and perchance his grave. Mothers, who had given their first-born, held not back their youngest now; the strongest first, and then the dearest. And the converse of this, the father following the son. Well might the lip of veteran quiver as his quick eye, scanning a squad of newcomers, caught the figure of some father, gray and grim, still so erect and eagle-eyed, straining for every semblance of youth, that he might be permitted to stand beside his boy whom he could not let come alone. Nor is this sympathy unmarked in higher grades. What has come over the spirit of that stern officer, pushing his column with relentless energy on the terrible forced march, that with furtive side-look as if half-ashamed, he draws the back of his sword-hand across his compressed eyelids, like the swift sign of the cross over the face of a prayer? He has turned in his saddle to order the ambulance, or his own headquarters' wagon to pick up from the trodden wayside some fallen, fainting boy, overweighted by the heavy armor of his country's defense, whose soul has carried him already far beyond his body's strength. Some home-loved boy; and so soon, so nearly lost! God help us all!

The exercise of thought that had been invited and sanctioned naturally fostered indulgence in some "free thinking." Some liberties were taken in canvassing the merits not only of commanders but rather more freely of campaigns,—particularly this *reductio ad absurdum* of the siege of Petersburg. And they would have been something less than rational human beings if they did not indulge in some criticisms. Too free expression of unfavorable opinion, it is true, might render one liable to the counter charge of conduct to "the prejudice of good order and military discipline." But wisdom was also brought to use. Our soldiers had well learned the lesson that it is sometimes necessary to reverse the maxim of public law, and subordinate civil rights to military rules.

Evil-minded people were trying to make our men believe that Grant and Lincoln were making this long delay in front of Petersburg in order to secure their continuance in office. But this was an outrage upon those noble characters, and an insult to the common sense of every man among us. We knew that the surest way for our high officials to hold their place was by no means to court delay, but to strike a quick, bold blow at the enemy.

Grant's change of base from the Rappahannock

to the James, and his immediate objective from the front of Richmond to its rear by way of Petersburg, called for no adverse criticism. There were deep-felt reasons for acquiescence. Nor could it be fairly criticized on purely military grounds. Although technically a change of base, it was not a change in his grand purpose,—"to fight it out on this line if it takes all summer." That meant there was to be no retreating. And this might justly be considered a master stroke of grand tactics in the continuous movement to turn Lee's right, and also cut his communications. When we understood the purpose of this move we believed it to be good tactics, and we took it up with hope and cheer. Sober second thought justified the first impression. It was a well-planned and well-executed movement. Our army was skilfully withdrawn from the front of a watchful and active enemy, and the main body of our army was before Petersburg before Lee knew it had crossed the James. The first blow was well delivered; but a series of shortcomings, for which it must be said neither the men nor their immediate commanders were responsible, brought all to nought. Successive assaults on the enemy's lines were made as corps after corps extended leftward; but gallant fighting left little to show but its cost. Especially did we hold in mind the last of these made by the Fifth Corps on the second day, when an assault was ordered, by my fine veteran Brigade on the strong entrenchments at Rives' Salient commanding the important avenue of communication, the

Norfolk Railroad and Jerusalem Plank Road. By this time it was too late; all Lee's army were up and entrenched. We encountered a far outnumbering force of veteran troops well entrenched and a cross-fire of twenty guns in earthworks planted with forethought and skill. Desperate valor could accomplish nothing but its own demonstration. Our veterans were hurled back over the stricken field, or left upon it—I, too, proud witness and sharer of their fate. I am not of Virginia blood; she is of mine. So ended the evening of the second day. And the army sat down to that ten months' symposium, from which twenty thousand men never rose.

The development of this campaign led many to compare Grant with McClellan. They marched their armies over much the same ground, with much the same result. Only McClellan was brought to Washington; Grant was permitted to remain at City Point and the Appomattox. The rumor ran that McClellan had also proposed to cut across the James and around Lee's flank. Many still believed in his soldiership, but broader elements now entered into the estimate. Something in the nature of the man and something in his environment caused his failure. With great organizing power, he failed in practical application. The realities of war seemed to daze him. He lacked dash, resolution; he hesitated to seize the golden moment, to profit by his own openings, to press his advantage, to solve doubt by daring. With all that marvelous magnetism which won the love and enthusiasm of his subordinates, he lacked the skill, or the will, to gain the sympathy of his superiors. It is as much the requisite in generalship to secure the confidence and co-operation of the Government as to command armies and over come opposing force. It was unfortunate for him, also, that he allowed himself to be drawn into politics, which paid him in its own kind. The foreshadowing thought of this created in his mind a "double objective," which confused his purpose and benumbed his fighting energy as against possible fellow citizens.

But many circumstances were against him. Few seemed to realize that this was war. And many who influenced his surroundings thought they knew as much of war as he. At that time the North was in a craze; nobody would accept the suggestion that it would be a long and costly task to put down the rebellion, or even to break up the Southern army. The North was as arbitrary as the South was arrogant. Strong in its conviction of right, proud of its sponsorship for the old flag; stung, too, by the sharp rebuff to its assumption and its authority, the North did not count patience as the chief of virtues. Its cry was "On to Richmond!" to capture the rebel capital so impudently set up in face of our own, and thus wipe out that pretended token of independence and sovereignty which gave pretext for foreign recognition. For this had become an element in the contest,—the hostility of the French Emperor, and the "nobility" of England with difficulty held back from recognizing the Southern Confederacy through the moral courage of John Bright and the royal wisdom of the Queen and Prince Consort of England.

The impatience of the North is perhaps to be pardoned for the reason of its impelling motive; but it demanded of General McClellan impossibilities. And these were created quite as much by forces in his rear as by those in his front.

As for Grant, he was like Thor, the hammerer; striking blow after blow, intent on his purpose to beat his way through, somewhat reckless of the cost. Yet he was the first one of our commanders who dared to pursue his policy of delay without apology or fear of overruling. He made it a condition of his acceptancy of the chief command that he should not be interfered with from Washington. That gave him more freedom and "discretion" than any of his predecessors. He had somehow, with all his modesty, the rare faculty of controlling his superiors as well as his subordinates. He outfaced Stanton, captivated the President, and even compelled acquiescence or silence from that dread source of paralyzing power,—the Congressional Committee on the conduct of the war.

The Government and the country had to exercise patience,—with us no doubt, and even with General Grant. He had to exercise it also, with himself. It must have been a sore trial to his pride, and a measure very foreign to his temperament to have to sit down so long before Petersburg; to abandon the tactics of main force and commence a series of sporadic harassments on the enemy's weak spots, and adopt for his main strategic plan the attempt to tire and starve him out. That was what things looked like now. There was all the while the ever increasing risk that, with this seeming long irresolution, influences from within might induce the country to concession and compromise at cost of the vital point of the whole contention, the supremacy of its proclaimed ideal,—the guaranty of human rights.

We all had to learn the bitter but salutary lesson, taught by adversity and humiliation,—that instant advantage is not always lasting achievement; that mere good intentions will not win victories, and that the conditions and cost of undertakings must be considered and prepared for body and spirit. We had the discipline of adversity. We found patience an active force and not merely an endurance of suffering. The brave Saint Paul declares that "tribulation worketh patience; and patience experience; and experience hope." But we found things turned a little otherwise; experience demanded patience, and both sorely tried hope. Those who believe there is a divine appointment or mysterious overruling purpose in the prolonged struggles of human history might see in these repeated reverses of ours an intimation that greater things were in issue here than the taking of Petersburg or Richmond, or the destruction of Lee's army, or even the quick overthrow of the rebellion. Should our success come according to our hopes there might be danger of too ready a compromise with the forces that had brought on the war, and so the winnowings of life and death must go on till the troubles be sifted to the core. Lincoln's proclamation, though looked upon by our old-school officers as unadvised and unwarranted by the Constitution, had sent thoughts wider and higher than the range of army regulations or text-books of the law. It was a time of travail with the new birth of the nation. Time and tide wait for no man; but man must wait for them.

With all Grant's reticence, we felt sure that he was preparing some great movement, and this must be still to the left, to cut Lee's communications and envelop his existing lines, or as the wiseacres said, to take Richmond in something like Joshua's way with Jericho,—sounding trumpets all around its walls. We had, indeed, been rehearsing for this performance from time to time all winter, and had already cut several of Lee's best communications. Our established line now extended some sixteen miles. Occasional dashes had broken in upon them for some four or five miles farther westward, to near Burgess' Mill on Hatcher's Run, at the junction of the Boydton Plank Road and the White Oak Road; but these points could not be strongly held by us, and were more strongly guarded by the enemy, as almost their last avenue of sea-coast communication. Lee had two railroads: the Richmond and Danville, leading to important connections in North Carolina; and the Petersburg and Lynchburg, known to us as the "Southside," making a junction with the former at Burkeville, about fifty miles from Petersburg, as also from Richmond.

On our part, as we gained ground we had unrolled a military railroad, up hill and down, without much grading, and hence exhibiting some remarkable exploits in momentum of mind and machinery. This terminated at the Vaughan Road on the north branch of Rowanty Creek.

Meantime Sherman had made his masterly march from the Great River to the Sea, and the even more masterly movement north to Gouldsboro, North Carolina, where with his alert and dashing army he threatened Lee's sea communication and also the flank and rear of his position. It was a curious element in the situation that the astute Confederate General "Joe Johnston" should come in north of Sherman and interpose his army between Sherman's and ours. This sort of "voltaic pile" generated some queer currents of conjecture and apprehension. Disquieting rumors came across the picket lines that Johnston was coming up to strike our flank and rear, and thus between his army and Lee's we should be caught in the jaws of a leviathan. But we believed Sherman would give Johnston something else to do. We were more troubled by the rumor that Lee, presuming on our inertness, was preparing to make a master movement; to occupy our attention by feints in front while he should withdraw his main army, pass around our left and join Johnston, knock Sherman out, then turn back and attend to the "sick lion" of the Army of the Potomac.

Grant was evidently anxious lest Lee should manage to get away from our front and effect a junction with Johnston for some bold stroke. That would be a shame for us. We would far rather fight, even if unsuccessful as usual. Then we were much annoyed by rumors coming around from Washington, that Sherman was coming up with his power and prestige to take our business out of our hands and the glory of success to his army. But in the depth of our doubts and apprehension word came that Grant had brought Sherman to a conference at his headquarters, and had invited Sheridan as a participant, on the evening of March 27th, and we knew now that something was to be done on a grand scale.

Soon came the thrilling General Order. It announced one more leftward movement, but it woke new courage and inspired confidence. Its very style and manner was new. It seemed to take us all into confidential relations with the commander; the whole object and plan set forth in a manner clear, circumstantial, and complete, so that each subordinate knew the part he was expected to take. The colonels, on whom the brunt of battle so heavily falls, felt that they were appreciated, and they were quickened in soldierly pride and manly resolution. And the younger generals, who had become veterans in experience, especially in the practical working of the felicitous provision in the Army Regulations that, while their proper position is habitually a hundred and fifty yards in rear of the center of their commands, they may, nevertheless, in time of action, "go to any place where they deem their presence necessary," and had found that was anywhere but in the rear, took new assurance now that permission was expressly given that when they got the enemy to "going" they might "push things" at their discretion.

So when on the last evening of the old dispensation we prepared to break camp before the dawn, silently and unseen, without blast of bugle or blow of axe, or sight of fire to betray unusual movements to the ever watchful foe so near, and each one who could dashed off his little farewell message home, there was in his heart a strange mingling of emotion, the vision of a great joy, in which, perhaps, he was to lie silent and apart, a little shadow on the earth, but overhead a great light filling the sky. This lifted him to the surpassing joy that, however it should be with him, his work and worth had entered into the country's life and honor.

Now the solemn notes of the last tattoo rang "Lights out!" through the deepening shades, echoed from point to point of wooded hill and earth-piled parapet, floating away northward over the awful powers lying hushed beneath the twilight semblance of peace,—northward, toward the homes our hearts reached after, the lingering echoes sweeping the heartstrings as they died away. But the same heart told that the evening bugle would not sound "Lights out!" again till the nights of the tremendous tragedy were over; that whatever of him or his should be of the returning, never would return that awful, long repeated scene: two armies, battered, broken, blood-bathed from brow to foot, but still face to face in unconquerable resolve. No, but in the far sky another vision: calm in triumph, thinking not of mastery over man, but of right for all; and in God's heaven the old flag redeemed from shame and scorn, standing for a regenerated people and a new covenant of brotherly love for the world's hereafter.

CHAPTER II

THE OVERTURE

GRANT'S general plan involved an alternative: to cut Lee's communications or turn the right flank of his entrenched line, and in case of the success of either, to take Petersburg by direct front attack. To carry out this plan he appointed Sheridan with the cavalry of the Army of the Shenandoah, two divisions, under General Merritt, and the cavalry division now commanded by General Crook, formerly belonging to the Army of the Potomac. He was to have the Fifth Corps as infantry support, to be followed, if necessary, by the Second Corps. General Meade, commanding the Army of the Potomac, was to accompany the movement. The former places of these corps on the left of our entrenchments before Petersburg, were to be taken by troops of the Army of the James. On the right of these, our Sixth and Ninth Corps were to hold their old positions in front of Petersburg, ready to break through the enemy's works if they should be stripped somewhat of troops by the necessity of meeting our assault on their right.

The scope of Grant's intentions may be understood from an extract from his orders to Sheridan, March 28, 1865:

The Fifth Army Corps will move by the Vaughan Road at three A.M. to-morrow morning. The Second moves at about nine A.M. . . . Move your cavalry at as early an hour as you can, . . and passing to or through Dinwiddie, reach the right and rear of the enemy as soon as you can It is not the intention to attack the enemy in his entrenched position, but to force him out, if possible. Should he come out and attack us, or get himself where he can be attacked, move in with your entire force in your own way, and with full reliance that the army will engage or follow the enemy as circumstances will dictate. I shall be on the field, and will probably be able to communicate with you. Should I not do so, and you find that the enemy keeps within his main entrenched line, you may cut loose and push for the Danville Road. If you find it practicable, I would like you to cross the Southside Road between Petersburg and Burkesville, and destroy it to some extent . . . After having accomplished the destruction of the two railroads, which are now the only avenues of supply to Lee's army, you may return to this army or go on into North Carolina and join General Sherman. . . .

General Grant evidently intended to rely more on tactics than strategy in this opening. In his personal letter to General Sherman, of March 22d, giving the details of his plans for Sheridan's movement, he adds: "I shall start out with no distinct view, further than holding Lee's forces from following Sheridan. But I shall be along myself, and will take advantage of anything that turns up."

The general plan was that Sherman should work

his way up to Burkesville, and thus cut off Lee's communications, and force him to come out of his entrenchments and fight on equal terms. Sherman says he and General Grant expected that one of them would have to fight one more bloody battle. He also makes the characteristic remark that his army at Goldsboro was strong enough to fight Lee's army and Johnston's combined, if Grant would come up within a day or two.[1]

It will be observed that we had abundance of commanders independent among each other,—Sheridan, Meade, and Ord commanding the Army of the James, subordinate only to Grant who was present in the field. The result of this the sequel will show.

We were all good friends,—those who were to constitute the turning column. Warren of our Fifth Corps had once commanded the Second; Humphreys of the Second had formerly commanded a division in the Fifth; Miles, division commander in the Second, had won his spurs in the Fifth; Meade, commanding the army, had been corps commander of the Fifth. Crook's cavalry division of our army, now about to go to Sheridan, had been our pet and pride; Sheridan was an object of admiration and awe.

[1] Sherman's *Memoirs*, vol. ii, p. 325. This seems to imply a reflection on the fighting qualities of the Army of the Potomac, as at that time Sherman's army did not exceed in number the Army of the Potomac but by six thousand men But it must be remembered that the Army of the Potomac confronted an enemy covered by entrenched works for sixteen miles,—a circumstance which gave the Confederates the great advantage of three to one in effective numbers

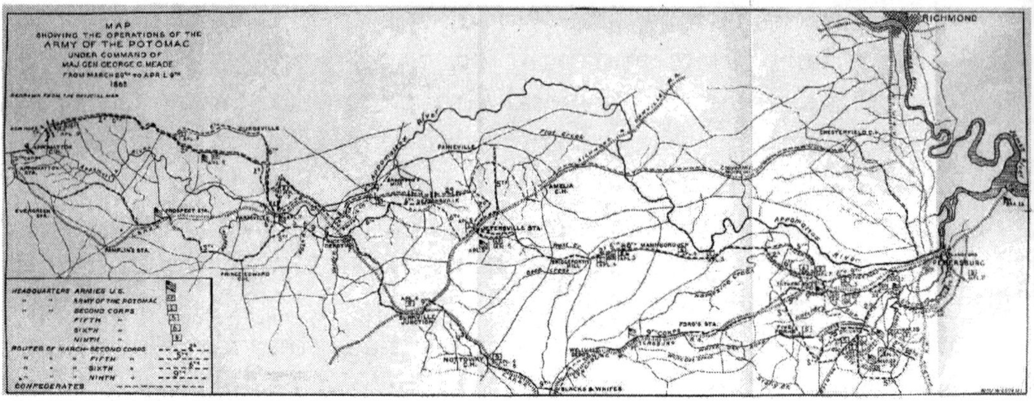
MAP
SHOWING THE OPERATIONS OF THE
ARMY OF THE POTOMAC
UNDER COMMAND OF
MAJ. GEN. GEORGE G. MEADE
FROM MARCH 29TH TO APRIL 9TH
1865
RICHMOND
CURDSVILLE
FARMVILLE
PAINESVILLE
AMELIA C.H.
CHESTERFIELD C.H.
JETERSVILLE STA.
PROSPECT STA.
EVERGREEN STA.
PAMPLIN'S STA.
PRINCE EDWARD
APPOMATTOX STA.
BURKEVILLE JUNCTION
NOTTOWAY C.H.
BLACKS & WHITES
FORD'S STA.
APPOMATTOX RIVER
HEADQUARTERS ARMIES U.S.
ARMY OF THE POTOMAC
SECOND CORPS
FIFTH
SIXTH
NINTH
ROUTES OF MARCH—SECOND CORPS
FIFTH
SIXTH
NINTH
CONFEDERATES

Of the Fifth Corps, the division commanders of the First and Second were Griffin and Ayres of the regular artillery, and veterans of the Mexican War, who had served with their batteries in the Fifth Corps early in its career; and Crawford of the Third, who was with Anderson at Fort Sumter, was identified with the Pennsylvania Reserves, whose whole history was closely connected with this Corps.

As for the First Division, the morning report for March 29, 1865, showed 6547 men present for duty. This number being on various duty elsewhere or sick in hospital was 4000 short of its full ranks. The remnants of the old First Division had been consolidated into the Third Brigade, formerly my own, consisting of about 3000 men, commanded by the able General Joseph J. Bartlett of the Sixth Corps. The Second Brigade, about 1750, commanded by the experienced and conscientious Colonel Edgar M. Gregory, of the 91st Pennsylvania Volunteers, Brevet Brigadier-General of Volunteers, consisted of three new regiments from New York, the 187th, the 188th, and 189th, new regiments but mostly old soldiers. My own brigade, the First, consisting of like new regiments, had about 450 short of its normal numbers, mustering 1750 men for duty. These regiments were the 198th Pennsylvania, composed of fourteen full companies, being a special command for a veteran and brave officer, Colonel Horatio G. Sickel, Brevet Brigadier-General, and the 185th New York, a noble body of men of high capability and character, and a well-disciplined regiment now commanded by Colonel Gustave Sniper, an able man and thorough soldier.

Gregory and Sickel had both ranked me formerly as Colonels, but accepted the new relations with sincerity and utmost courtesy.

The ground about to be traversed by us is flat and swampy, and cut up by sluggish streams which, after every rain, become nearly impassable. The soil is a mixture of clay and sand, quite apt in wet weather to take the character of sticky mire or of quicksands. The principal roads for heavy travel have to be corduroyed or overlaid with plank. The streams for the most part find their way south-easterly into the tributaries of the Chowan River. Some, however, flow northeasterly into the waters of the Appomattox. Our available route was along the divide of these waters.

The principal road leading out westerly from Petersburg is the Boydton Plank Road, for the first ten miles nearly parallel with the Appomattox, and distant from it from three to six miles. The Southside Railroad is between the Boydton Road and the river. South of the Boydton is the Vaughan Road; the first section lying in rear of our main entrenchments, but from our extreme left at Hatcher's Run inclining towards the Boydton Road, being only two miles distant from it at Dinwiddie Court House. Five miles east of this place the Quaker Road, called by persons of another mood, the "Military Road," crosses the Vaughan and leads northerly into the Boydton

Road midway between Hatcher's Run and Gravelly Run, which at this junction became Rowanty Creek.

A mile above the intersection of the Quaker Road with the Boydton is the White Oak Road, leading off from the Boydton at right angles westerly, following the ridges between the small streams and branches forming the headwaters of Hatcher's and Gravelly Runs, through and beyond the "Five Forks." This is a meeting-place of roads, the principal of which, called the Ford Road, crosses the White Oak at a right angle, leading from a station on the Southside Railroad, three miles north, to Dinwiddie Court House, six miles south.

The enemy's main line of entrenchments west from Petersburg covered the important Boydton Plank Road, but only so far as Hatcher's Run, where at Burgess' Mill their entrenchments leave this and follow the White Oak Road for some two miles, and then cross it, turning to the north and following the Claiborne Road, which leads to Sutherland's Station on the Southside Railroad ten miles distant from Petersburg, covering this road till it strikes Hatcher's Run about a mile higher up. This "return" northerly forms the extreme right of the enemy's entrenched line.

When the instructions for this campaign reached us, all were animated with confidence of quick success. If Lee's lines before Petersburg were held in place, it would be easy work to cut his communications, turn his right, and roll him back upon

Petersburg or Richmond; if, on the other hand, his main lines were stripped to resist our attack, our comrades in the old lines would make short work of Lee's entrenchments and his army.

At daylight on the twenty-ninth of March the Fifth Corps moved out toward the enemy's right. As the movement was intended to mask its destination by a considerable detour to the rear, our column first moved southward to Arthur's Swamp, crossing the Rowanty at Monk's Bridge, and thence by way of the Old Stage Road into and down the Vaughan. My brigade, being the advance of the First Division, reached the Chapple House, about two miles from Dinwiddie, early in the forenoon, encountering only a few cavalry pickets. Sheridan with the cavalry, moving by a still exterior route, was pushing on towards Dinwiddie Court House.

At about noon General Griffin directed me to return upon the Vaughan Road to the junction of the Quaker Road, and push up this road to develop the enemy's position in that quarter. This direction we knew led towards the very strong salient of the enemy's works near Burgess' Mill on Hatcher's Run: but we did not know where, nor with what force, Lee might see fit to push out a counter movement to thwart ours. We soon found this road better entitled to its military than its Quaker appellation. A spirited advanced line of the enemy had destroyed the bridge over Gravelly Run and were posted behind some defenses on the north bank intending to give serious check to our advance. Evidently there was something nearby which they deemed it important to cover; and which accordingly we felt an interest to uncover. I formed a plan which I communicated to General Griffin, who approved it and directed General Gregory to support me on the left as I should instruct him, and also directed General Bartlett to be ready to take part as circumstances should require. Things being thus arranged, I placed General Sickel with eight companies on the right below the ruined bridge, with instructions to pour a hot fire upon the enemy opposite when with the rest of the brigade I would ford the stream waist-deep above the bridge and strike the enemy's right flank obliquely. This led to a hand-to-hand encounter. The attack was impetuous; the musketry hot. Major Glenn with his six companies in skirmishing order dashed through the stream and struck the enemy's breastworks front and flank. In a moment everything started loose. The entire brigade forded the stream and rolled forward, closing upon Glenn right and left, and the whole command swept onward like a wave, carrying all before it a mile or more up the road, to the buildings of the Lewis Farm. The enemy now re-enforced made a decided stand, and the fight became sharp. But our enveloping line pressed them so severely that they fell back after each struggle to the edge of a thick wood, where a large body had gathered behind a substantial breastwork of logs and earth.

A withering volley breaks our line into groups. Courage and resolution are great, but some other sentiment mightier for the moment controls our men; a backward movement begins, but the men retire slowly, bearing their wounded with them, and even some of their dead. The enemy, seeing this recoil, pour out of their shelter and make a dash upon our broken groups, but only to be dashed back in turn hand to hand in eddying whirls. And seized by our desperate fellows, so many are dragged along as prisoners in the receding tide that it is not easy to tell which side is the winning one. Much of the enemy's aim is unsteady, for the flame and murk of their thickening fire in the heavy moist air are blown back into their eyes by the freshening south wind. But reinforcements are coming in, deepening and broadening their line beyond both our flanks. Now roar and tumult of motion for a fierce pulse of time, then again a quivering halt. At length one vigorous dash drives the assailants into the woods again with heavy loss. We had cleared the field, and thought it best to be content with that for the present. We reform our lines each side the buildings of the Lewis Farm, and take account of the situation. We had about a hundred prisoners from Wise's and Wallace's Brigades, who said nearly all Anderson's Division were with them, and that more were coming, and they were bound to hold this outpost covering the junction of two roads which are main arteries of their vital hold,—the White Oak and the Boydton Plank.

We found General Griffin there, and were relieved to see that he did not find fault with us, although we had not done all that we expected—perhaps not all that was expected of us. We had been repulsed, no doubt. But there was more to be done. I wondered why Gregory had not attacked on the enemy's right flank when they were driving us back, but found he had difficulty with the streams, which were almost impassable.

But our work was still before us. I saw that General Griffin was anxious to carry the enemy's position, and I as anxiously formed a new line for the assault. So we were in for it again and almost in cavalry fashion. Giving the right of the line to General Sickel and the left to Colonel Sniper on each side the road, I took Major Glenn with his six companies for a straight dash up the Quaker Road, our objective point being a heap of sawdust where a portable mill had stood, now the center of the enemy's strong advanced line. We received a hot fire which we did not halt to return as that would expose us to heavy loss, but advanced at the double quick to go over the enemy's works with the bayonet. At close quarters the sharpshooters in the tree-tops cut us up badly, but we still pressed on, only now and then, here and there, delivering fire ourselves. In the full crescendo of this, now close to the sawdust pile, my horse, wild for the front, all his pulses aglow, was exceeding the possible pace of the men following and I gave him a vigorous check on the curb. Resenting this, he touched his fore feet to earth only to rebound head-high to the level of my face. Just at that instant a heavy blow struck me on the left breast just below the heart. I fell forward on my horse's neck and lost all consciousness. The bullet at close range had been aimed at my breast, but the horse had lifted his head just in time to catch it, so that, passing through the big muscle of his neck (and also I may say through a leather case of field orders and a brass-mounted hand-mirror in my breast-pocket—we didn't carry towels in this campaign), demolished the pistol in the belt of my aide Lieutenant Vogel, and knocked him out of the saddle. This, of course, I only knew afterwards. The shock had stopped my horse, and I must have been for some little time unconscious. The first thing I knew an arm was around my waist and words murmured in my ear, "My dear General, you are gone," the kindly voice of General Griffin who had ridden up beside me. At that moment also a very different strain struck my ear on the other hand,—a wild rebel yell. As I lifted my head a glance showed me the right of our line broken and flying before the enemy like leaves before the wind. This explains my answer to Griffin, "Yes, General, I am,"—that is, "gone" in another sense.

The bullet had riddled my sleeve to the elbow and bruised and battered my bridle arm so that it was useless, and the obstructions it met had slightly deflected it so that, instead of striking the point of my heart, it had followed around two ribs so as to come out at the back seam of my coat. The horse was bleeding profusely and my falling on his neck brought a blood relationship of which I was not ashamed. Everybody around thought I was "gone" indeed, and that is why a telegram went to the New York morning papers reporting me as killed. In the shock my cap had fallen to the ground, and I must have been a queer spectacle as I rose in the saddle tattered and battered, bareheaded and blood-smeared. I swung the rein against my horse's wounded neck and lightly touching his flank with my heel, we made a dash for the rally of our right. Pushing in among our broken ranks or our 198th Pennsylvania, the men might well have thought me a messenger from the other world. That rally was sharp work—and costly. Down at the extreme right, in the maddened whirl, I found the brave Sickel, his face aflame, rallying his men with an appeal none could resist. In a moment after he fell by my side with a shattered arm. With him was that heroic boy Major McEuen who high above all thought of self was dashing into the seething crest of battle and was shot from his saddle within touch of my unavailing hand; so passed a noble spirit, a sweet soul, only son of his proud father and last of his race on earth. By such appeal and offering this gallant regiment, forced back by overpowering onset, straightened up into line again, and with a thrilling, almost appalling cheer, turned the tide of battle, and rolled it fairly back inside the enemy's works.

Aware of some confusion near the sawdust pile I thought it fitting to return to my place at the center. I was astonished at the greeting of cheers which marked my course. Strangest of all was that when I emerged to the sight of the enemy, they also took up the cheering. I hardly knew what world I was in.

By the time I got back to the center the loss of blood had exhausted the strength of my horse, and his nose came to earth. I had to send him back and become a foot soldier. It was a critical time there, with much confusion. Glenn was having a hard time at the sawdust pile, and I worked myself forward in the crowd to get at the state of things in front. By a sudden backset I found myself surrounded by Confederates, who courteously lowered their muskets and locked their bayonets around me to indicate a reception not easily to be declined, and probably to last some time. The old coat was dingy almost to gray; I was bareheaded, and rather a doubtful character anyway. I thought it warrantable to assume an extremely friendly relation. To their exhortation I replied: "Surrender? What's the matter with you? What do you take me for? Don't you see these Yanks right onto us? Come along with me and let us break 'em." I still had my right arm and my light sword, and I gave a slight flourish indicating my wish and their direction. They did follow me like brave fellows,—most of them too far; for they were a long time getting back.

There was a little lull shortly afterwards, but quite a curious crowd around the sawdust pile. Colonel Spear of my old 20th Maine, who charged himself with a certain care for me, came up now and with a mysterious and impressive look, as if about to present a brevet commission, drew from his breast-pocket an implement or utensil somewhat resembling a flask, which he confidentially assured me contained some very choice wine, of which he invited me to take a swallow. Now that word is a very indeterminate and flighty term. As I took the instrument in hand, I perceived it to be a Jamaica-ginger bottle frugally indented on all sides. I elevated it at the proper angle of incidence without, perhaps, sufficiently observing that of reflection; but I thought masonic courtesy would be observed if I stopped when the bubble indicated "spirit-level." I returned the equitable remainder to him with commendation and grateful thanks. But the melancholy, martyr-like look on his face as he held it up to the light, revealed his inward thought that in appropriating his courtesy I had availed myself to the extreme of my privilege. My friend in later years seeks to get even with me by recalling this story on festive occasions for the entertainment of friends. I do not like to admit the charge against myself, but have no hesitation in entering the plea on behalf of my accessory, the bottle, of extremely extenuating circumstances. I was glad the Colonel was not on my staff then, and I did not have to meet him at evening.

We were soon parted. A hoarse yell rose through the tumult on the left, where the impetuous Sniper had tried to carry the breastworks in the woods, and now, badly cut up, his regiment was slowly falling back, closely followed by the enemy pouring out from their works. They were soon pressed back to a line perpendicular to their proper front, and the flight was fierce. Meantime, I scarcely know how, nor by whom helped, I found myself mounted on the back of a strange, dull-looking white horse, that had been bespattered by the trodden earth, and as I rode down among my fine New Yorkers, I must have looked more than ever like a figure from the Apocalypse.

There I found the calm, cold-steel face of Sniper, who had snatched his regimental colors from the dead hands of the third color-bearer that had gone down under them in the last half-hour, and was still holding his shattered ranks facing the storm; himself tossing on the crest of every wave, rolling and rocking like a ship laying to in the teeth of a gale. I dispatched a staff-officer for Gregory to attack where I supposed him to be, in position to enfilade the enemy's newly gained alignment. In response up rode Griffin, anxious and pale, his voice ringing with a strange tone, as of mingled command and entreaty: "If you can hold on there ten minutes, I will give you a battery." That was a great tonic: Griffin's confidence and his guns. There was quite an eminence a little to our rear, behind which I was intending to re-form my line should it be driven from the field. I changed my plan. Pushing through to Sniper, I shouted in his ear in a voice the men should hear: "Once more! Try the steel! Hell for ten minutes and we are out of it!"

I had no idea we could carry the woods, or hold them if we did. My real objective was that knoll in the rear. I wanted to keep the enemy from pressing over it before we could get our guns up. A desperate resort was necessary.

While a spirit as it were superhuman took possession of minds and bodies; energies of will, contradicting all laws of dynamics, reversed the direction of the surging wave, and dashed it back upon the woods and breastworks within them. Having the enemy now on the defensive, I took occasion to let Sniper know my purpose and plan, and to instruct his men accordingly: to demoralize the enemy by a smashing artillery fire, and then charge the woods by similar bolt-like blast of men. They took this in with calm intelligence, and braced assent. I knew they would do all possible to man. All the while I was straining eyes and prayers for a sight of the guns. And now they come—B of the 4th Regulars, Mitchell leading with headlong speed, horses smoking, battery thundering with jolt and rattle, wheeling into action front, on the hillock I had been saving for them, while the earth flew beneath the wheels,—magnificent, the shining, terrible Napoleons. I rode out to meet them, pointing out the ground. Mitchell's answering look had a mixed expression, suggestive of a smile. I did not see anything in the situation to smile at, but he evidently did. I should have remembered my remarkable personal appearance. He did not smile long. The colloquy was short: "Mitchell, do you think you can put solid shot or percussion into those woods close over the rebels' heads, without hurting my men?"—"Yes, Sir! if they will keep where they are."—"Well then, give it to them the best you know. But stop quick at my signal, and fire clear of my men when they charge."

It was splendid and terrible: the swift-served, bellowing, leaping big guns, the thrashing of the solid shot into the woods; the flying splinters and branches and tree-tops coming down upon the astonished heads; shouts changing into shrieks at the savage work of these unaccustomed missiles; then answering back the burst of fire oblique upon the left front of the battery, where there was a desperate attempt to carry it by flank attack; repulsed by Sniper drawing to the left, and thus also leaving clear range for closer cutting projectiles, when now case shot and shell, now a blast of canister, poured into the swarming, swirling foe.

My right wing was holding itself in the line of woods they had carried, reversing the breastworks there. The strain was on the left now. I was at the guns, where danger of disaster centered, so closely were they pressed upon at times. Mitchell, bravely handling his imperilled battery,—I had just seen him mounting a gun-carriage as it recoiled, to observe the effect of its shot,—went down grievously wounded. It was thunder and lightning and earthquake; but it was necessary to hold things steady. Now, thank Heaven! comes up Griffin, anxious and troubled. I dare say I too looked something the worse for wear, for Griffin's first word was: "General, you must not leave us. We cannot spare you now." "I had no thought of it, General," was all I had to say. He brought up Colonel Doolittle (not named by a prophet, surely) with the 189th New York, from Gregory's Brigade, and Colonel Partridge (a trace of the bird of Jove on his wing), with the 1st and 16th Michigan, to my support. These I placed on Sniper's right; when up came that handsome Zouave regiment, the 155th Pennsylvania, the gallant Pearson at their head, regimental colors in hand, expecting some forward work, sweeping so finely into line that I was proud to give them the center, joining on the heroic Glenn, holding there alone.

It is soon over. Woods and works are cleared, and the enemy sent flying up the road towards their main entrenchments. The 185th New York is drawn back and placed in support of the battery, right and left. The 198th Pennsylvania is gathered on the right, in front of the farm buildings. Gregory takes the advanced line, and soon Bartlett comes up and presses up the road to near the junction of the Boydton and White Oak, reminded of the enemy's neighborhood by a few cannon shots from their entrenchments near Burgess' Mill bridgehead. At about this time word comes that the Second Corps is on our right, not far away. By our action a lodgment had been effected which became the pivot of the series of undulations on the left, which after three days resulted in turning the right flank of Lee's army. We had been fighting Gracie's, Ransom's, Wallace's, and Wise's Brigades, of Johnson's Division, under command of General R. H. Anderson, numbering, as by their last morning reports, 6277 officers and men "effective" for the field.

My own brigade in this engagement numbered less than 1700 officers and men. Mitchell's battery and Gregory's and Bartlett's regiments assisting in the final advance added to this number probably 1000 more. Their total loss in this engagement was slight in numbers. The loss in my brigade was a quarter of those in line.

My fight was over, but not my responsibilities. The day and the field are ours; but what a day, and what a field! As for the day, behind the heavy brooding mists the shrouded sun was drawing down the veil which shrined it in the mausoleum of vanished but unforgotten years. And for the field: strown all over it were a hundred and fifty bodies of the enemy's dead, and many of the hundred and sixty-seven of my own men killed and wounded. Both my personal aides had been severely wounded, and every officer of my staff unhorsed. The casualties among officers were especially beyond the ratio in other battles. Captain Mitchell, commanding the battery, was lying behind it severely wounded. It may be proper to add that as he was serving away from his immediate superiors, I saw to it that his gallant and most effective service was faithfully reported, and fairly recognized by the Government. There was a sequel to this in the widowhood of after years. Sometimes we can do for others what we cannot do for ourselves. And this is the law of richest increase.

With the declining day I slowly rode over the stricken field. Around the breastworks lay a hundred and fifty of the enemy's dead and desperately wounded. We had taken also in the countercharges and eddies of the strife nearly two hundred prisoners—happier than they knew. These we sent away for safe-keeping. But we had with us, to keep and to care for, more than five hundred bruised bodies of men,—men made in the image of God, marred by the hand of man, and must we say in the name of God? And where is the reckoning for such things? And who is answerable? One might almost shrink from the sound of his own voice, which had launched into the palpitating air words of order—do we call it?—fraught with such ruin. Was it God's command we heard, or His forgiveness we must forever implore?

For myself, though hardly able to move erect for soreness and weakness, I was thankful to have come out holding together as well as I did. For one little circumstance, which, I suppose, has interest only for myself, I felt very grateful for the kindness, and possibly the favor, of General Griffin in so ordering my reinforcements as not to deprive me of the command of the field till my fight was over. In the exigency of the situation, instead of sending me four regiments from the other two brigades of the division, he might very properly have put in Bartlett, with his fine brigade, and that gallant officer would doubtless have carried all before him. But that noble sense of fairness, that delicate recognition of honorable sensibilities, in thoughtfully permitting, and even helping, a subordinate to fight his fight through, if he could, and receive whatever credit might belong to it, shows not only the generous traits of General Griffin's character, but shows also how strange a bond it is to hold a body of soldiers together, each and each to all, when men can feel what they have wrought with the best that is in them is safe in the hands of their commander, whose power over the "ways of putting things" has so much effect to make or mar their reputation. Some commanders more than others have commanded love. That too has reason. Justice is said to be an attribute of the divine: in our imperfect world, missing that, we count one thing noblest,—and that is soul.

One other thing I may mention. General Warren, our Corps commander, came up to me with pleasant words. "General," he says, "you have done splendid work. I am telegraphing the President. You will hear from it." Not long afterwards I received from the Government a brevet commission of Major-General, given, as it stated, "for conspicuous gallantry in action on the Quaker Road, March 29, 1865." I had previously received this brevet of the date of March 13th, purporting to be for meritorious services during that Virginia campaign. I begged permission to decline this and to accept the later one.

First looking after the comfort of my wounded horse in one of the farmsheds, I walked out alone over the field to see how it was faring for the "unreturning brave." It was sunset beyond the clouds; with us the murky battle-smoke and thickening mists wrapped the earth, darklier shaded in many a spot no light should look on more. Burials were even now begun; searchings, questionings, reliefs, recognitions, greetings, and farewells; last messages tenderly taken from manly lips for breaking hearts; insuppressible human moan; flickerings of heart-held song; vanishing prayer heavenward. But what could mortal do for mortal or human skill or sympathy avail for such deep need? I leaned over one and spoke to another as I passed, feeling how little now I could command. At length I kneeled above the sweet body of McEuen, where God's thought had folded its wing; and near by, where wrecks were thickly strewn, I came upon brave old Sickel lying calm and cheerful, with a shattered limb, and weakened by loss of blood while "fighting it through," but refusing to have more attention than came in his turn. Still pictured on my mind his splendid action where I had left him rallying his men, I sat down by him to give him such cheer as I could. He seemed to think I needed the comforting. The heroic flush was still on his face. "General," he whispers, smiling up, "you have the soul of the lion and the heart of the woman." "Take the benediction to yourself," was the reply; "you could not have thought that, if you had not been it." And that was our thought at parting for other trial, and through after years. For so it is: might and love, —they are the all;—fatherhood and motherhood of God himself, and of every godlike man.

Still we are gathering up our wounded; first filling the bleak old Quaker meeting-house with those requiring instant attention and tenderest care, then giving our best for the many more, sheltering them as we could, or out under the brooding rain, where nature was sighing her own requiem, but even this grateful to some parched lip or throbbing wound. Still, after the descending night had wrapped the world in its softening shroud the burials were going on (for we had other things for the morrow),—strange figures on some far edge, weirdly illumined by the lurid lanterns holding their light so close, yet magnifying every form and motion of the scene, all shadow-veiled and hooded like the procession of the "misericordia." Seeking also the wounded of the enemy, led mostly by moans and supplications,—souls left so lonely, forlorn, and far away from all the caring; caring for these too, and partly for that very reason; gathering them out of the cold and rain when possible,—for "blood is thicker than water,"—we treated them as our own. "How far that little candle throws its beams!" Indeed, in the hour of sorrow and disaster do we not all belong to each other? At last, having done all possible, our much-enduring men lay down under the rain and darkness descending so close, so stifling, so benumbing,—to sleep, to dream.

For my own part, I was fain to seek a corner of the sorrow-laden Lewis house, sinking down drenched and torn in that dark, unwholesome, scarcely vital air, fitting companion of the weakest there. But first of all, drawing near a rude kitchen box, by the smouldering light of a sodden candle, steadying my nerves to compose a letter to dear, high-souled Doctor McEuen of Philadelphia, remembering his last words commending to my care his only son, with the beseeching, almost consecrating hands laid on my shoulder,—to tell him how, in the forefront of battle and in act of heroic devotion, his noble boy had been lifted to his like, and his own cherished hope merged with immortal things.

Never to be forgotten,—that night of March twenty-ninth, on the Quaker Road. All night the dismal rain swept down the darkness, deep answering deep, soaking the fields and roads, and drenching the men stretched on the ground, sore with overstrain and wounds,—living, dead, and dying all shrouded in ghastly gloom. Before morning the roads were impassable for artillery and army-wagons, and nearly so for the ambulances, of our Corps and the Second, that crept up ghostlike through the shuddering mist. Under the spectral light of hovering lanterns hundreds of helpless patient sufferers were loaded in; to be taken from this scene of their manly valor, now so barren of all but human kindness, in long procession for the nearest hospital or railroad station,—and for what other station and what other greeting, what could they, or we, foreknow?

CHAPTER III

THE WHITE OAK ROAD

WITH customary cognizance of our purposes and plans, Lee had on the 28th of March ordered General Fitzhugh Lee with his division of cavalry—about 1300 strong—from the extreme left of his lines near Hanover Court House, to the extreme right in the vicinity of Five Forks, this being four or five miles beyond Lee's entrenched right, at which point it was thought Sheridan would attempt to break up the Southside Railroad. Longstreet had admonished him that the next move would be on his communications, urging him to put a sufficient force in the field to meet this. "Our greater danger," he said, "is from keeping too close within our trenches."[1] Such despatch had Fitzhugh Lee made that on the evening of the twenty-ninth he had arrived at Sutherlands Station, within six miles of Five Forks, and about that distance from our fight that afternoon on the Quaker Road. On the morning of the 29th, Lee had also despatched General R. H. Anderson with Bushrod Johnson's Division—

[1] *Manassas to Appomattox*, p. 588.

Gracie's, Ransom's, Wise's, and Wallace's Brigades —to reinforce his main entrenchments along the White Oak Road. It was these troops which we had encountered on the Quaker Road. Pickett's Division, consisting of the brigades of Stuart, Hunton, Corse, and Terry, about five thousand strong, was sent to the entrenchments along the Claiborne Road, and Roberts's Brigade of North Carolina cavalry, to picket the White Oak Road from the Claiborne, the right of their entrenchments, to Five Forks.

On the thirtieth, the Fifth Corps, relieved by the Second, moved to the left along the Boydton Road, advancing its left towards the right of the enemy's entrenchments on the White Oak Road. Lee, also, apprehensive for his right, sent McGowan's South Carolina Brigade and McRae's North Carolina, of Hill's Corps, to strengthen Bushrod Johnson's Division in the entrenchments there; but took two of Johnson's brigades—Ransom's and Wallace's—with three brigades of Pickett's Division (leaving Hunton's in the entrenchments), to go with Pickett to reinforce Fitzhugh Lee at Five Forks. W. H. F. Lee's Division of cavalry, about one thousand five hundred men, and Rosser's, about one thousand, were also ordered to Five Forks. These reinforcements did not reach Five Forks until the evening of the thirtieth.

The precise details of these orders and movements were, of course, not known to General Grant nor to any of his subordinates. But enough had been developed on the Quaker Road to lead

Grant to change materially his orginal purpose of making the destruction of the railroads the principal objective of Sheridan's movements. At the close of our fight there, Grant had despatched Sheridan: "Our line is now unbroken from Appomattox to Dinwiddie. I now feel like ending the matter, if possible, before going back. I do not want you, therefore, to cut loose and go after the enemy's roads at present. In the morning push around the enemy, if you can, and get on to his right rear. The movements of the enemy's cavalry may, of course, modify your action. We will act together as one army here, until it is seen what can be done with the enemy." Grant also telegraphed President Lincoln: "General Griffin was attacked near where the Quaker Road intersects the Boydton, but repulsed it easily, capturing about 100 prisoners." But on the morning of the 30th, he telegraphed the President again: "I understand the number of dead left by the enemy yesterday for us to bury was much greater than our own dead. Our captures also were larger than reported. This morning all our troops have been pushed forward." For the morning of the 30th in spite of the sodden earth and miry roads, we managed to pull through to the Boydton Plank Road, which the Fifth Corps occupied as far as its crossing of Gravelly Run. Meantime, Humphreys with the Second Corps, advanced on the right of the road, and pressing the Confederate pickets behind their entrenchments, held his line close up to them.

The effect of this message to Sheridan reached to something more than a measure of tactics. It brought him at once to Grant. It will be borne in mind that he was not under the orders of Meade, but an independent commander, subject to Grant alone. His original orders contemplated his handling his command as a flying column, independently of others—all the responsibility and all the glory being his own. The new instructions would bring him to act in conjunction with the Army of the Potomac, and render quite probable under army regulations and usages his coming under temporary command of General Meade, his senior in rank,—a position we do not find him in during this campaign. The logic of the new situation involved some interesting corollaries beyond the direct issue of arms.

In that dismal night of March 29th on the Quaker Road Sheridan was holding long and close conference with Grant, having ridden up through the mud and rain immediately on receiving the message announcing the change of plan, to Grant's headquarters a little in rear of us on Gravelly Run. All that was known of this interview to those outside was that at the close of it, Sheridan was directed to gain possession of Five Forks early in the morning. We could not help feeling that he should have taken possession of this before. For all the afternoon and night of the 29th, there was nothing to oppose him there but the right wing of Roberts' slender brigade, picketing the White Oak Road. But when he received a positive order to secure that point on the morning of the 30th, he seems to have moved so late and moderately that Fitzhugh Lee had time to march from Sutherland's Station to Five Forks, and thence half-way to Dinwiddle Court House to meet him; and even then, attacking with a single division, although this outnumbered the enemy by a thousand men,[1] he permitted his demonstration on Five Forks to be turned into a reconnaissance half-way out,[2] his advance being checked at the forks of the Ford and Boisseau Road, where it remained all night and until itself attacked the next morning.[3] It is true that the roads and fields were heavy with rain; but this did not prevent our two infantry corps from moving forward and establishing themselves in front of the White Oak Road, in face of considerable opposition; nor hinder Lee from zealously strengthening the right of his lines and pressing forward his reinforcements of infantry and cavalry to Fitzhugh Lee at Five Forks, where they arrived about sunset. What we cannot understand is why previous to that time General Sheridan, with thirteen thousand cavalry, had not found it practicable to make an effective demonstration on Five Forks, covered all the morning only by what few men Roberts had there picketing the White Oak Road, and after that

[1] General Devin's Division numbered, according to returns of March 30, 169 officers and 2830 men, present for duty.

[2] General Merritt's despatch of March 30th. *Rebellion Records*, Serial 97, p. 326.

[3] General Fitzhugh Lee's testimony. *Warren Court Records*, vol. i, p. 469.

time, all day, only by Fitzhugh Lee with eighteen hundred cavalry.

Early on the morning of the 31st the Fifth Corps had all advanced northerly beyond the Boydton Road towards the enemy at the junction of the White Oak and Claiborne Roads: Ayres, with the Second Division, in advance, about six hundred yards from this junction; Crawford, with the Third Division, on Ayres' right rear in echelon with him, about six hundred yards distant; and Griffin, with the First Division, in position about thirteen hundred yards in rear of a prolongation of Crawford's line to the left, entirely out of sight of both, owing to woods and broken ground, but within what was thought to be supporting distance. This position was along the southeast bank of a swampy branch of Gravelly Run, half a mile north of the Boydton Road, and a mile and a half south of the White Oak Road. Miles' Division of the Second Corps had extended to the left on the Boydton Road to connect with Griffin.

My command was the extreme left of our lines; my own brigade along the difficult branch of Gravelly Run, facing towards Ayres. Gregory, who had been directed by General Griffin to report to me for orders with his brigade for the rest of this campaign, was placed on the left, his line bent back at right angles along a country road leading from Boydton to the Claiborne Road. A portion of the artillery of the division was placed also in my lines to strengthen the defense of that flank, where we had reason to believe the enemy, after their old fashion, were very likely to make a dash upon our left while we were manœuvring to turn their right.

General Grant, understanding from General Sheridan that he was on the White Oak Road near Five Forks, on the afternoon of the 30th, had replied to him that his position on this road was of very great importance, and concluded this answer with these words: "Can you not push up towards Burgess' Mills on the White Oak Road?"[1]

General Grant's wishes, as now understood, were that we should gain possession of the White Oak Road in our front. This was indicated in a despatch from him March 30th, to General Meade, the purport of which was known to us and had much to do with shaping our energies for action. The despatch was the following:

> As Warren and Humphreys advance, thus shortening their line, I think the former had better move by the left flank as far as he can stretch out with safety, and cover the White Oak Road if he can. This will enable Sheridan to reach the Southside Road by Ford's Road, and, it may be, double the enemy up, so as to drive him out of his works south of Hatcher's Run

In accordance with this understanding, Ayres had made a careful examination of the situation in his front, upon the results of which General

[1] Sheridan's despatch to Grant, March 30th, 2.45 P.M., and Grant's reply thereto, Records, *Warren Court of Inquiry*, vol. ii., p 1309 It afterwards transpired that Sheridan's cavalry did not long hold this position. Grant's despatch to Meade, March 31st, *Rebellion Records*, Serial 97, p. 339.

Warren had reported to Generals Meade and Grant that he believed he could, with his whole corps, gain possession of the White Oak Road. This proposition was made in face of the information of Grant's order of 7.40 this morning, that owing to the heavy rains the troops were to remain substantially as they were, but that three days' more rations should be issued to the Fifth Corps; an intimation of a possible cutting loose from our base of supplies for a time.

Griffin's Division, being entrusted with a double duty—that of guarding the exposed left flank of the Fifth and Second Corps, and that of being in readiness to render prompt assistance in case of trouble arising from the demonstrations against the White Oak Road front—our adjustments had to be made for what in familiar speech is termed a "ticklish situation." Vague rumors from the direction of Five Forks, added to what we knew of the general probabilities, justified us in considerable anxiety. There was a queer expression on Griffin's face when he showed me a copy of a message from Grant to Sheridan, late the evening before, which gave us the comical satisfaction of knowing that our inward fears had good outside support. This was what we thus enjoyed: "From the information I have sent you of Warren's position, you will see that he is in danger of being attacked in the morning. If such occurs, be prepared to push up with all your force to assist him." The morning had now come. It is needless to remark that there was no lethargy in the minds of any on that left flank of ours in a situation so critical, whether for attack or defense.

It may seem strange that in such a state of things Warren should have made the suggestion for a movement to his front. But he was anxious, as were all his subordinates, to strike a blow in the line of our main business, which was to turn Lee's right and break up his army. Wet and worn and famished as all were, we were alive to the thought that promptness and vigor of action would at all events determine the conditions and chances of the campaign. And if this movement did not involve the immediate turning of Lee's right in his entrenchments, it would secure the White Oak Road to the west of them, which Grant had assured Sheridan was of so much importance, and would enable us to hold Lee's right in check, so that Sheridan could either advance on the White Oak Road toward us and Burgess' Mills, as Grant had asked him to do, or make a dash on the Southside Railroad, and cut their communications and turn their right by a wider sweep, as Grant had also suggested to him to do.

Late in the forenoon Warren received through General Webb, chief of staff, the following order: "General Meade directs that should you determine by your reconnaissance that you can gain possession of, and hold, the White Oak Road, you are to do so, notwithstanding the order to suspend operations to-day." This gave a sudden turn to dreams. In that humiliation, fasting, and prayer, visions arose like prophecy of old. We felt the swing and sweep; we saw the enemy turned front and flank across the White Oak Road; Sheridan flashing on our wheeling flank, cutting communications, enfilading the Claiborne entrenchments; our Second Corps over the main works, followed up by our troops in the old lines seizing the supreme moment to smash in the Petersburg defenses, scatter and capture all that was left of Lee's army, and sweep away every menace to the old flag between us and the James River,—mirage and glamour of boyish fancy, measuring things by its heart; daydreams of men familiar with disaster, drenched and famished, but building, as ever, castles of their souls above the level river of death.

It was with mingled feelings of mortification, apprehension, and desperation that, in the very ecstasy of these visions, word came to us of Sheridan's latest despatch to Grant the evening before, that Pickett's Division of infantry was deployed along the White Oak Road, his right reaching to Five Forks, and the whole rebel cavalry was massing at that place, so that Sheridan would be held in check by them instead of dashing up, as was his wont, to give a cyclone edge to our wheeling flank. Grant's despatch to Meade, transmitting this, was a dire disenchantment. The knell rang thus: "From this despatch Warren will not have the cavalry support on his left flank that I expected. He must watch closely his left flank."

Although Grant had given out word that there should be no movement of troops that day, Lee seems not so to have resolved. Driven to seize every advantage or desperate expedient, he had ordered four brigades, those of Wise, Gracie, and Hunton, with McGowan's South Carolina Brigade, to move out from their entrenchments, get across the flank of the Fifth Corps and smash it in. We did not know this, but it was the very situation which Grant had made the occasion for attacking ourselves. It was a strange coincidence, and it was to both parties a surprise.

This was the condition of things and of minds when the advance ordered for the White Oak Road was put into execution. Ayres advanced soldier-like, as was his nature; resolute, firm-hearted, fearing nothing, in truth not fearing quite enough. Although he believed his advance would bring on a battle, he moved without skirmishers, but in a wedgelike formation guarding both flanks. His First Brigade, commanded by the gallant Winthrop, had the lead in line of battle, his right and rear supported by the Third Brigade, that of Gwyn, who was accounted a good fighter; and Denison's Maryland Brigade formed in column on Winthrop's left and rear, ready to face outward by the left flank in case of need; while a brigade of Crawford's was held in reserve in rear of the center. This would seem to be a prudent and strong formation of Ayres' command. The enemy's onset was swift and the encounter sudden. The blow fell without warning, enveloping Ayres' complete front. It appears that McGowan's Brigade struck squarely on Winthrop's left flank, with an oblique fire also on the Maryland Brigade, while the rest of the attacking forces struck on his front and right. General Hunton[1] says they were not expecting to strike our troops so soon and that the attack was not made by usual order, but that on discovering our advance so close upon them a gallant lieutenant in his brigade sprang in front of his line, waving his sword, with the shout, "Follow me, boys!" whereupon all three brigades on their right dashed forward to the charge. Winthrop was overwhelmed and his supports demoralized. All he could hope for was to retire in good order. This he exerted himself to effect. But this is not an easy thing to do when once the retreat is started before a spirited foe superior in numbers, or in the flush of success. In vain the sturdy Denison strove to stem the torrent. A disabling wound struck down his brave example, and the effect of this shows how much the moral forces have to do in sustaining the physical. Brigade after brigade broke, that strange impulse termed a "panic" took effect, and the retreat became a rout.

Ayres, like a roaring lion, endeavors to check this disorder, and makes a stand on each favoring crest and wooded ravine. But in vain. His men stream past him. They come back on Crawford's veteran division and burst through it in spite of all the indignant Kellogg can do, involving this also in the demoralization; and the whole crowd comes back reckless of everything but to get behind the lines on the Boydton Road, plunging through the swampy run, breaking through Griffin's

[1] *Records, Warren Court*, p. 623.

right where he and Bartlett re-form them behind the Third Brigade. The pursuing enemy swarming down the opposite bank are checked there by the sharp musketry from our line. Not knowing but the enemy were in force sufficient to smash through us on the left, I prepared for action. Griffin authorized me to use a portion of the artillery, and I swung two pieces to the right front, while he himself with great exertion got a battery into position along Bartlett's front. The enemy were gathering force, although in much confusion.

I was apprehensive of an attempt to take us in flank on the left in Gregory's front, and was about giving my attention to this, when General Warren and General Griffin came down at full speed, both out of breath, with their efforts to rally the panic-stricken men whose honor was their own, and evidently under great stress of feeling. Griffin breaks forth first, after his high-proof fashion: "General Chamberlain, the Fifth Corps is eternally damned." I essayed some pleasantry: "Not till you are in heaven." Griffin does not smile nor hear, but keeps right on: "I tell Warren you will wipe out this disgrace, and that's what we're here for." Then Warren breaks out, with stirring phrase, but uttered as if in a strangely compressed tone: "General Chamberlain, will you save the honor of the Fifth Corps? That's all there is about it." That appeal demanded a chivalrous response. Honor is a mighty sentiment, and the Fifth Corps was dear to me. But my answer was not up to the keynote—I confess that. I was expecting every moment an attack on my left flank now that the enemy had disclosed our situation. And my little brigade had taken the brunt of things thus far, but the day before the last, winning a hard-fought field from which they had come off grievously thinned and torn and worn, and whence I had but hardly brought myself away. I mentioned Bartlett, who had our largest and best brigade, which had been but little engaged. "We have come to you; you know what that means," was the only answer. "I'll try it, General; only don't let anybody stop me except the enemy." I had reason for that protest as things had been going. "I will have a bridge ready here in less than an hour. You can't get men through this swamp in any kind of order," says Warren. "It may do to come back on, General; it will not do to stop for that now. My men will go straight through." So at a word the First Battalion of the 198th Pennsylvania, Major Glenn commanding, plunges into the muddy branch, waist deep and more,[1] with cartridge-boxes borne upon the bayonet sockets above the turbid waters; the Second Battalion commanded now by Captain Stanton, since Sickel and McEuen were gone, keeping the banks beyond clear of the enemy by their well-directed fire, until the First has formed in skirmishing order and pressed up the bank. I then pushed through to support Glenn and formed

[1] General Warren states in his testimony before the Court of Inquiry that this stream was sixty feet wide and four or five feet deep. *Records*, p. 717.

my brigade in line of battle on the opposite bank, followed by Gregory's in column of regiments. The enemy fell back without much resistance until finding supports on broken strong ground they made stand after stand. Griffin followed with Bartlett's Brigade, in reserve. In due time Ayres' troops got across and followed up on our left rear, while Crawford was somewhere to our right and rear, but out of sight or reach after we had once cleared the bank of the stream. It seems that General Warren sent to General Meade the following despatch: "I am going to send forward a brigade from my left, supported by all I can get of Crawford and Ayres, and attack. . . . This will take place about 1.45, if the enemy does not attack sooner." This was the only recognition or record we were to have in official reports; it was not all we were to achieve in unwritten history.

At about this time, Miles, of the Second Corps, had, after the fashion of that corps, gone in handsomely in his front, somewhat to the right of our division, and pressed so far out as to flank Wise's Brigade on the left of the troops that had attacked Ayres, and drove them back half-way to their starting-point. This had the effect to induce the enemy in my front to retire their line to a favorable position on the crest of a ravine where they made another determined stand. After sharp fighting here we drove them across an extensive field into some works they seemed to have already prepared, of the usual sort in field operations—logs and earth,—from which they delivered a severe fire which caused the right of my line to waver. Taking advantage of the slight shelter of a crest in the open field I was preparing for a final charge, when I received an order purporting to be Warren's, to halt my command and hold my position until he could reconnoitre conditions in my front. I did not like this much. It was a hard place to stay in. The staff officer who brought me the order had his horse shot under him as he delivered it. I rode back to see what the order meant. I found General Griffin and General Warren in the edge of the woods overlooking the field, and reported my plans. We had already more than recovered the ground taken and lost by the Second and Third Divisions. The Fifth Corps had been rapidly and completely vindicated, and the question was now of taking the White Oak Road, which had been the object of so much wishing and worrying. It was evident that things could not remain as they were. The enemy would soon attack and drive me back. And it would cost many men even to try to withdraw from such a position. The enemy's main works were directly on my right flank, and how the intervening woods might be utilized to cover an assault on that flank none of us knew. I proposed to put Gregory's Brigade into those woods, by battalion in echelon by the left, by which formation he would take in flank and reverse in succession any attacks on my right. When Gregory should be well advanced I would charge the works across the field with my own brigade. My plan being approved, I instructed Gregory to keep in the woods, moving forward with an inclination towards his left to keep him closed in toward me, and at the same time to open the intervals in his echelons so that he would be free to deliver a strong fire on his own front if necessary, and the moment he struck any opposition to open at once with full volleys and make all the demonstration he could, and I would seize that moment to make a dash at the works in my front. Had I known of the fact that General Lee himself was personally directing affairs in our front,[1] I might not have been so rash, or thought myself so cool.

Riding forward I informed my officers of my purpose and had their warm support. Soon the roar of Gregory's guns rose in the woods like a whirlwind. We sounded bugles "Forward!" and that way we go; mounted officers leading their commands, pieces at the right shoulder until at close quarters. The action and color of the scene were supported by my horse Charlemagne, who, though battered and torn as I was, insisted on coming up. We belonged together; he knew that as well as I. He had been shot down in battle twice before; but his Morgan endurance was under him, and his Kentucky blood was up.

What we had to do could not be done by firing. This was foot-and-hand business. We went with a rush, not minding ranks nor alignments, but with open front to lessen loss from the long-range rifles. Within effective range, about three hun-

[1] Testimony of General Hunton and General McGowan, *Warren Court Records*, vol. i., pp. 625 and 648.

dred yards, the sharp, cutting fire made us reel and shiver. Now, quick or never! On and over! The impetuous 185th New York rolls over the enemy's right, and seems to swallow it up; the 198th Pennsylvania, with its fourteen companies, half veterans, half soldiers "born so," swing in upon their left, striking Hunton's Brigade in front, and for a few minutes there is a seething wave of countercurrents, then rolling back, leaving a fringe of wrecks,—and all is over. We pour over the works, swing to the right and drive the enemy into their entrenchments along the Claiborne Road, and then establish ourselves across the White Oak Road facing northeast, and take breath.[1]

Major Woodward in his history of the 198th Pennsylvania, giving a graphic outline of the last dash, closes with an incident I had not recorded. "Only for a moment," he says, "did the sudden and terrible blast of death cause the right of the line to waver. On they dashed, every color flying, officers leading, right in among the enemy, leaping the breastworks,—a confused struggle of firing, cutting, thrusting, a tremendous surge of force, both moral and physical, on the enemy's breaking lines,—and the works were carried. Private Augustus Ziever captured the flag of the 46th Virginia in mounting one of the parapets, and handed it to General Chamberlain in the midst of the mêlée, who immediately gave it back to him, telling him

[1] General Hunton, since Senator from Virginia, said in his testimony before the Warren Court, speaking of this charge, "I thought it was one of the most gallant things I had ever seen."—*Records*, Part 1, p. 625.

to keep it and take the credit that belonged to him. Almost that entire regiment was captured at the same time." It scarcely need be added that the man who captured that battle flag was sent with it in person to General Warren, and that he received a medal of honor from the Government.

In due time Gregory came up out of the woods, his face beaming with satisfaction at the result, to which his solid work, so faithfully performed, had been essential. His brigade was placed in line along the White Oak Road on our right, and a picket thrown out close up to the enemy's works. This movement had taken three hours, and was almost a continuous fight, with several crescendo passages, and a final cadence of wild, chromatic sweeps settling into the steady keynote, thrilling with the chords of its unwritten overtones. It had cost us a hundred men, but this was all too great, of men like these,—and for oblivion. It was to cost us something more—a sense of fruitlessness and thanklessness.

It seems that in the black moment, when our two divisions were coming back in confusion, Meade had asked Grant to have Sheridan strike the attacking force on their right and rear, as he had been ordered to do in case Warren was attacked. For we have Grant's message to Meade, sent at 12.40, which is evidently a reply: "It will take so long to communicate with Sheridan that he cannot be brought to co-operation unless he comes up in obedience to orders sent him last night. I understood General Forsyth to say that as soon as another division of cavalry got up, he would send it forward. It may be there now. I will send to him again, at once."

So far, to all appearance, all was well. The Fifth Corps was across the White Oak Road. General Grant's wish that we should extend our left across this road as near to the enemy as possible, so that Sheridan could double up the enemy and drive him north of Hatcher's Run, had been literally fulfilled. It had cost us three days' hard work and hard fighting, and more than two thousand men. It had disclosed vital points. General Grant's notice of all this, as given in his *Memoirs* (vol. ii., p. 435), representing all these movements as subordinated to those of General Sheridan, is the following: "There was considerable fighting in taking up these new positions for the Second and Fifth Corps, in which the Army of the James had also to participate somewhat, and the losses were quite severe. This is what was known as the battle of the White Oak Road."[1]

The understanding of this affair has been confused by the impression that it was the Second

[1] Contrasts are sometimes illumining. When our assault on the enemy's right, March 31st, was followed by General Miles' attack on the Claiborne entrenchments on the second of April, after the exigency at Five Forks had called away most of its defenders,—Generals Anderson and Johnson, with Hunton, Wise, Gracie, and Fulton's Brigades being of the number,—and the whole rebel army was demoralized, General Grant, now free to appreciate such action, despatches General Meade at once: "Miles has made a big thing of it, and deserves the highest praise for the pertinacity with which he stuck to the enemy until he wrung from him victory." Verily, something besides circumstances can "alter cases."

Corps troops which attacked and drove back the forces of the enemy that had driven in the Second and Third Divisions of the Fifth Corps. In the complicated rush and momentous consummation of the campaign, and particularly in the singular history of the Fifth Corps for those days, in which corps and division and brigade commanders were changed, there was no one specially charged with the care of seeing to it that the movements of this corps in relation to other corps were properly reported as to the important points of time as well as of place. General Miles, doubtless, supposed he was attacking the same troops that had repulsed part of the Fifth Corps. He moved promptly when Griffin, with infantry and artillery, was checking the onrushing enemy now close upon our front; and, attacking in his own front—that of the Second Corps,—fought his way valiantly close up to the enemy's works in that part of their line. Miles reported to Humphreys that he was "ahead of the Fifth Corps," which subsequently bore off to the left of him and left a wide interval. This expression must not be understood as direction in a right line. It is used rather as related to the angular distance between the Boydton and the White Oak Roads, this being less where Miles was, on the right, and widening by a large angle towards the left, where the Fifth Corps was. It is as one line is ahead of another when advanced in echelon; or as a ship tacking to windward with another is said to be "ahead" of the latter when she is on the weather beam of it. Miles did not come in contact with a single regiment that had attacked the Fifth Corps. He struck quite to the right of us all, attacking in his own front. But it got into the reports otherwise, and "went up." Grant accepted it as given; and so it has got into history, and never can be gotten out. General Miles did not get ahead of the Fifth Corps that day, but he came up gallantly on its flank and rendered it great assistance by turning the flank of General Wise and keeping the enemy from massing on our front. He reports the capture of the flag of the 47th Alabama, a regiment of Law's old brigade of Longstreet's Corps, which was nowhere near the front of the Fifth Corps on this day.

In the investigations before the Court of Inquiry, General Warren felt under the necessity of excusing himself from the responsibility of the disastrous results of Ayres' advance on the morning of the thirty-first. He is at pains to show that he did not intend an attack there, although he had suggested the probable success of such movement.[1] What then was this advance? Surely not to create a diversion in favor of Sheridan before Dinwiddie. At all events, there was an endeavor to get possession of the White Oak Road. And that could not be done without bringing on a battle, as Ayres said he knew, beforehand,[2] and afterwards knew still better, and we also, unmistakably. Warren was evidently impressed with Grant's desire to gain the White Oak Road in order to strike the

[1] *Records, Warren Court*, Part ii., p. 1525.
[2] Testimony, *Warren Court Records*, Part i., p. 247.

enemy's right as soon as possible; and he was not aware of any change of intention.

But however this may have been, when Ayres' advance was repulsed, why was it felt necessary to recover that field and "the honor of the Fifth Corps"? Unless it was the intention to take forcible possession of the White Oak Road, the recovery of that field was not a tactical necessity, but only—if I may so speak—a sentimental necessity. And there was no more dishonor in this reconnaissance—if it was only that—being driven back than in Sheridan's reconnaissance toward Five Forks being driven back upon Dinwiddie, for his conduct in which he received only praise. It is evident that General Grant thought an attack was somehow involved; for hearing of Ayres' repulse, he blames General Warren for not attacking with his whole corps, and asks General Meade, "What is to prevent him from pitching in with his whole corps and attacking before giving him time to entrench or retire in good order to his old entrenchments?" This is exactly what was done, before receiving this suggestion; but it did not elicit approval, or even notice, from Grant or Meade, or Warren. As things turned, Warren was put under a strong motive to ignore this episode; and as for Grant, he had other interests in mind.

In our innocence we thought we had gained a great advantage. We had the White Oak Road, and were across it, and as near to the enemy as possible, according to Grant's wish. Now we were ready for the consummate stroke, the achievement of the object for which all this toil and trial had been undergone. It needed but little more. The splendid Second Corps was on our right, close up to the enemy's works. We were more than ready. If only Sheridan with but a single division of our cavalry could disengage himself from his occupation before Dinwiddie, so far away to our rear, and now so far off from any strategic point, where he had first been placed for the purpose of raiding upon the Danville and Southside Railroads,—which objective had been distinctly given up in orders by General Grant,—if with his audacity and insistance Sheridan could have placed himself in position to obey Grant's order, and come to Warren's assistance when he was attacked, by a dash up between us and Five Forks, we would have swiftly inaugurated the beginning of the end,—Grant's main wish and purpose latest expressed to Sheridan, of ending matters here before he went back. But another, and by far minor, objective interposed. Instead of the cavalry coming to help us complete our victories at the front, we were to go to the rescue of Sheridan at the rear.

Little did we dream that on the evening of the 30th, Grant had formed the intention of detaching the Fifth Corps to operate with Sheridan in turning the enemy's right. This was consistent, however, with the understanding in the midnight conference on the 29th. The proposition to Sheridan was this: "If your situation in the morning is such as to justify the belief that you can turn the enemy's right with the assistance of a corps of infantry entirely detached from the balance of the army, I will so detach the Fifth Corps and place the whole under your command for the operation. Let me know early in the morning as you can your judgment in the matter, and I will make the necessary orders. . . ." Precisely what Warren had proposed to do at that very time on Gravelly Run, only Sheridan would not have been in chief command. His assistance had, however, been promised to Warren in case he was attacked. Sheridan replies to this on the morning of the 31st. " . . . If the ground would permit, I believe I could, with the Sixth Corps, turn the enemy's right, or break through his lines; but I would not like the Fifth Corps to make such an attempt." By "turning the enemy's right," and "breaking through his lines," he meant only the isolated position at Five Forks, where for two days past there was nothing to prevent his handling them alone, and easily cutting the Southside Railroad. Fortunately for our cause, Lee was so little like himself as to allow the detachment of a considerable portion of his infantry from the entrenchments on the evening of the 30th to reinforce this position, for the sake, probably, of covering the Southside Road, to which, however, this was not the only key.

Asking for the Sixth Corps shows a characteristic intensity of self-consciousness and disregard of the material elements of the situation wholly unlike the habits of our commanders in the Army of the Potomac. The Sixth Corps was away on the right center of our lines, even beyond Ord with the Army of the James, and the roads were impracticable for a rapid movement like that demanded. Grant's predilection for his forceful and brilliant cavalry commander could not overcome the material difficulty of moving the Sixth Corps from its place in the main line before Petersburg: he could only offer him the Fifth. And Meade, with meekness quite suggestive of a newly regenerate nature, seems to have offered no objection to this distraction from the main objective, and this inauguration of proceedings which repeatedly broke his army into detachments serving under other commanders, and whereby, in the popular prestige and final honors of the campaign, the commander of the Army of the Potomac found himself subordinated to the militant cavalry commander of the newly made "Middle Military Division."

So while Warren was begging to be permitted to take his corps through fields sodden saddle-girth deep with rain and mire, and get across the right of Lee's entrenched position, the purpose had already been formed of sending him and his corps to try to force the enemy from the position where they were gathering for a stand after having forced Sheridan's cavalry back upon its base at the Boisseau Cross Road, and holding his main body inactive at Dinwiddie a whole day through. And after Warren had accomplished all that he had undertaken in accordance with the expressed wishes of his superiors, this purpose was to be put into execution.

Minds accustomed to consider evidence could not resist the impression that at the midnight conference on the rainy night of March 29th, when Grant had announced that they would act together as one army, one item of the arrangement was that nothing should be allowed to interfere with Sheridan's being the leading spirit, and so actual field-commander in this enterprise. I am not sure that we can blame Sheridan or Grant for this if it were so. But it was at least a good working hypothesis on which to explain facts.

I do not know that Warren was then aware of General Grant's loss of interest in this movement for the White Oak Road since the new plan for Sheridan and the Fifth Corps. Let us recall: at eight o'clock on the evening before, Meade had sent Grant a despatch from Warren, suggesting this movement. Meade forwarded it to Grant, with the remark: "I think his suggestion the best thing we can do under existing circumstances—that is, let Humphreys relieve Griffin, and let Warren move on to the White Oak Road, and endeavor to turn the enemy's right." To this Grant replied at 8.35: "It will just suit what I intended to propose—to let Humphreys relieve Griffin's Division, and let that move further to the left. Warren should get himself strong to-night." Orders being sent out accordingly, and reported by Meade, General Grant replies late that evening: "Your orders to Warren are right. I do not expect him to advance in the morning. I supposed, however, that he was now up to the White Oak Road. If he is not, I do not want him to move up without further orders."[1] Meade replies: "He will not be allowed to advance unless you so direct."[2]

It is impossible to think that Warren knew of this last word of Grant on the subject of the White Oak Road, but, as we read it now, it throws light on many things then "dark." It was consistent with Grant's new purpose, but it must have perplexed Meade. And at the turn things took—and men also—during the next forenoon and midday, what must have been the vexation in Grant's imperturbable mind, and the ebullition of the few unsanctified remnants in Meade's strained and restrained spirit, those who knew them can freely imagine. And as for Warren, when all this light broke upon him, in the midst of his own hardly corrected reverses, into what sullen depths his spirit must have been cast, to find himself liable to a suit for breach of promise for going out to an open-handed meeting with Robert Lee of the White Oak Road when he was already clandestinely engaged to Philip Sheridan of Dinwiddie.

A new anxiety now arose. Just as we had got settled in our position on the White Oak Road, heavy firing was heard from the direction of Sheri-

[1] *Records, Warren Court*, vol. ii., p. 1242.

[2] This is to be compared with Meade's order of 10.30 A.M., March 31st through General Webb: see *ante*.

dan's supposed position. This attracted eager attention on our part as, with that open flank, Sheridan's movements were all important to us. At my headquarters we had dismounted, but had not ventured yet to slacken girths. I was standing on a little eminence, wrapped in thoughts of the declining day and of these heavy waves of sound, which doubtless had some message for us, soon or sometime, when Warren came up with anxious earnestness of manner, and asked me what I thought of this firing,—whether it was nearing or receding. I believed it was receding towards Dinwiddie; that was what had deepened my thoughts. Testing the opinion by all tokens known to us, Warren came to the same conclusion. He then for a few minutes discussed the situation and the question of possible duty for us in the absence of orders. I expressed the opinion that Grant was looking out for Sheridan, and if help were needed, he would be more likely to send Miles than us, as he well knew we were at a critical point, and one important for his further plans as we understood them, especially as Lee was known to be personally directing affairs in our front. However, I thought it quite probable that we should be blamed for not going to the support of Sheridan even without orders, when we believed the enemy had got the advantage of him. "Well, will you go?" Warren asked. "Certainly, General, if you think it best; but surely you do not want to abandon this position." At this point, General Griffin came up and Warren asked him to send

Bartlett's Brigade at once to threaten the rear of the enemy then pressing upon Sheridan. That took away our best brigade. Bartlett was an experienced and capable officer, and the hazardous and trying task he had in hand would be well done.

Just after sunset Warren came out again, and we crept on our hands and knees out to our extreme picket within two hundred yards of the enemy's works, near the angle of the Claiborne Road. There was some stir on our picket line, and the enemy opened with musketry and artillery, which gave us all the information we wanted. That salient was well fortified. The artillery was protected by embrasures and little lunettes, so that they could get a slant- and cross-fire on any movement we should make within their range.

I then began to put my troops into bivouac for the night, and extended my picket around my left and rear to the White Oak Road, where it joined the right of Ayres' picket line. It was an anxious night along that front. The darkness that deepened around and over us was not much heavier than that which shrouded our minds, and to some degree shadowed our spirits. We did not know what was to come, or go. We were alert—Gregory and I—on the picket line nearly all the night, and Griffin came up to us at frequent intervals, wide-awake as we were.

In the meantime many things had been going on, and going back. It came to us now, in the middle of the night, that Sheridan had been attacked by Fitzhugh Lee and Pickett's infantry and driven pell-mell into Dinwiddie. He could hardly hold himself there. The polarities of things were reversed. Instead of admitting the Fifth Corps to the contemplated honor of turning Lee's right, or breaking through his lines, between Dinwiddie and Five Forks, orders and entreaties came fast and thick, in every sense of these terms, for the Fifth Corps to leave the White Oak Road, Lee's company, and everything else, and rush back five miles to the rear, floundering through the mire and dark, to help Sheridan stay where Pickett and Fitzhugh Lee had put him. Indeed, the suggestive information had leaked out from Grant's headquarters that Sheridan might be expected to retreat by way of the Vaughan Road, quite to the rear of our entire left. This would leave all the forces that had routed Sheridan at perfect liberty to fall upon our exposed flank, and catch the Fifth Corps to be bandied to and fro between them and the enemy in their fortifications near at hand. By the time the Fifth Corps began to be picked to pieces by divisions and brigades, and finally made a shuttle-cock as an entire organization, the situation of things and of persons had very much changed.

At 6.30 P.M., General Warren received an order to send a brigade to Sheridan's relief by the shortest road threatening the rear of the enemy then in his front. Soon other orders followed,—the last of these being to send the brigade by the Boydton Road. This would have been quite a different matter. But Bartlett had already been gone an hour when this order came, and to the Crump Road, reaching this by aid of a cart track through woods and mire. Of course, Warren could not recall Bartlett. But to comply as nearly as possible with the order, he at once directed General Pearson, who with three of Bartlett's regiments was guarding the trains on the Boydton Road, to move immediately down towards Dinwiddie. Pearson got to the crossing of the main stream of Gravelly Run, and finding that the bridge was gone, and the stream not fordable, halted for orders. But things were crowding thick and fast. Pearson's orders were countermanded, and orders came from army headquarters for Griffin's Division to go.

On the news of Sheridan's discomfiture, Grant seems first to have thought of Warren's predicament. In a despatch to Meade early in the evening he says: "I would much rather have Warren back on the Plank Road than to be attacked front and rear where he is. He should entrench, front and rear of his left, at least, and be ready to make a good fight of it if he is attacked in the morning. We will make no offensive movement ourselves to-morrow."

That was on the evening before the battle of Five Forks.

This was a significant despatch; showing among other things Grant's intention of holding on, if possible, for the present at least, to the White Oak Road, at the Claiborne salient; for that was where our two advanced brigades of the Fifth

Corps were holding. This evidence has not been well appreciated by those who have formed their judgment, or written the history, of those three days' battles. And Meade had been trying all day to get up entrenching tools and implements for making the roads passable for wheels. A thousand men had been working at this for the two days past.

At 8.30 came the notice,—communicated confidentially, I remember,—that the whole army was going to contract its lines. At nine o'clock came the order from Grant to Meade: "Let Warren draw back at once to his position on the Boydton Road, and send a division of infantry to Sheridan's relief. The troops to Sheridan should start at once, and go down the Boydton Road." Meade promptly sent orders for the corps to retire, and for Griffin to go to Sheridan, and go at once.

Apparently nobody at general headquarters seems to have remembered two incidents concerning the selection of Griffin's Division for this movement: first, that Bartlett of this division was already by this time down upon the enemy's rear, by another more direct though more difficult road, and in a far more effective position for the main purpose than could be reached by the Boydton; and secondly, that the two remaining brigades of this division were with me on and across the White Oak Road,—the farthest off from the Boydton Road, and most impeded by difficult ground, of any troops remaining on our lines. Another circumstance, forgotten or ignored, was that the bridge at the Plank Road crossing of Gravelly Run was gone,[1] and that the stream was not fordable for infantry. Warren, in reporting his proceeding to comply with the order, reported also the destruction of the bridge and his intention to repair it; but this seems somehow, from first to last, to have added to the impatience felt toward him at those headquarters.

Grant had experienced a change of mind—a complete and decided one. His imperative order now received meant giving up entirely the position we had just been ordered to entrench, across the hard-won White Oak Road. Within ten minutes from the receipt of this order, Warren directed his division commanders to gather up their pickets and all outlying troops, and take position on the Boydton Road. Griffin was directed to recall Bartlett and then move down the Plank Road and report to Sheridan. But as it would take time for Griffin to get his scattered division together and draw back through the mud and darkness to the Boydton Road, ready to start for Sheridan, Warren, anxious to fulfill the spirit and object of the order, rather than render a mechanical obedience to the letter of it, sends his nearest division, under Ayres, the strong, stern old soldier of the Mexican War, to start at once for Sheridan. Meantime, the divisions of Griffin and Crawford were

[1] Colonel Theodore Lyman, aid-de-camp on the staff of General Meade, wrote in his diary on the night of March 30th: "Roads reduced to a hopeless pudding, Gravelly Run swollen to treble its usual size, and Hatcher's Run swept away its bridges and required pontoons."—*Records, Warren Court of Inquiry*, vol. i., p. 519.

taking steps to obey the order to mass on the Boydton Road. For my own part, I did not move a man, wishing to give my men all possible time to rest, until Bartlett should arrive, who must come past my rear.

This was the situation when at half-past ten in the evening came an order throwing everything into a complete muddle. It was from Meade to Warren: "Send Griffin promptly as ordered by the Boydton Plank Road, but move the balance of your command by the road Bartlett is on, and strike the enemy in rear, who is between him and Dinwiddie. Should the enemy turn on you, your line of retreat will be by J. M. Brooks' and R. Boisseau's on Boydton Road. You must be very prompt in this movement, and get the forks of the road at Brooks' so as to open to Boisseau's. Don't encumber yourself with anything that will impede your progress, or prevent your moving in any direction across the country." The grim humor of the last suggestion was probably lost on Warren, in his present distraction. "Moving in any direction" in the blackness of darkness across that country of swamps and sloughs and quicksands, would be a comedy with the savage forces of nature and of man in pantomime, and a spectacle for the laughter of the gods. Nor was there much left to encumber ourselves with, more especially in the incident of food. Grant had been very anxious about rations for us ever since early morning, when he had said that although there were to be no movements that day, the Fifth Corps must be supplied with three days' rations more. But all the day nothing had been gotten up. Indeed, I do not know how they could have found us, or got to us if they had. Grant had repeated imperative orders to Meade to spare no exertions in getting rations forward to the Fifth Corps; whereupon Meade, who had himself eaten salt with this old Corps, gave orders to get supplies to us anyway—if not possible for trains, then by pack-mules. The fortunate and picturesque conjuncture was that some few rations were thus got up by the flexible and fitting donkey-train, while we were floundering and plunging from every direction for our rendezvous on the Boydton Road or elsewhere, just at that witching hour of the night when the flying cross-shuttle of oscillating military orders was weaving such a web of movements between the unsubstantial footing of earth and the more substantial blackness of the midnight sky, matched only by the benighted mind.

By this last order the Corps was to be turned end for end, and inside out. Poor Warren might be forgiven if at such an order his head swam and his wits collapsed. He responds thus, and has been much blamed for it by those under canvas, then and since: "I issued my orders on General Webb's first despatch to fall back; which made the divisions retire in the order of Ayres, Crawford, and Griffin, which was the order they could most rapidly move in. I cannot change them to-night without producing confusion that will render all my operations nugatory. I will now send General

Ayres to General Sheridan, and take General Griffin and General Crawford to move against the enemy, as this last despatch directs I should. I cannot accomplish the object of the orders I have received."[1]

But what inconceivable addition to the confusion came in the following despatch from General Meade to Warren at one o'clock at night: "Would not time be gained by sending troops by the Quaker Road? Sheridan cannot maintain himself at Dinwiddie without reinforcements, and yours are the only ones that can be sent. Use every exertion to get the troops to him as soon as possible. If necessary, send troops by both roads, and give up the rear attack."

Rapidly changing plans and movements in effecting the single purpose for which battle is delivered are what a soldier must expect; and the ability to form them wisely and promptly illustrates and tests military capacity. But the conditions in this case rendered the execution of these peculiarly perplexing. Orders had to pass through many hands; and in the difficulties of delivery owing to distance and the nature of the ground, the situation which called for them had often entirely changed. Hence some discretion as to details in executing a definite purpose must be accorded to subordinate commanders.

[1] See this despatch of 10.55 P.M., March 31st. *War Records*, Serial 97, p. 367. General Warren, in his testimony before the Court of Inquiry, claimed that the word "Otherwise" should be prefixed to the last sentence of this order, as it was dictated.—*Records*, p. 730, note.

Look for a moment at a summary of the orders Warren received that evening, after we had reached the White Oak Road, affecting his command in detail:

1. To send a brigade to menace the enemy's rear before Sheridan.

But he had already of his own accord sent Bartlett's Brigade, of Griffin's Division, the nearest troops, by the nearest way.

2. To send this brigade by the Boydton Road instead of the Crump.

This was a very different direction, and of different tactical effect. It being impossible to recall Bartlett, Warren sent Pearson, already on the Boydton Road, with a detachment of Bartlett's Brigade.

3. To send Griffin's Division by the Boydton Road to Sheridan, and draw back the whole corps to that road.

Griffin's Division being widely and far scattered and impossible to be collected for hours, Warren sends Ayres' Division, nearest, and most disengaged.

4. To send Ayres and Crawford by the way Bartlett had gone, and insisting on Griffin's going by Boydton Road.

This would cause Ayres and Bartlett to exchange places—crossing each other in a long, difficult, and needless march.

5. Ayres having gone, according to Warren's orders, Griffin and Crawford to go by Bartlett's way.

But Griffin had sent for Bartlett to withdraw

from his position and join the division ready to mass on the Boydton Road.

It is difficult to keep a clear head in trying to see into this muddle now: we can imagine the state of Warren's mind. But this was not all. Within the space of two hours, Warren received orders involving important movements for his entire corps, in four different directions. These came in rapid succession, and in the following order:

1. To entrench where he was (on the White Oak Road), and be ready for a fight in the morning. This from Grant.

2. To fall back with the whole corps from the White Oak Road to the Boydton, and send a division by this road to relieve Sheridan. This from Grant.

3. Griffin to be pushed down the Boydton Road, but the rest of the corps—Ayres and Crawford—to go across the fields to the Crump Road, the way Bartlett had gone, and attack the enemy in rear who were opposing Sheridan. This from Meade.

This required a movement in precisely the opposite direction from that indicated in the preceding order,—which was now partly executed. Ayres had already started.

4. Meade's advice to send these troops by the Quaker Road (ten miles around), and give up the rear attack.

5. To these may be added the actual final movement, which was that Ayres went down the

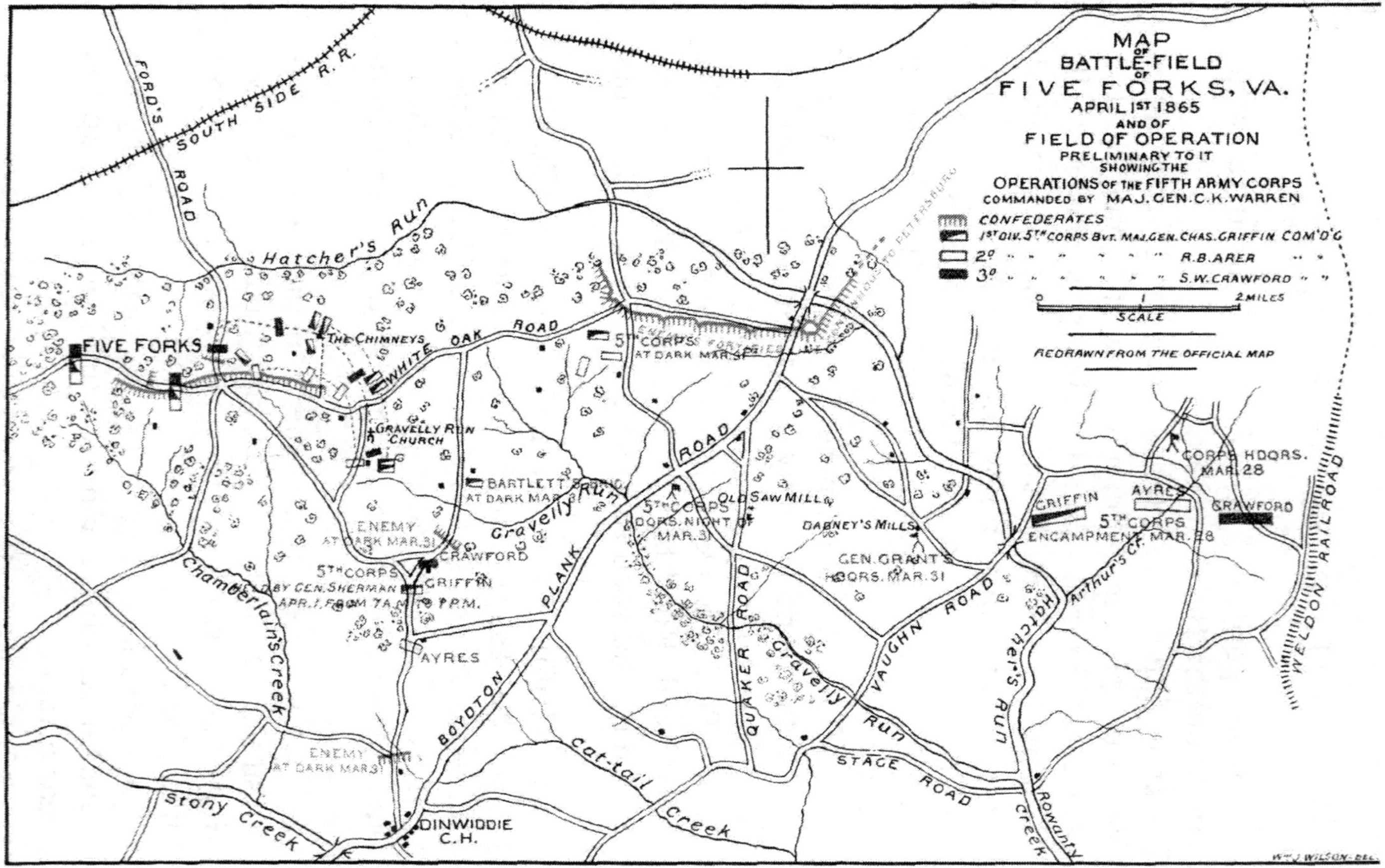
MAP
OF
BATTLE-FIELD
OF
FIVE FORKS, VA.
APRIL 1ST 1865
AND OF
FIELD OF OPERATION
PRELIMINARY TO IT
SHOWING THE
OPERATIONS OF THE FIFTH ARMY CORPS
COMMANDED BY MAJ. GEN. C. K. WARREN
CONFEDERATES
1ST DIV. 5TH CORPS BVT. MAJ.GEN. CHAS. GRIFFIN COM'D'G
2D " " " " " R.B.AYRES " "
3D " " " " " S.W.CRAWFORD " "
0 1 2 MILES
SCALE
REDRAWN FROM THE OFFICIAL MAP
FORD'S ROAD
SOUTH SIDE R.R.
Hatcher's Run
FIVE FORKS
THE CHIMNEYS
WHITE OAK ROAD
GRAVELLY RUN CHURCH
5TH CORPS AT DARK MAR. 31
BARTLETT AT DARK MAR. 31
Gravelly Run
ENEMY AT DARK MAR. 31
CRAWFORD
GRIFFIN
5TH CORPS
AYRES
Chamberlain's Creek
BOYDTON PLANK ROAD
ENEMY AT DARK MAR. 31
DINWIDDIE C.H.
Stony Creek
Cat-tail Creek
5TH CORPS HDQRS. NIGHT OF MAR. 31
OLD SAW MILL
DABNEY'S MILLS
GEN. GRANT'S HDQRS. MAR. 31
QUAKER ROAD
Gravelly Run
STAGE ROAD
VAUGHN ROAD
Hatcher's Run
Rowanty Creek
Arthur's Cr.
GRIFFIN
AYRES
CRAWFORD
5TH CORPS ENCAMPMENT MAR. 28
CORPS HDQRS. MAR. 28
WELDON RAILROAD
WM J. WILSON. DEL.

Boydton Road, and Griffin and Crawford went by the "dirt" road across the country to the Crump Road as indicated in Meade's previous orders.

There is one thing more. General Grant thought it necessary, in order to make sure that Sheridan should have complete and absolute command of these troops, to send a special message asking Meade to make that distinct announcement to Sheridan. (Despatch of 10.34 P.M., March 31st.) To this Meade replies that he had ordered the Fifth Corps to Sheridan, and adds: "The messenger to Sheridan has gone now, so that I cannot add what you desire about his taking command, but I take it for granted he will do so, as he is senior. I will instruct Warren to report to him."

So General Grant's solicitude lest Sheridan should forget to assume command, as the regulations clearly provided, was faithfully ministered to by that expert in nervous diseases,—Meade.

The orders which came to General Warren that night were to an amazing degree confused and conflicting. This is charging no blame on any particular person. We will call it, if you please, the fault of circumstances. But of course many evil effects of such conditions must naturally fall upon the officer receiving them. Although the responsibility according to military usage and ethics rests upon the officer originating the order, yet the practical effects are apt to fall upon the officer trying to execute it. And when he is not allowed to use his judgment as to the details of his own command, it makes it very hard for him sometimes. Indeed it is not very pleasant to be a subordinate officer, especially if one is also at the same time a commanding officer.

But in this case I think the trouble was the result of other recognizable contributory circumstances,—if I might not say causes.

1. The awkwardness of having in the field so many superior, or rather co-ordinate, commanders: Grant, commanding the United States Armies, with his headquarters immediately with those of the commander of the Army of the Potomac; unintentionally but necessarily confusing authority and detracting from the dignity and independence of this subordinate; Meade, commanding the Army of the Potomac, only two corps of which were with him,—and one of these half the time under Sheridan,—the two others being on the extreme right of our entrenched lines, with Ord and the Army of the James between them; Sheridan, maintaining an independent cavalry command, but in such ticklish touch with the Fifth Corps that it hardly knew from moment to moment whether it was under Meade or Sheridan.

2. A double objective: one point being Sheridan's independent operations to cut the enemy's communications; the other, the turning of Lee's right and breaking up his army by our infantry. It is true this double objective was in terms given up when Sheridan was informed all were to "act together as one army"; but the trouble is, this precept was never strictly carried into effect; inas-

much as General Sheridan was not inclined to serve under any other commander but Grant, and it became difficult to humor him in this without embarrassing other operations. And, as a matter of fact, the communications were not cut, either on the Southside or the Danville Roads, until our infantry struck them,—Sheridan, however, contributing in his own way to this result.

3. These two supreme commanders being at such distance from the fields of operation on the 31st of March, that it was impossible to have a complete mutual understanding at the minute when orders were to be put into effect. Nor could they make themselves alike familiar with material conditions, such as grounds and bridges, or with the existing state of things at important junctures, owing to rapid, unforeseen changes.

4. Time lost, and sequence confused, by the difficulty of getting over the ground to carry orders or to obey them, owing to the condition of the roads, or lack of them, and the extreme darkness of the night.

We had very able officers of the general staff at each headquarters; otherwise things might have been worse. The responsibilities, labors, tests, and perils—physical and moral—that often fall upon staff officers in the field are great and trying. Upon their intelligence, alertness, accuracy of observation and report, their promptitude, energy, and endurance, the fate of a corps or a field may depend.

The frictions, mischances, and misunderstandings of all these circumstances falling across Warren's path, might well have bewildered the brightest mind, and rendered nugatory the most faithful intentions.

Meantime, it may well be conceived we who held that extreme front line had an anxious night. Griffin was with me most of the time, and in investigating the state of things in front of our picket lines some time after midnight, we discovered that the enemy were carefully putting out their fires all along their own visible front. Griffin regards this as evidence of a contemplated movement on us, and he sends this information and suggestion to headquarters, and thus adds a new element to the already well-shaken mixture of uncertainty and seeming cross-purposes. But with us, the chief result was an anxiety that forbade a moment's relaxation from intense vigilance.

Meantime Ayres had kept on, according to Warren's first orders to him, getting a small installment of rations on the way, and arriving at Warren's "Bridge of Sighs" on the Gravelly Run just as it was ready, at about two o'clock in the morning, whence he pushed down the Plank Road and reported to Sheridan before Dinwiddie at the dawning of day. Whereupon he was informed that he had advanced two miles farther than General Sheridan desired, and he had to face about his exhausted men and go back to a cross-road which he had passed for the very sufficient reason that Sheridan had no staff-officer there to guide him where he was wanted.

At three o'clock I had got in my pickets, which were replaced by Crawford's, and let my men rest as quietly as possible, knowing there would be heavy burdens laid on them in the morning. For, while dividing the sporadic mule-rations, word came to us that the Fifth Corps, as an organization, was to report to Sheridan at once and be placed under his orders. We kept our heads and hearts as well as we could; for we thought both would be needed. It was near daylight when my command —all there was of Griffin's Division then left on the front—drew out from the White Oak Road; Crawford's Division replacing us, to be brought off carefully under Warren's eye. We shortly picked up Bartlett's returning brigade, halted, way-worn and jaded with marching and countermarching, and struck off in the direction of the Boisseau houses and the Crump Road, following their heavy tracks in the mud and mire marking a way where before there was none; one of those recommended "directions across the country," which this veteran brigade found itself thus compelled to travel for the third time in lieu of rest or rations, churning the sloughs and quicksands with emotions and expressions that could be conjectured only by a veteran of the Old Testament dispensation.

I moved with much caution in approaching doubtful vicinities, throwing forward an advance guard which, as we expected to encounter the enemy in force, I held immediately in my own hand. Griffin followed at the head of my leading brigade, ready for whatever should happen. Arrived at the banks of the south branch of Gravelly Run, where Bartlett had made his dispositions the night before, from a mile in our front the glitter of advancing cavalry caught my eye, saber-scabbards and belt-brasses flashing back the level rays of the rising sun. Believing this to be nothing else than the rebel cavalry we expected to find somewhere before us, we made dispositions for instant attack. But the steady on-coming soon revealed the blue of our own cavalry, with Sheridan's weird battle-flag in the van. I reduce my front, get into the road again, and hardly less anxious than before move forward to meet Sheridan.

We come face to face. The sunlight helps out the expression of each a little. I salute: "I report to you, General, with the head of Griffin's Division." The courteous recognition is given. Then the stern word, more charge than question: "Why did you not come before? Where is Warren?"—"He is at the rear of the column, sir."—"That is where I expected to find him. What is he doing there?"—"General, we are withdrawing from the White Oak Road, where we fought all day. General Warren is bringing off his last division, expecting an attack." Griffin comes up. My responsibility is at an end. I feel better. I am directed to mass my troops by the roadside. We are not sorry for that. Ayres soon comes up on the Brooks Road. Crawford arrives at length, and masses his troops also, near the J. Boisseau house, at the junction of the Five Forks Road. We were on the ground the enemy had occupied the evening before. It was Bartlett's outstretched line in their rear, magnified by the magic lens of night into the semblance of the whole Fifth Corps right upon them, which induced them to withdraw from Sheridan's front and fall back upon Five Forks.[1] So after all Bartlett had as good as fought a successful battle, by a movement which might have been praised as Napoleonic had other fortunes favored.

General Warren has been blamed, and perhaps justly, for attacking with a single division on the White Oak Road. As he denies that he intended this for an attack, we will put it that he is blamed for not sufficiently supporting a reconnaissance; so that the repulse of it involved the disorderly retreat of two divisions of his corps. It is to be said to this that he very shortly more than recovered this ground, driving the enemy with serious loss into his works. But at the worst, was that a fault hitherto unknown among corps or army commanders? Sheridan attacked with a single division when he was ordered to take Five Forks on the day before, and was driven back by a force very inferior to that he had in hand. He was not blamed, although the result of this failure was the next day's dire misfortunes. And on this very day, driven back discomfited into Dinwiddie, he was not blamed; he was praised,—and in this high fashion. General Grant in his official report and subsequent histories, speaking of this repulse, says: "Here General Sheridan displayed great general-

[1] Testimony of General Fitzhugh Lee, *Warren Court*, vol. i., pp. 475 and 481.

ship. Instead of retreating with his whole command on the main army, to tell the story of superior forces encountered, he deployed his cavalry on foot, leaving only mounted men enough to take charge of the horses. This compelled the enemy to deploy over a vast extent of wooded and broken country and made his progress slow."

This definition of great generalship was intended, no doubt, to reassure Sheridan; but it was encouraging all around. It would let quite a number of modest colonels, of both sides, into the temple of fame.

Warren was deposed from his command the next day, mainly, I have no doubt, under the irritation at his being slow in getting up to Sheridan the night before from the White Oak Road. But he was working and fighting all day to hold the advanced left flank of Grant's chosen position, and harassed all night with conflicting and stultifying orders, while held between two threatening forces: his left, with nothing to prevent Lee's choice troops disengaged from Sheridan from striking it a crushing blow; and on the other hand, Lee himself in person, evidently regarding this the vital point, with all the troops he could gather there, ready to deliver on that little front a mortal stroke. For it is not true, as has been stated by high authority, that any troops that had fought us on the White Oak Road had gone to Pickett's support at Five Forks that day. And when in the gray of the morning he moved out to receive Sheridan's not overgracious welcome to the Fifth Corps,

Warren withdrew under the very eyes of Lee, his rear division faced by the rear rank, ready for the not-improbable attack, himself the last to leave the field that might have been so glorious, now fated to be forgotten.

I enliven this somber story by a brief personal reference. Somehow—I never quite understood it—General Griffin, in the confusion of that dashing and leaping about, lost his sword—scabbard and all. Seeing him ride up to me in that way, I instantly unhooked my belt and sheathing my sword handed it to the General with the assurance that I should be proud if he would accept it, as a token of what I could not then fully set forth in words. He did accept it and outdid me in the expression of sentiments. One of the noble captains (Rehfuss) of the 198th Pennsylvania instantly handed me one that lay on the line we had carried, —I should say, perhaps, he had carried,—and which was a fine sword with a "Palmetto" engraved scabbard. I took it until our muster out, when I returned it to Captain Rehfuss, with words of remembrance which he seemed to appreciate.

This sword of mine has a peculiar history since that time. General Griffin at the close of the war was ordered to a command in Texas, and took this sword with him. Here the yellow fever breaking out he was advised by the War Department to take a leave of absence and return to his home for a season. He declined; saying that his duty was where his command was, and that he would stay by his men. He took the fever and died before friends could reach him. Sometime afterwards I received through the War Department a box containing this sword and General Griffin's cap worn by him in the Civil War, and familiar to all his soldiers, together with the last division battle-flag we carried in the field, and the division bugle, which had sounded all the calls during the last two years of the war. I could not express the regard in which these relics are held.

It may be presumption to offer opinions on the operations of that day under such commanders. But having ventured some statements of fact that seem like criticism, it may be required of me to suggest what better could have been done, or to show reason why that which was done was not the best. I submit therefore, the following remarks:

1. Five Forks should have been occupied on the thirtieth as Grant had ordered, and when there was nothing formidable to oppose. The cavalry could then easily strike the Southside Railroad, and the Fifth and Second Corps be extended to envelop the entire right of the enemy's position, and at the opportune moment the general assault could be successfully made, as Grant had contemplated when he formed his purpose of acting as one army with all his forces in the field.

2. This plan failing, there were two openings promising good results: one, to let the cavalry linger about Dinwiddie and threaten Lee's communications, so as to draw out a large body of his troops from the entrenchments into the open where they could be attacked on equal ground,

and his army be at least materially crippled; the other, to direct the assault immediately on the right of Lee's entrenched lines on the Fifth Corps front,—the cavalry, of course, sweeping around their flank so as to take them in reverse, while the infantry concentrated on their weakest point.

A third thing was to do a little of both; and this is what we seem to have adopted, playing from one to the other, fitfully and indecisively, more than one day and night.

Beyond doubt it was Grant's plan when he formed his new purpose on the night of the twenty-ninth, to turn the enemy on their Claiborne flank, and follow this up sharply by vigorous assault on the weakest point of their main line in front of Petersburg. The positions taken up by the Fifth and Second Corps are explained by such a purpose, and the trying tasks and hard fighting required of them for the first three days are therein justified. The evidence of this purpose is ample.

Everything was made ready, but the attack was suspended. I am not upon the inquiry whether this was postponed until Sheridan should have done something; my point is that if, or when, this purpose was abandoned for another line of action, other dispositions should have been promptly made, and information given to officers charged with responsibilities, and environed with difficulties as Warren was, so that they could catch the change of key. Grant had set the machinery in motion for the White Oak Road, and it was hard and slow work to reverse it when he suddenly changed his tactics, and resolved to concentrate on Sheridan. Why was the Fifth Corps advanced after Ayres' repulse? The "reconnaissance" had been made; the enemy's position and strength ascertained, and our party had returned to the main line. There was no justification in pressing so hard on that point of the White Oak Road, at such costs, unless we meant to follow up this attack to distinct and final results. This may possibly be laid to Warren's charge in his anxiety and agony to "save the honor of the Fifth Corps." But this was not essential to the grander tactics of the field. I sometimes blame myself,—if I may presume to exalt myself into such high company,—for going beyond the actual recovery of Ayres' lost field, and pressing on for the White Oak Road, when it was not readily permitted me to do so. It may be that my too youthful impetuosity about the White Oak Road got Warren into this false position across this road, where all night, possessed with seven devils, we tried to get down to Sheridan and Five Forks. But I verily believed that what we wanted was the enemy's right, on the White Oak Road. How could we then know Grant's change of purpose? However, it was all a mistake if we were going to abandon everything before morning. We should have been withdrawn at once, and put in position for the new demonstration. That order to mass on the Boydton Road, received at about ten o'clock at night, should have been given much earlier, as soon as we could safely move away from the presence of the enemy, if we were to reinforce Sheridan on his own lines.

3. But better than this, as things were, it would have been to leave a small force on the White Oak Road to occupy the enemy's attention, and move the whole Fifth Corps to attack the rear of the enemy then confronting Sheridan, as Meade suggested to Grant at ten o'clock at night. It would have been as easy for us all to go, as for Bartlett. With such force we would not have stopped on Gravelly Run, but would have struck Pickett's and Fitzhugh Lee's rear, and compelled them to make a bivouac under our supervision on that ground where they had "deployed." They would not have been able to retire in the morning, as they were constrained to do by Bartlett's demonstration.

4. No doubt it was right to save the honor of the cavalry before Dinwiddie, as of the Fifth Corps before the White Oak Road; and Sheridan's withdrawal to that place having lured out so large a force—six thousand infantry and four thousand cavalry—from a good military position to the exposed one at Five Forks, it was good tactics to fall upon them and smash them up. Lee, strangely enough, did not think we would do this; so he held himself at the right of his main line on the White Oak Road, as the point requiring his presence; and sent reinforcements from there for his imperiled detachment only so late that they did not report until after the struggle at Five Forks was all over.

But we owe much to fortune. Had the enemy on the afternoon of the 31st let Fitzhugh Lee with his cavalry reinforcements occupy Sheridan, and rushed Pickett's Division with the two brigades of Johnson's down the White Oak Road upon the flank of the momentarily demoralized Fifth Corps, while Hunton and Gracie and Wallace and Wise were on its front, we should have had trouble. Or had they, after repulsing Sheridan towards evening, left the cavalry deployed across his front to baffle his observation, while Pickett should anticipate and forestall the movement of Bartlett's Brigade, and come across conversely from that Crump Road to fall upon our untenable flank position, it would have opened all eyes to the weakness and error of our whole situation. What would have become of us, only some higher power than any there could say.

So we part, after this strangely broken acquaintance,—Sheridan, the Fifth Corps, and White Oak Road. Whether the interventions that brought intended purposes and effects to nought were through the agency of supernal or infernal spirits, we must believe that it was by one of those mysterious overrulings of Providence, or what some might call poetic justice, and some the irony of history, that it befell Sheridan to have with him at Five Forks and at Appomattox Court House—not slow nor inconspicuous—the deprecated, but inexpugnable, old Fifth Corps.

CHAPTER IV

FIVE FORKS

AFTER such a day and night as that of the 31st of March, 1865, the morning of April 1st found the men of the Fifth Corps strangely glad they were alive. They had experienced a kaleidoscopic regeneration. They were ready for the next new turn—whether of Fortunatus or Torquemada. The tests of ordinary probation had been passed. All the effects of "humiliation, fasting, and prayer," believed to sink the body and exalt the spirit, had been fully wrought in them. At the weird midnight trumpet-call they rose from their sepulchral fields as those over whom death no longer has any power. Their pulling out for the march in the ghostly mists of dawn looked like a passage in the transmigration of souls—not sent back to work out the remnant of their sins as animals, but lifted to the "third plane" by those three days of the underworld,—eliminating sense, incorporating soul.

The vicissitudes of that day, and the grave and whimsical experiences out of which we emerged into it, exhibited the play of that curious law of the universe seen in tides, reactions, or reversals of polarities at certain points of tension or extremes of pressure, and which appears also in the mixed relations of men and things. There are pressure-points of experience at which the insupportably disagreeable becomes "a jolly good time." When you cannot move in the line of least resistance, you take a very peculiar pleasure in crowding the point of greatest resistance. No doubt there is in the ultimate reasons of human probation special place for that quality of manhood called perseverance, patience, pluck, push, persistence, pertinacity, or whatever name beginning with this "explosive mute," the excess of which, exhibited by persons or things, is somewhat profanely referred to as "pure cussedness."

The pleasantries associated with April 1st were not much put in play: none of those men were going to be "fooled" that day.

When we joined the cavalry, some of us were aware of a little shadow cast between the two chief luminaries,—him of the cavalry and him of the infantry; but that by no means darkened our disks. If not hale fellows, we were well met. The two arms of the service embraced each other heartily, glad to share fortunes. Particularly we; for the cavalry had the habit of being a little ahead, and so, as the Germans said, "got all the pullets." And we thought the cavalry, though a little piqued at our not going down and picking up what they had left at Dinwiddie the night before, were quite willing we should share whatever they should get to-day. Sheridan had also come to the opinion that infantry was "a good thing to have around,"—however by some queer break in the hierarchy of honor subordinated to the chevaliers, the biped to the quadruped, and by some freak of etymology named "infantry"—the speechless—whether because they had nothing to answer for, or knew too much and mustn't tell. We were glad to be united to Sheridan, too, after the broken engagements of the day before, perhaps renewed reluctantly by him; glad to fight under him, instead of away from him, hoping that when he really struck, the enemy would hurt more than friends.

We cannot wonder that Sheridan might not be in the best of humor that morning. It is not pleasant for a temperament like his to experience the contradiction of having the ardent expectations of himself and his superior turned into disaster and retreat. It was but natural that he should be incensed against Warren. For not deeply impressed with the recollection that he had found himself unable to go to the assistance of Warren as he had been ordered to do, his mind retained the irritation of vainly expecting assistance from Warren the moment he desired it, without considering what Warren might have on hand at the same time. Nor could Warren be expected to be in a very exuberant mood after such a day and night. Hence the auguries for the cup of loving-kindness on this crowning day of Five Forks were not favorable. Each of them was under the shadow of yesterday: one, of a mortifying repulse; the other, of thankless success. Were Warren a mind-reader he would have known it was a time to put on a warmer manner towards Sheridan,—for a voice of doom was in the air.

That morning, two hours after the head of the Fifth Corps column had reported to General Sheridan, an officer of the artillery staff had occasion to find where the Fifth Corps was, evidently not knowing that under orders from superiors it had been like "all Gaul," divided into three parts,—and went for that purpose to the point where Warren had had his headquarters the night before. Warren, in leaving at daybreak, had not removed his headquarters' material; but in consideration for his staff, who had been on severe duty all night, told Colonel Locke, Captain Melcher, and a few others to stay and take a little rest before resuming the tasking duties of the coming day. It was about nine o'clock in the morning when the artillery officer reached Warren's old headquarters, and suddenly rousing Colonel Locke asked where the Fifth Corps was. Locke, so abruptly wakened, his sound sleep bridging the break of his last night's consciousness, rubbed his eyes, and with dazed simplicity answered that when he went to sleep the Fifth Corps was halted to build a bridge at Gravelly Run on the Plank Road. No time was lost in reporting this at headquarters, without making further inquiries as to the whereabouts of the Fifth Corps, now for three hours with Sheridan on the Five Forks Road. Thereupon General Grant forthwith sends General Babcock to tell

General Sheridan that "if he had any reason to be dissatisfied with General Warren," or as it has since been put, "if in his opinion the interests of the service gave occasion for it," he might relieve him from command of his corps.[1]

"So do we walk amidst the precipices of our fate."

Griffin's and Crawford's Divisions were massed near the house of J. Boisseau, on the road leading from Dinwiddie Court House to Five Forks. Ayres was halted a mile back at the junction of the Brooks Road, which he had reached by his roundabout, forced march during the night. We were waiting for Sheridan, at last. And he was waiting until the cavalry should complete one more "reconnoissance," to determine the enemy's position and disposition at Five Forks, three miles northward.

Although the trains which had got up were chiefly ammunition wagons, a considerable halt was indicated and the men seized the occasion to eat, to rest, to sleep,—exercises they had not much indulged in for the last three days,—and to make

[1] *Records, Warren Court*, testimony of Captain Warner, p. 38, of General Babcock, p. 901, also of General Sheridan, p. 93, and General Grant, p. 1028.

General Grant afterwards stated that although this information about the bridge was the occasion, it was not the reason, of his authorization of General Sheridan to depose General Warren from his command. *Ibid.*, p. 1030.

That bridge—for a non-existent one—had a strange potency. Considering how various were the tests of which it was made the instrument, it well rivals that other "*pons asinorum*" of Euclid, and certainly the associated triangle was of surpassing attributes, for the squares described on the two "legs" of it were far more than equal to that so laboriously executed on its hypothenuse.

their toilets, which means to wring out their few articles of clothing, seriatim, and let the sun shine into the bottom of their shoes; and also—those who could—to make up their vital equation of three days' rations—hard-tack, pork, coffee, and sugar—by stuffing their haversacks with twenty rounds extra ammunition.

Meantime those of us who were likely to have some special responsibilities during the approaching battle, had anxious thoughts. We had drawn away from the doubly confused conflict of yesterday; we were now fairly with Sheridan, cut off from reach of other wills, absolved from the task of obeying commands that made our action seem like truants driving hoops,—resulting mostly in tripping up dignitaries, and having a pretty hard time ourselves, without paternal consolations when we got home. We expected something out of the common order now. General Griffin came and sat by me on the bank-side and talked quite freely. He said Sheridan was much disturbed at the operations of the day before, as Grant's language to him about this had been unwontedly severe, and that all of us would have to help make up for that day's damage.[1]

[1] This was in a despatch sent by Grant to Sheridan at about 2 P.M. on the 31st of March, just as I was advancing, after Ayres' repulse. This read: "Warren's and Miles' Divisions are now advancing. I hope your cavalry is up where it will be of assistance. Let me know how matters stand now with the cavalry; where they are, what their orders, etc. If it had been possible to have had a division or two of them well up on the right-hand road taken by Merritt yesterday, they could have fallen on the enemy's rear as they were pursuing Ayres and Crawford"—*Records, Warren Court*, p. 1313.

He told me also that Grant had given Sheridan authority to remove Warren from command of the corps, when he found occasion, and that we should see lively times before the day was over. We remarked how these things must affect Sheridan: Grant's censure of his failures the day before; the obligation to win a decisive battle to-day; and the power put in his hands to remove Warren. We could not but sympathize with Sheridan in his present perplexities, and, anxious for Warren, were resolved to do our part to make things go right.[1]

[1] The mental attitude of the parties concerned will be understood by reference to the despatches of the Hon Charles A Dana to the War Office during the previous summer. They were doubtless known to Sheridan, as to the higher officers of the Fifth Corps Those of May 9th and 12th, 1864, referring to Warren's movements as slow and piecemeal, so as to fail of the desired effect in the plans of the general commanding the army. He accuses him of not handling his corps in a mass, and even implies a positive disobedience of orders on his part in attacking with a division when ordered by Grant to attack with his whole corps. (Serial No 67, pp. 64, 68.)

Still the Fifth Corps "got in" enough to lose ten thousand six hundred and eighty-six men in the first two fights. (Dana's report, *War Records*, Serial 64, p. 71)

Even more light is turned on. For no despatch of Dana's concerning Warren compares in severity with Dana's to the Secretary of War, July 7, 1864, denouncing General Meade, and advising that he be removed from the command of the army. (Serial No. 80, p. 35.)

It now appears that Warren was in great disfavor with Meade also, after arriving before Petersburg. Meade called upon Warren to ask to be relieved from command of his corps on the alternative that charges would be preferred against him. (Dana's despatch, June 20, 1864, *War Records*, Serial No. 80, p. 26)

Meade was much displeased, too, with Warren for his characteristic remark to the effect that no proper superior commanding officer was present at the time of the Mine explosion, to take control of the whole affair.

And now, with Sheridan against him, poor Warren may well have

The troops had enjoyed about four hours of this unwonted rest when, the cavalry having completed its reconnoissance, we were ordered forward. We turned off on a narrow road said to lead pretty nearly to the left of the enemy's defenses at Five Forks on the White Oak Road. Crawford led, followed by Griffin and Ayres,—the natural order for prompt and free movement. The road had been much cut up by repeated scurries of both the contending parties, and was even yet obstructed by cavalry led horses, and other obstacles, which it would seem strange had not been got off the track during all this halt. We who were trying to follow closely were brought to frequent standstill. This was vexatious,—our men being hurried to their feet in heavy marching order, carrying on their backs perhaps three days' life for themselves and a pretty heavy installment of death for their antagonists, and now compelled every few minutes to come to a huddled halt in the muddy road, "marking time" and marking place also with deep discontent. In about two hours we get up where Sheridan wants us, in some open ground and thin woods near the Gravelly Run Church, and form as we arrive, by brigades in column of regiments. The men's good nature seems a little ruffled on account of their manner of marching or being marched. They have their own way of expressing their wonder why we could not have taken a shorter

---

wished at least for David's faculty of putting his grievances into song, with variations on the theme "Many bulls have compassed me about; yea, many strong bulls of Bashan."

road to this cavalry rendezvous, rather than to be dragged around the two long sides of an acute-angled triangle to get to it,—why the two-legged animals might not have taken the short route and the four-legged ones the long one,—in short, what magic relics there were about "J. Boisseau's," that we should be obliged to make a painful pilgrimage there before we were purified enough to die at Five Forks.

It is now about four o'clock. Near the church is a group of restless forms and grim visages, expressing their different tempers and temperaments in full tone. First of all the chiefs: Sheridan, dark and tense, walking up and down the earth, seeking—well, we will say—some adequate vehicle or projectile of expression at the prospect of the sun's going down on nothing but his wrath; evidently having availed himself of some incidental instrumentalities to this end, more or less explicit or expletive. Warren is sitting there like a caged eagle or rather like a man making desperate effort to command himself when he has to obey unwelcome orders,—all his moral energies compressed into the nerve centers somewhere behind his eyes and masked pale cheek and compressed lip. Griffin is alert and independent, sincere to the core, at his ease, ready for anything,—for a dash at the enemy with battery front, or his best friend with a bit of satire when his keen sense of the incongruous or pretentious is struck; Bartlett, with drawn face, like a Turkish cimetar, sharp, springy, curved outward, damascened by various experience and in the flame and whirl of battle, leading his brigade like a demigod, as in a chariot of fire he was lifted to his like.

The corps formation was: Ayres on the left, west of the Church Road, the division in double brigade front in two lines, and Winthrop with the First Brigade in reserve, in rear of his center; Crawford on the right, east of the road, in similar formation; Griffin in rear of Crawford, with Bartlett's Brigade in double column of regiments, three lines deep; my own brigade next, somewhat in echelon to the right, with three battalion lines in close order, while Gregory at first was held massed in my rear. General Mackenzie's cavalry, of the Army of the James, had been ordered up from Dinwiddie, to cross the White Oak Road and move forward with us covering our right flank. Nevertheless, just as we were moving, General Griffin cautioned me: "Don't be too sure about Mackenzie; keep a sharp lookout for your own right." Accordingly I had Gregory throw out a small battalion as skirmishers and flankers, and march another regiment by the flank on our right, ready to face outwards, and let his other regiment follow in my brigade column.

At four o'clock we moved down the Gravelly Run Church Road, our lines as we supposed nearly parallel to the White Oak Road, with Ayres directed on the angle of the enemy's works. Just as we started there came from General Warren a copy of a diagram of the proposed movement. I was surprised at this. It showed our front of

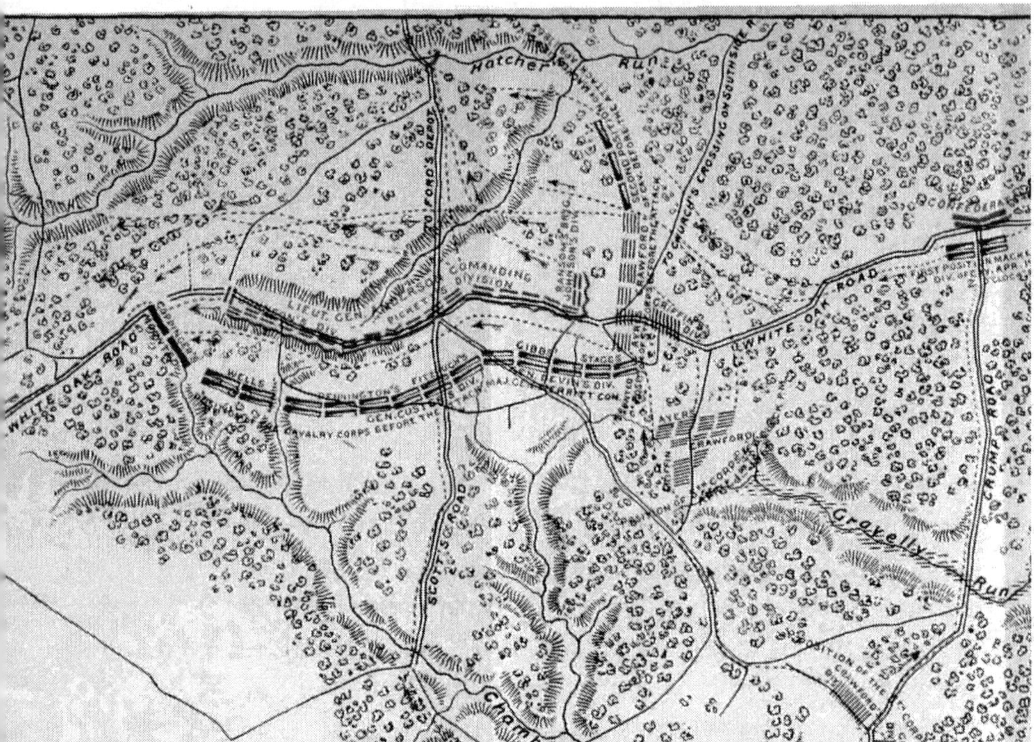
THE
BATTLE-FIELD
OF
FIVE FORKS, VA.
FOUGHT APRIL 1ST 1865
REDRAWN FROM THE MAP
PREPARED UNDER
DIRECTION OF
BRVT MAJ. G.L. GILLESPIE, U.S.A.
JULY, 1865
SCALE
0
1/4
1/2
3/4
1 MILE
U.S. INFANTRY
U.S. CAVALRY
CONFEDERATES
Hatcher
Run
WHITE OAK ROAD
WHITE OAK ROAD
TO FORD'S DEPOT
TO CHURCH'S CROSSING ON SOUTHSIDE R.R.
LIEUT. GEN.
COMANDING
PICKETT'S DIVISION
CRAWFORD'S DIV.
GRIFFIN'S DIV.
AYRES
GEN. CUSTER'S DIV.
CAVALRY CORPS BEFORE THE
SCOTT'S ROAD
Gravelly
Run
CRUMP'S ROAD
Chamberlain's
Creek
GEN. AYRES' DIV.
MACKENZIE'S DIV.
DINWIDDIE
C.H.
Stony
Creek
FLAT FOOT ROAD
ONE REGT OF DAVIES' BRIG.
GUARDING
BRIDGE

movement to be quite oblique to the White Oak Road,—as much as half a right angle,—with the center of Crawford's Division directed upon the angle, and Ayres, of course, thrown far to the left, so as to strike the enemy's works halfway to Five Forks. Griffin was shown as following Crawford; but the whole direction was such that all of us would strike the enemy's main line before any of us could touch the White Oak Road. The diagram, far from clearing my mind, added confusion to surprise. The order read: "The line will move forward as formed till it reaches the White Oak Road, when it will swing around to the left, perpendicular to the White Oak Road. General Merritt's and General Custer's cavalry will charge the enemy's line as soon as the infantry get engaged." This was perfectly clear. The whole corps was to reach the White Oak Road before any portion of it should change direction to the left; Ayres was to attack the angle, and the rest of us swing round and sweep down the entrenchments along the White Oak Road.

The diagram showed the Gravelly Run Church Road as leading directly to and past the angle of the enemy's works. The formation shown led us across the Church Road and not across the White Oak Road at all, which at the point of direction was behind the enemy's entrenched lines. According to this, Crawford and not Ayres would strike the angle. Ayres would strike the breastworks well up toward the cavalry,—quite a way from any support Griffin's division could give him.

Ill at ease in such uncertainty I rode over to General Griffin, who with General Warren was close on my left at this early stage of the movement, and asked for an explanation. Griffin answers quickly: "We will not worry ourselves about diagrams. We are to follow Crawford. Circumstances will soon develop our duty." In the meantime we were moving right square down the Church Road, and not oblique to it as the diagram indicated. However, I quieted my mind with the reflection that the earth certainly was a known quantity, and the enemy susceptible to discovery, whatever might be true of roads, diagrams, or understandings.

Crawford crossed the White Oak Road, his line nearly parallel to it, without encountering the expected angle. This road, it is to be remarked, made a considerable bend northerly at the crossing of the Church Road, so that Ayres had not reached it when Crawford and even Griffin were across. We naturally supposed the angle was still ahead. Crawford immediately ran into a sharp fire on his right front, which might mean the crisis. I had been riding with Griffin on the left of my front line, but now hastened over to the right, where I found Gregory earnestly carrying out my instructions to guard that flank. I caught a glimpse of some cavalry in the woods on our right, which I judged to be Roberts' North Carolina Brigade, that had been picketing the White Oak Road, and so kept Gregory on the alert. The influence of the sharp skirmish fire on Crawford's right tended to draw the men towards it; but I used all my efforts to shorten step on the pivot and press the wheeling flank, in order to be ready for the "swing" to the left. Still, the firing ahead kept me dubious. It might mean Fitzhugh Lee's cavalry making a demonstration there; but from the persistence of it was more likely to mean infantry reinforcements sent the enemy from the Claiborne entrenchments where we had left them the day before. It was afterwards seen how near it came to being that.[1]

It was, in fact, Fitzhugh Lee's cavalry, commanded now by the experienced and able Munford who had dismounted his men and posted them at the junction of the Church Road and the White Oak Road, behind some light rail defenses which they had hastily thrown up. From this they were being slowly driven by Crawford's advance. We crossed the White Oak Road without hearing anything from Ayres, a circumstance which troubled me very much, as our division was supposed to be in supporting distance of both Crawford and Ayres. It was now apparent that the road-crossing Crawford had struck was not at the angle of the enemy's entrenched line, but at least a gunshot to the east of this,—in fact it was a thousand yards away.

[1] Wise, Gracie, and Hunton's Brigades had been ordered out of the Claiborne entrenchments that afternoon to attack the right flank of the Fifth Corps; but being obliged to take a roundabout way and getting entangled among the streams and marshes north of the White Oak Road, they were too late to reach the scene of action until all was over.—*Records, Warren Court*, Lee's testimony, p. 473; McGowan's, p 651, Hunton's, p. 626.

Mackenzie had crowded off Roberts' cavalry towards its right near Burgess' Mill,—this cavalry not being under Fitzhugh Lee or Munford but taking orders directly from the infantry general R. H. Anderson. My orders were in general to follow Crawford.

I had managed, however, to gain towards the left until we had fairly got past Crawford's left rear. Some firing we had heard in the supposed direction of our cavalry, but it did not seem heavier than that in Crawford's front. We were moving rapidly, and had been out about twenty minutes from the church, and perhaps nearly a mile distant, when a sudden burst of fire exactly on our left roused very definite thoughts. This could only be from Ayres' attack. I halted my line and rode ahead through the woods to some high, cleared ground, the southeastern corner of a large field, known as the "Sydnor field," along the opposite edge of which I could see strong skirmishing along Crawford's front; and turning southerly, looking across broken, scrubby ground, could see Ayres' troops engaged in a confused whirl of struggling groups, with fitful firing. This was about as far away, I judged, as Crawford's skirmishing, about six hundred yards. The great gap between these engagements made me feel that something was "all wrong." I was anxious about my duty. My superiors were not in sight. Bartlett had closely followed Crawford, away to my right. But I could see the corps flag in the Sydnor field, moving towards Crawford, and on the other side, in a ravine half-way to Ayres, I saw the division flag. There was Ayres fighting alone, and that was not in the program. There was Griffin down there; that was order enough for me, and I took the responsibility of looking out for the left instead of the right, where my last orders committed me. I pulled my brigade out of the woods by the left flank, telling Gregory to follow; and, sending to Bartlett to let him know what I was doing, pushed across a muddy stream and up a rough ravine towards Ayres. Half-way up, Griffin came to meet me,—never more welcome. He gave the look I wanted, and without coming near enough for words waved me to follow up to the head of the ravine and to attack on my right, along the bank where, hidden by brush and scrub, the enemy had a line perpendicular to their main one on the White Oak Road, and were commencing a slant fire in Ayres' direction. Griffin rode past me towards Warren and Bartlett.

At the head of the gully all we had to do was to front into line of battle, and scramble up the rough brambly steep. The moment we showed our heads, we were at close quarters with the enemy. We exchanged volleys with good will, and then came the rush. Our lines struck each other obliquely, like shutting jaws. It was rather an awkward movement; for we had to make a series of right half-wheels by battalion to meet the fire, and all the while gain to the left. Thus we stopped that cross-fire on Ayres, who was now lost from sight by intervening scrubby woods. The brunt

9

of this first fell on my stalwart 185th New York, Colonel Sniper; but Gregory[1] soon coming in by echelon on their right took the edge off that enfilading fire.

Ayres' fitful fire was approaching, and I rode over towards it. Somewhere near the angle of the "return" I met Sheridan. He had probably seen me putting my men in, and hence I escaped censure for appearing. Indeed his criticism seemed to be that there was not more of me, rather than less. "By G—, that's what I want to see!" was his greeting, "general officers at the front. Where are your general officers?" I replied that I had seen General Warren's flag in the big field north of us, and that seeing Ayres in a tight place I had come to help him, and by General Griffin's order. "Then," cried he, with a vigor of utterance worthy of the "army in Flanders," "you take command of all the infantry round here, and break this dam—" I didn't wait to hear any more. That made good grammar as it stood. I didn't stand for anything, but spurred back to some scattered groups of men, demoralized by being so far in the rear, and not far enough to do them any good, yet too brave to go back. Captain Laughlin of Griffin's staff came along, and I took him with me down among these men to get them up. I found one stalwart fellow on his hands and knees behind a stump, answering with whimsical grimaces to the bullets coming pretty thick and near. "Look here, my good fel-

[1] His regiments were the 187th, 188th, and 189th New York; thus the four New York regiments constituted the right of my command.

low," I called down to him, "don't you know you'll be killed here in less than two minutes? This is no place for you. Go forward!" "But what can I do?" he cried; "I can't stand up against all this alone!" "No, that's just it," I replied. "We're forming here. I want you for guide center. Up, and forward!" Up and out he came like a hero. I formed those "reserves" on him as guide, and the whole queer line—two hundred of them—went in right up to the front and the thick of it. My poor fellow only wanted a token of confidence and appreciation to get possession of himself. He was proud of what he did, and so I was for him.

I let the staff officers take these men in, for I had caught sight of Ayres' Third Brigade coming out of the woods right behind me, and standing in the further edge of the scrubby field. The men were much excited, but were making a good line. General Gwyn was riding up and down their front in a demonstrative manner, but giving no sign of forward movement. I thought this strange for him and bad for us all, in the pinch things then were at, and with the warrant Sheridan had given me galloped down to him and asked him if he was acting under any particular orders from General Ayres. "No, General," he replied with an air of relief, "I have lost Ayres. I have no orders. I don't know what to do." "Then come with me," I said; "I will take the responsibility. You shall have all credit. Let me take your brigade for a moment!" His men gave me good greeting as I rode down their front and gave the order, "Forward, right oblique!" On they came, and in they went, gallantly, gladly, just when and where they were needed, with my own brigade fighting the "return," and ready to take touch with Ayres. His fire was advancing rapidly on my left, and I rode over to meet him. Sheridan was by my side in a moment, very angry. "You are firing into my cavalry!" he exclaims, his face darkening with a checked expletive. I was under a little pressure, too, and put on a bold air. "Then the cavalry have got into the rebels' place. One of us will have to get out of the way. What will you have us do, General?" "Don't you fire into my cavalry, I tell you!" was the fierce rejoinder. I felt a little left out in the cold by General Sheridan's calling them "my cavalry," as if we were aliens and did not belong to him also; but, whosesoever they were, I could not see what business they had up here at the "angle." This was our part of the field. The plan of the battle put them at the enemy's right and center, a mile away on the Dinwiddie Road and beyond.

Fortunately for me, Ayres comes up, his troops right upon the angle—the right, the Maryland Brigade on the "return"—brave Bowerman down—and Winthrop's Brigade—gallant Winthrop gone—reaching beyond, across the White Oak Road, driving a crowd before them. I have only time to say to Ayres, "Gwyn is in on the right"; for Sheridan takes him in hand. "I tell you again, General Ayres, you are firing into my cavalry!" "We are firing at the people who are firing at us!" is the quick reply. "These are not carbine shot. They are minie-balls. I ought to know."

But I felt the point of Sheridan's rebuke. As my oblique fire across the "return" was now so near the enemy's main line on the White Oak Road, it was not unlikely that if any of the cavalry were up here on their front, I might be firing into them and they into me. There was a worse thing yet: if we continued advancing in that direction, in another minute we should be catching Ayres' fire on our left flank. He was already in, with his men. Griffin, coming up, detains me a moment. Sheridan greets him well. "We flanked them gloriously!" he exclaims, with a full-charged smile, implying that all was not over yet. After a minute's crisp remark, Griffin wheels away to the right, and I am left with Sheridan. He was sitting right in the focus of the fire, on his horse "Rienzi," —both about the color of the atmosphere, his demon pennon, good or ill, as it might bode, red and white, two-starred, aloft just behind him. The stream of bullets was pouring so thick it crossed my mind that what had been to me a poet's phrase—"darkening the air"—was founded on dead-level fact. I was troubled for Sheridan. We could not afford to lose him. I made bold to tell him so, and begged him not to stay there;—the rest of us would try to take care of things, and from that place he could be spared. He gave me a comical look, and answered with a peculiar twist in the toss of his head, that seemed to say he didn't care much for himself, or perhaps for me. "Yes, I think I'll go!" and away he dashed, right down through Ayres' left, down the White Oak Road, into that triple cross-fire we had been quarreling about. I afterwards learned that Sheridan did order his cavalry to cease firing in the direction of our advancing infantry.

I plunged into my business, to make up for this minute's lost time. My men were still facing too much across Ayres' front, and getting into the range of his fire. We had got to change that, and swing to the right, down the rear of the enemy's main works. It was a whirl. Every way was front, and every way was flank. The fighting was hand to hand. I was trying to get the three angles of the triangle into something like two right angles, and had swung my left well forward, opening quite a gap in that direction, when a large body of the enemy came rushing in upon that flank and rear. They were in line formation, with arms at something like a "ready," which looked like "business." I thought it was our turn to be caught between two fires, and that these men were likely to cut their way through us. Rushing into the ranks of my left battalion I shouted the order, "Prepare to fire by the rear rank!" My men faced about at once, disregarding the enemy in front; but at this juncture our portentous visitors threw down their muskets, and with hands and faces up cried out, "We surrender," running right in upon us and almost over us. I was very glad of it, though more astonished, for they outnumbered us largely.[1] I was a little afraid of them, too, lest they might find occasion to take arms again and revoke the "consent of the governed." They were pretty solid commodities, but I was very willing to exchange them for paper token of indebtedness in the form of a provost-marshal's receipt. So getting my own line into shape again, I took these well-mannered men, who had been standing us so stiff a fight a few minutes before, with a small escort out over the "return," into the open field in rear, and turned them over to one of Sheridan's staff, with a request for a receipt when they were counted.[2]

In the field I find Ayres, who is turning over a great lot of prisoners. The "angle" and the whole "return" are now carried, but beyond them the routed enemy are stubbornly resisting. I have time for a word with Ayres now, and to explain my taking up Gwyn so sharply. He is not in the mood to blame me for anything. He explains also. He had been suddenly attacked on his left, and

[1] These were Colonel Hutter of the 11th Virginia Infantry of Mayo's Brigade and part of the 3d Virginia Cavalry dismounted which Munford had sent to reinforce Ransom.

[2] The receipt sent me bore the whole number of prisoners turned over by me during the battle; but most of them were taken in this encounter. This acknowledges from my command two colonels, six captains, eleven lieutenants, and a thousand and fifty men sent in by my own brigade; and four hundred and seventy men by Gregory's It is not impossible that some of these prisoners turned over to General Sheridan's provost marshal, may have been counted twice,—with the cavalry captures as well as my own. It should be said that the prisoners taken by us were due to the efficiency and admirable behavior of all the troops in our part of the field near the "angle," and not alone to that of my immediate command.

had been obliged to change front instantly with two of his brigades. Their two commanders, Winthrop and Bowerman, falling almost at the first stroke, he had taken these brigades in person, and put them in, without sending any word to Gwyn on his right. I could see how it was. Losing connection, Gwyn was at a loss what to do, and in the brief time Ayres was routing the enemy who had attacked him, I had come upon Gwyn and had put him in, really ahead of the main line of Ayres, who soon came up to him. So it all came about right for Ayres.[1]

General Bartlett now came appealing for assistance. Two of his regiments had gone off with Crawford, and Bartlett had more than he could do to make head against a stout resistance the enemy were making on a second line turned back near the Ford Road. I helped him pick up a lot of stragglers and asked Gregory to give him the 188th New York for assistance.

Meanwhile Warren, searching for Crawford, had come upon his First Brigade, Kellogg's, and had faced it southerly towards the White Oak

[1] To complete this reference, I will mention that Brevet Brigadier-General Gwyn was colonel of the 118th Pennsylvania Volunteers, in Griffin's Division, and had been assigned to command one of Ayres' Brigades. Not long afterwards I came in command of the division, and, a general court-martial being convened, charges were preferred against Gwyn by some who did not understand the facts of this occurrence as well as I did. When the papers reached me, I disapproved them and sent them back with the endorsement that General Gwyn had done his best under peculiarly perplexing circumstances, and had gone in with his brigade handsomely, under my own eye at a critical moment of the battle. I believed this to be justice to a brave officer.

Road, as a guide for a new point of direction for that division, and had then gone off in search of the rest of these troops to bring them in on the line. Thereupon one of Sheridan's staff officers came across Kellogg standing there, and naturally ordered him to go forward into the "fight." Kellogg questioned his authority, and warm words took the place of other action, till at length Kellogg concluded it best to obey Sheridan's representative, and moved promptly forward, striking somewhere beyond the left of the enemy's refused new flank. It seems also that Crawford's Third Brigade, Coulter's, which was in his rear line, had anticipated orders or got Warren's, and moved by the shortest line in the direction Kellogg was taking. So Crawford himself was on the extreme wheeling flank, with only Baxter's Brigade and two regiments of Bartlett's of the First Division immediately in hand. His brigades were now moving in echelon by the left, which was in fact about the order of movement originally prescribed, and that which the whole corps actually took up, automatically as it were, or by force of the situation. Our commands were queerly mixed; men of every division of the corps came within my jurisdiction, and something like this was probably the case with several other commanders. But that made no difference; men and officers were good friends. There was no jealousy among us subordinate commanders. We had eaten salt together when we had not much else This liveliness of mutual interest and support, I may remark, is sometimes of great importance in the developments of a battle.

The hardest hold-up was in front of my left center, the First Battalion of the 198th Pennsylvania. I rode up to the gallant Glenn, commanding it, and said, "Major Glenn, if you will break that line you shall have a colonel's commission!" It was a hasty utterance, and the promise unmilitary, perhaps; but my every energy was focused on that moment's issue. Nor did the earnest soldier need a personal inducement; he was already carrying out the general order to press the enemy before him, with as much effect as we could reasonably expect. But it was deep in my mind how richly he already deserved this promotion, and I resolved that he should get it now. It was this thought and purpose which no doubt shaped my phrase, and pardoned it. Glenn sprung among his men, calling out, "Boys, will you follow me?" wheeled his horse and dashed forward, without turning to see who followed. Nor did he need. His words were a question; his act an order. On the brave fellows go with a cheer into the hurricane of fire. Their beautiful flag sways gracefully aloft with the spring of the brave youth bearing it, lighting the battle-smoke; three times it goes down to earth covered in darkening eddies, but rises ever again passing from hand to hand of dauntless young heroes. Then bullet-torn and blood-blazoned it hovers for a moment above a breastwork, while the regiment goes over like a wave. This I saw from my position to the left of them where I was pressing on the rest of my command. The sight so wrought upon me that I snatched time to ride over and congratulate Glenn and his regiment. As I passed into a deeper shadow of the woods, I met two men bearing his body, the dripping blood marking their path. They stopped to tell me. I saw it all too well. He had snatched a battle flag from a broken regiment trying to rally on its colors, when a brute bullet of the earth once pronounced good, but since cursed for man's sin, struck him down to its level. I could stop but a moment, for still on my front was rush and turmoil and tragedy. I could only bend down over him from the saddle and murmur unavailing words. "General, I have carried out your wishes!"—this was his only utterance. It was as if another bullet had cut me through. I almost fell across my saddle-bow. My wish? God in heaven, no more my wish than thine, that this fair body, still part of the unfallen "good," should be smitten to the sod, that this spirit born of thine should be quenched by the accursed!

What dark misgivings searched me as I took the import of these words! What sharp sense of responsibility for those who have committed to them the issues of life and death! Why should I not have let this onset take its general course and men their natural chances? Why choose out him for his death, and so take on myself the awful decision into what home irreparable loss and measureless desolation should cast their unlifted burden? The crowding thought choked utterance. I could only bend my face low to his and answer: "*Colonel*, I will remember my promise; I will remember *you*!" and press forward to my place, where the crash and crush and agony of struggle summoned me to more of the same. War!—nothing but the final, infinite good, for man and God, can accept and justify human work like that!

I feared most of all, I well remember,—such hold had this voice on me,—that it might not be given me to be found among the living, so that I could fulfill my word to him. But divine grace and pity granted me this. As soon as the battle was over, I sent forward by special messenger my recommendation for two brevets for him, in recognition of his conspicuous gallantry and great service in every battle of this campaign, up to this last hour. These were granted at once, and Glenn passed from us to other recognition, "Brevet Colonel of United States Volunteers,"—and that phrase, so costly won, so honorable then, made common since, has seemed to me ever after, tame and something like travesty.[1]

[1] I sought for him from the Governor of Pennsylvania lineal promotion in his regiment, though he had but few hours to live. But that grade was held by an accomplished gentleman detached from his regiment on office duties in the cities, and there was no place for Glenn The colonel, dear old Sickel, was in hospital with an amputated arm, shattered at the Quaker Road three days before. Within that time this regiment had now lost in battle colonel, major, and adjutant, and all we could secure for the rest of the service, that great regiment of fourteen companies, was a major's rank. This, indeed, was worthily bestowed. It came to Captain John Stanton, who after the fall of Sickel and MacEuen

By this time Warren had found Crawford, who with Baxter's Brigade had been pursuing Munford's dismounted cavalry all the way from where we had crossed the White Oak Road, by a wide detour reaching almost to Hatcher's Run, until he had crossed the Ford Road, quite in rear of the breaking lines which Ransom and Wallace and Wood were trying to hold together.[1] Hence he was in position to do them much damage, both by cutting off their retreat by the Ford Road and taking many prisoners, and also by completing the enemy's envelopment. To meet this, the enemy, instead of giving up the battle as they would have been justified in doing, stripped still more their main works in front of our cavalry by detaching nearly the entire brigade of General Terry, now commanded by Colonel Mayo, and facing it quite to its rear pushed it down the Ford Road and across the fields to resist the advance of Warren with Crawford.

We, too, were pressing hard on the Ford Road from the east, so that all were crowded into that whirlpool of the fight. Just as I reached it, Captain Brinton of Griffin's staff dashed up at

---

had acted as a field officer with fidelity and honor, and had distinguished himself in the struggle for the flag snatched by Glenn with more than mortal energy and at mortal cost.

[1] To my grief over the costs of this struggle was added now another, when, borne past me on the right, came the form of Colonel Farnham of the 16th Maine, now on Crawford's staff, who, sent to bear an order into this thickening whirl, was shot through the breast and fell, as we thought, mortally wounded, but the courage and fortitude which never forsook him carried him through this also.

headlong speed and asked if I knew that Griffin was in command of the corps. I was astonished at first, and incredulous afterwards. I had heard nothing from General Warren since I saw his flag away in the Sydnor field when I was breaking out from the column of march to go to Ayres' support. My first thought was that he was killed. I asked Brinton what he meant. He told me the story. General Warren, when he got to the rear of the Ford Road, sent an enthusiastic message by Colonel Locke, his chief of staff, to Sheridan, saying that he was in the enemy's rear, cutting off his retreat, and had many prisoners. This message met scant courtesy. Sheridan's patience was exhausted. "By G—, sir, tell General Warren he wasn't in the fight!" Colonel Locke was thunderstruck. "Must I tell General Warren that, sir?" asked he. "Tell him that, sir!" came back, the words like hammer-blows. "I would not like to take a verbal message like that to General Warren. May I take it down in writing?"—"Take it down, sir; tell him, by G—, he was not at the front!" This was done. Locke, the old and only adjutant-general of the Fifth Corps, himself just back from a severe wound in the face on some desperate front with Warren, never felt a blow like that. Soon thereafter Sheridan came upon General Griffin, and, without preface or index, told the astonished Griffin, "I put you in command of the Fifth Corps!" This was Brinton's story; dramatic enough, surely; pathetic too. I hardly knew how to take it. I thought it possible Sheridan had told every general officer he met, as he had told me, to take command of all the men he could find on the field and push them in. I could not think of Warren being so wide-off an exception.

Pressing down towards the Forks, some of Ayres' men mingled with my own, I saw on emerging into a little clearing, Sheridan riding beside me like an apparition. Yet he was pretty certain flesh and blood. I felt a little nervous, not in the region of my conscience, nor with any misgiving of the day's business, but because I was alone with Sheridan. His expression was at its utmost bent; intent and content, incarnate will. But he greeted me kindly, and spoke freely of the way things had been going. We were riding down inside the works in the woods covering the Forks and Ford Road, now the new focus of the fight. Just then an officer rode flightily up from that direction, exclaiming to General Sheridan, "We are on the enemy's rear, and have got three of their guns." "I don't care a d— for their guns, or you either, sir! What are you here for? Go back to your business, where you belong! What I want is that Southside Road." The officer seemed to appreciate the force of the suggestion, and the distant attraction of the Southside Road. I looked to see what would happen to me. There were many men gathered round, or rather we had ridden into the midst of them, as they stood amazed, at the episode. The sun was just in the tree-tops; it might be the evening chill that was creeping over us. Then Sheridan, rising in his stirrups, hat in hand waving aloft at full arm's length, face black as his horse, and both like a storm-king, roared out: "I want you men to understand we have a record to make, before that sun goes down, that will make hell tremble!—I want you there!" I guess they were ready to go; to that place or any other where death would find them quickest; and the sooner they got there, the safer for them.

Griffin came down now from the right, dashed ahead of me and jumped his horse over the works. I thought myself a pretty good rider, but preferred a lower place in the breastworks. My horse saw one and made for it. Just as he neared the leap, a bullet struck him in the leg, and gave him more impetus than I had counted on. But I gave him free rein and held myself easy, and over we went, and down we came, luckily feet-foremost, almost on top of one of the enemy's guns, which we were fortunate enough not to "take." In truth the gun was so hot from its rapid recent fire that we could not bear our hands on it.

There was a queer "parliament of religions" just then and there, at this Five Forks focus. And it came in this wise. As Ransom and Wallace and Wood's reinforced but wasting lines had fallen back before us along the north and east side of their works, our cavalry kept up sharp attacks upon their right across the works, which by masterly courage and skill they managed to repel, replacing as best they could the great gaps made in their defenses by the withdrawal of so many of Stewart's and Terry's Brigades, to form the other sides of their retreating "hollow square." Driven in upon themselves, and over much "concentrated," they were so penned in there was not a fair chance to fight. Just as Ayres' and Griffin's men struck the brave fellows holding on around the guns at the Forks, from which Pegram, the gifted young commander, had been borne away mortally wounded,—and spirits as well as bodies were falling,—two brigades of our cavalry, Fitzhugh's and Pennington's of Devins' and Custer's commands, seizing the favorable moment, made a splendid dash, dismounted, over the works in their front, passing the guns and joining with our men in pressing back the broken ranks scattering through the thick woods. Bartlett, also, with some of Crawford's men following, came down nearly at the same time from the north on the Ford Road. All, therefore, centered on the three guns there; so that for a moment there was a queer colloquy over the silent guns. The cavalry officers say that they captured the guns, but Griffin would not let them "take" them. Crawford and Bartlett afterwards also both report the capture of the guns; but as the enemy had abandoned them before these troops struck them, the claimants of the capture should be content to rank their merits in the order of their coming. There were, however, some guns farther up the Ford Road,—whether those at first under Ransom on the "refused" flank, or those hurried from Pegram's command on the White Oak Road to the support of the breaking lines vainly essaying to cover the Ford Road. Of the capture of these there is no doubt. These Major West Funk—a strange misnomer, but a better name in German than in English, showing there is some "sparkle" in his blood—actually "took," by personal touch, —both ways. First dodging behind trees before their canister, then shooting down the horses and mules attached to the limbers, as well as the gunners who stood by them, his two little regiments made a rush for the battery, overwhelmed it, unmanned it, and then swept on, leaving the guns behind them, making no fuss about it, and so very likely to get no credit for it. This little episode, however, was not unobserved by me; for this resolute young commander had been a member of my personal staff, and these two regiments—the 121st and 142d Pennsylvania, now attached to Crawford's Division, were all that was left to us of the dear lost old First Corps, and of my splendid brigade from it in Griffin's Division, in the ever memorable charge of "Fort Hell," June 18, 1864.

"Taking guns" is a phrase associated with very stirring action. But words have a greater range than even guns. There is the literal, the legal, the moral, the figurative, the poetic, the florid, the transcendental. All these atmospheres may give meaning and color to a word. But dealing with solid fact, there is no more picturesque and thrilling sight, no more telling, testing deed, than to "take a battery" in front. Plowed through by booming shot; torn by ragged bursts of shell; riddled by blasts of whistling canister; straight ahead to the guns hidden in their own smoke; straight on to the red, scorching flame of the muzzles, the giant grains of cannon-powder beating, burning, sizzling into the cheek; then in upon them!—pistol to rifle-shot, saber to bayonet, musket-butt to hand-spike and rammer; the brief frenzy of passion; the wild "hurrah!" then the sudden, unearthly silence; the ghastly scene; the shadow of death; the aureole of glory; much that is telling here, but more that cannot be told. Surely it were much better if guns must be taken, to take them by flank attack, by skillful manœuvre, by moral suasion, by figure of speech, or even by proxy.

But this is digression, or reminiscence. For the matter in hand, the guns taken at the Forks and on the Ford Road, with due acknowledgments of individual valor, were taken by all the troops who closed in around them, front, flank, and rear; by the whole movement, indeed, from the brain of the brilliant commander who planned, to the least man who pressed forward to fulfill his high resolve.

We had pushed the enemy a mile from the left of their works—the angle, their tactical center—and were now past the Forks. Something remained to be done, according to Sheridan's biblical intimation. But the enemy made no more resolute, general stand. Only little groups, held back and held together by individual character, or the magnetism of some superior officer, made front and gave check. For a moment, after the deafening din and roar, the woods seemed almost given back to nature, save for the clinging smoke and broken bodies and breaking moans which betokened man's intervention.

Our commands were much mixed, but the men well moving on, when in this slackening of the strain, Griffin and Ayres, who were now riding with me, spoke regretfully, sympathizingly, of Warren. They thought he had sacrificed himself for Crawford, who had not proved equal to the demands of the situation. "Poor Warren, how he will suffer for this!" they said with many variations of the theme. Griffin did not say a word about his being placed in command of the corps. He was a keen observer, a sharp critic, able and prompt to use a tactical advantage, but he was not the man to take pleasure which cost another's pain, or profit from another's loss. It was high promotion, gratifying to a soldier's ambition; it was special preferment, for he was junior to Crawford. But he took it all modestly, like the soldier and man he was, thinking more of duty and service than of self.

Sheridan came upon us again, bent to his purpose. "Get together all the men you can," he says, "and drive on while you can see your hand before you!" The men were widely scattered from their proper commanders. Griffin told me to gather the men of the First Division and bring them to the White Oak Road. Riding along the ground of the wide pursuit, I kept my bugler sounding the brigade calls of the division. This brought our officers and men to the left. Among others, General Warren came riding slowly from the right. I took pains to greet him cheerfully, and explained to him why I was sounding all the bugle calls. "You are doing just right," he replies, "but I am not in command of the corps." That was the first authoritative word I had heard spoken to this effect. I told him I had heard so, but that General Sheridan had been putting us all in command of everything we could get in hand, and perhaps after the battle was over we would all get back where we belonged. I told him I was now moving forward under Sheridan's and Griffin's order, and rode away from him towards the left with my gathered troops, shadowed in spirit for Warren's sake. I could not be sorry for the corps, nor that Griffin was in command of it—he had the confidence of the whole corps. And however sharp was Griffin's satire, he had the generosity which enables one to be truly just, and never made his subordinates vicarious victims of his own interior irritations.

We had now come to the edge of a wide field across the road and the works on the enemy's right, known as the Gilliam field. Here I came to Sheridan and Griffin, my troops all up, and well in hand. A sharp cavalry fight was going on, in which some of Ayres' men and my own had taken part. On the right, along the White Oak Road, were portions of Crawford's infantry that had swung around so quickly as to get ahead of us and they were the ones now principally engaged.

Here Warren took his leave of the corps, himself under a shadow as somber as the scene and with a flash as lurid as the red light of the battle-edge rolling away into the darkness and distance of the deep woods. When our line was checked at this last angle, Griffin had ordered one of Crawford's colonels to advance. The colonel, a brave and well-balanced man, replied that where soldiers as good as Griffin's men had failed, he did not feel warranted in going in without proper orders. "Very well I order you in!" says Griffin, without adding that he did it as commander of the corps. The gallant colonel bows,—it is Richardson, of the 7th Wisconsin,—grasps his regimental colors in his own hand, significant of the need and his resolution in face of it, and rides forward in advance of his men. What can they do but follow such example? General Warren, with intensity of feeling that is now desperation, snatches his corps flag from the hands of its bearer, and dashes to Richardson's side. And so the two leaders ride, the corps commander and his last visible colonel,—colors aloft, reckless of the growing distance between them and their followers, straight for the smoking line, straight for the flaming edge; not hesitating at the breastworks, over they go: one with swelling tumult of soul, where the passion of suffering craves outburst in action; the other with obedience and self-devotion, love-like, stronger than death. Over the breastworks, down among the astonished foe, one of whom, instinct overmastering admiration, aims at the foremost a deadly blow, which the noble youth rushes forward to parry, and shielding with his own the breast of his uncaring commander, falls to earth, bathing his colors with his blood. Need more be told? Do men tarry at such a point? One crested wave sweeps on; another, broken, rolls away. All is lost; and all is won. Slowly Warren returns over the somber field. At its forsaken edge a staff officer hands him a crude field order. Partly by the lurid flashes of the last guns, partly by light of the dying day, he reads: "Major-General Warren, commanding the Fifth Army Corps, is relieved from duty and will at once report for orders to Lieutenant-General Grant, commanding Armies of the United States. By command of Major-General Sheridan."

With almost the agony of death upon his face, Warren approaches Sheridan and asks him if he cannot reconsider the order. "Reconsider. Hell! I don't reconsider my decisions. Obey the order!" fell the last thunderbolt on Warren's heart.

The battle has done its worst for him. The iron has entered his soul. With bowed head and without a word, he turns from the spectral groups of friend and foe mingled in the dark, forbidding cloud of night, to report to the one man on earth who held power over what to him was dearer than life, and takes his lonely way over that eventful field, along that fateful White Oak Road, which for him had no end on earth.

After nightfall the corps was drawn in around Five Forks, for a brief respite. We were all so worn out that our sinking bodies took our spirits with them. We had reasons to rejoice so far as victory gives reasons; but there was a strange weight on the hearts of us all. Of things within? or things without? We could not tell. It was not wholly because Warren had gone, although in the sundering of old ties there is always a strain, and Warren had been part of the best history of the Fifth Corps from the beginning. Even victory is not for itself; it looks to a cause and an end. We thought of this, pondering on the worth and cost, and to what that end might unfold, of which this was the beginning. There are other emotions, too, which will arise when night draws over a scene like that, and with it the thoughts come home.

We grouped ourselves around Griffin at the Forks, center of the whirling struggle, we who were left of those once accustomed to gather about him in field or bivouac,—alas for those who came no more!—half-reclining against the gloomy tree-trunks and rudely piled defenses so gallantly lost and won, torn by splintering shot and rush of men; half-stretched on the ground moistened by the dews of night and the blood of the mingled brave; hushed at heart, speaking but in murmurs answering to the whispers of the night; with a tremulous sensitiveness, an awe that was not fear. Few things we said; but they were not of the history that is told.

Suddenly emerged from the shadows a compact form, with vigorous stride unlike the measure and mood of ours and a voice that would itself have thrilled us had not the import of it thrilled us more. "Gentlemen," says Sheridan, as we half started to our feet, "I have come over to see you. I may have spoken harshly to some of you to-day; but I would not have it hurt you. You know how it is: we had to carry this place, and I was fretted all day till it was done. You must forgive me. I know it is hard for the men, too; but we must push. There is more for us to do together. I appreciate and thank you all."

And this is Phil Sheridan! A new view of him, surely, and amazing. All the repressed feeling of our hearts sprang out towards him. We were ready to blame ourselves if we had been in any way the cause of his trouble. But we thought we had borne a better part than that.

We had had a taste of his style of fighting, and we liked it. In some respects it was different from ours; although this was not a case to test all qualities. We had formed some habits of fighting too. Most of us there had been through Antietam, Fredericksburg, Chancellorsville, Gettysburg, Mine Run, the Wilderness, Spottsylvania, Cold Harbor, Bethesda Church, the North Anna, Petersburg:—we had formed habits. We went into a fight with knowledge of what it meant and what was to be done. We went at things with dogged resolution; not much show; not much flare; not much accompaniment of brass instruments. But we could give credit to more brilliant things. We could see how this voice and vision, this swing and color, this vivid impression on the senses, carried the pulse and will of men. This served as the old "fife and drum," and "Hail Columbia," that used to stir men's souls. We had a habit, perhaps, drawn from dire experience, and for which we had also Grant's quite recent sanction,[1] when we had carried a vital point or had to hold one, to entrench. But Sheridan does not entrench. He pushes on, carrying his flank and rear with him,—rushing, flashing, smashing. He transfuses into his subordinates the vitality and energy of his purpose; transforms them into part of his own mind and will. He shows the power of a commander,—inspiring both confidence and fear He commanded our admiration, but we could discriminate: we reserved room for question whether he exhibited all the qualities essential to a chief commander in a campaign, or even in the complicated movements of an extensive field of battle.

As a rule, our corps and army commanders were men of brains rather than of magnetism. Warren was one of these. He was well capable of organizing an entire plan of battle on a great field. He would have been an admirable chief of staff of the army, where brains outweigh temperament. He could see the whole comprehensively and adjust the parts subordinate to it. But he had a certain ardor of temperament which, although it brought him distinction as a subordinate commander, seemed to work against him as corps commander. It led him to go in personally with a single division or brigade, when a sharp fight came on. Doing this when having a larger command, one takes the risk of losing grasp of the whole. That was what

[1] The order to entrench on the White Oak Road, March 31st. See *War Papers*, vol. 1, p 235.

he did in trying to change front with Crawford's Division under fire. It was a difficult thing. He put his personality into it; just as Sheridan would do and did in this very fight. It was the cruelest thing to say of him that he "was not in the fight." This blamed him for the very opposite of what had been complained of as his chief fault; and this time the accusation was not true. He *was* in the fight; and that in fact was his fault; at any rate it was his evil fate. That he felt this accusation keenly was manifest in that last reckless onset in the charge in the Gilliam field: he would let Sheridan see whether he was in the fight or not. But this did no good. If he had brought Crawford in where Griffin came, he might have saved himself. But that long labor of his out of Sheridan's sight missed the moment. It was too late. The day was done. So he rode through into the night.

In the later dispositions of the corps the several divisions were moved out in directions which would best guard against sudden attack, not unexpected: Crawford, down the Ford Road, half-way to the Run; Ayres out the White Oak Road on the right, and Bartlett on the left, facing towards the enemy, supposed to be gathered in their last stronghold where we had left their main body the day before,—the Claiborne entrenchments. It fell to me to be held in reserve, and by midnight my command was left alone on the field over which the sweeping vision of power had passed. The thunder and tumult of the day had died with it. Now only the sighing of the night winds through the pine tops took up the ghostly refrain; and moans from the darkened earth beneath told where we also belonged. So the night was not for sleep, but given to solemn and tender duties, and to thoughts that passed beyond that field.

This is the story of Five Forks within my knowledge of what was done and suffered there. It shows confusions and struggles besides those of the contending lines. It shows extent and complexity quite beyond what would appear from an outside view of the movement or the orders concerning it. The story that went out early, and has taken lodgment in the public mind, is more simple. Taking its rise and keynote from Sheridan's report, somewhat intensified by his staff officers, and adopted by Grant without feeling necessity of further investigation, this story is that Sheridan and his cavalry, with the assistance of a part of Ayres' Division, carried Five Forks with all its works, angles, and returns, its captives, guns, and glory.

The widely drawn and all-embracing testimony before the Warren Court of Inquiry in 1879 and 1880, although in some instances confused and even contradictory,—the result, however, in no small degree of the preoccupation in the witnesses' minds by the accounts so early and abundantly put forth, and without rectification for so long a time,—yet reveals some spreading of the plan of battle, a steadfast, well-connected, and well-executed conformity to the ideas under which the battle was ordered. It also affords ample means of understanding the confusions and frictions which were actual passages in the battle, and not artificial and intensified in statement under the necessity of sustaining a thesis or vindicating an act of authority. The light shed by these records and the official *War Records* lately published enables us now, by some effort of attention it is true, to see in proper perspective, sequence, and comprehension the complex details of that battle.

There was some very remarkable testimony before the court in regard to the fight at Dinwiddie, resulting from anything but "infirmity of mind." There were also many inconsistencies concerning the fight at Five Forks. But all these must be accepted as a part of human conditions.[1]

The whole trouble and the disturbance of Sheridan's preconceived image of the battle arose from a wide misunderstanding of the enemy's position, and the consequent direction of the attack by the Fifth Corps. The general plan was well understood by us all, and the specific written orders were in perfect accordance with the idea in our minds. It was to be mainly a flank and rear attack,—a cyclone sweep. The intention evidently was that

[1] See, for instance, Sheridan's statement before the Warren Court, *Records*, p. 118, and those of his officers all through this investigation. Also Grant's account of this battle, *Memoirs*, vol. ii., pp 443-446, the details of which, however, are so erroneous as to movements, their time and place and bearing on the result, that they would not be recognized as pertaining to that battle by anyone who was there,—an observation which adds to our sorrow at the distressing circumstances under which the distinguished writer was compelled to conclude his last volume without opportunity for examining the then existing evidence in that case.

our cavalry should engage the enemy's attention by vigorous demonstrations on their right and center, while the left of the Fifth Corps—Ayres' Division—should strike the left of the enemy's entrenched line at the angle or return on the White Oak Road, and on this pivot the whole corps should make a great left turn and flank and envelop the enemy's entire position.[1] It was a brilliant piece of tactics, and if properly carried out its success was as certainly predicted as anything in warfare can be. There was no lack of loyalty and earnestness. The importance of the battle was felt, and Sheridan's impatience shared by all.

But our actual movement was based on an imperfect reconnoissance, and a diagram made therefrom greatly misled us. This showed Crawford, the extreme right of the corps, directed on the angle, instead of Ayres, the extreme left. By this, not a man of the Fifth Corps could reach the White Oak Road without doing so on top of the enemy entrenched upon it. Swinging to the left on reaching it would have to be done inside the enemy's lines, or in front of them at close touch, presenting the right of each subdivision to their raking fire.

The diagram placed the angle of the enemy's works at the crossing of the White Oak Road and the road we were formed on,—the Gravelly Run Church Road; while as matter of fact, the angle was one thousand yards west of this crossing. So that "the line as formed" moving forward,

[1] See map.

instead of its right striking the angle, as the diagram indicated, the left of the line would pass it at the distance of nearly five hundred yards, as Ayres did.

It is now perfectly shown, although not clearly held in mind by all, even at the Warren investigation, that the celebrated "angle" and "return" were not the extreme left of the enemy's lines, nor of his fortified position, as would appear by the diagram. East of the angle as given there, was an extended work of similar character, but across the White Oak Road—south of it—extending a hundred and fifty yards, facing south. This seems to have been intended to cover the "return" which ran north from its right for some two hundred yards. This was the vicinity of the veritable "angle" where the severe fight took place when our infantry struck Ransom's and Wallace's Brigades on the return.[1] There had been a good deal of hard fighting north of the White Oak Road before reaching this angle at all.

Nor were the troops in the main works and about the "angle" and the "return"—as both the orders and the diagram indicated—by any means all the force we had to contend with that day. Fitzhugh Lee's cavalry, dismounted, now commanded by Munford,—among them Stuart's old brigade, and as their officers said, "as good marksmen as ever fired a gun,"—were confronting our advance, all the way round, not less than

[1] It was from this that our advance, Ayres and Crawford, was first struck. Testimony of General Munford, *Warren Court Records*, p. 442.

fifteen hundred skilled and veteran soldiers,—no sort of people to be ignored by us, nor by those reporting the battle to be wholly on the angle and on our cavalry front.

Now this was a very different state of facts from that anticipated and pictured by us, and we had to rectify all our lines under heavy fire in the midst of battle. Who was responsible for this misapprehension? It would appear that the staff officer making the reconnoissance had not examined the whole field or all of the enemy's position. Possibly Munford's cavalry had not then reached that portion of the field. But a discrepancy of a thousand yards in a report of such consequence is a pretty wide error. It might be said that Warren was responsible for assuring himself perfectly of the conditions in his front of attack. But Sheridan saw and approved the diagram; and if anybody is to be blamed, he must be considered ultimately, and in a military sense, responsible for these misapprehensions. At any rate there was a very imperfect reconnoissance, from which we all suffered; but it would be very unjust to place the blame on the Fifth Corps or its commander.

It was charged by General Sheridan and some of his staff that the right of Ayres' line, which they call skirmishers, behaved badly on receiving the first fire,—that they threw themselves on the ground and fired into the air; that they even broke and ran; and that General Warren did not exert himself to correct the confusion. As if the corps commander's duty was to be on a brigade skirmish line in a great wide-sweeping movement of his entire corps! Sheridan and Ayres would seem to be assistance enough for Gwyn in handling his little skirmish line. But Sheridan says more deliberately and explicitly before the Warren Court: "Our skirmish line lay down; the fire of the enemy was very slight. The line became confused, and commenced firing straight in the air." A somewhat difficult operation, it may be remarked parenthetically, for men lying down,—unless the resultant of two such compound forces as the enemy in front and Sheridan behind made them roll over flat on their backs, calling on heaven for aid. "The poor fellows," he continues, "had been fighting behind breastworks, for a long period, and when they got out to attack breastworks, they seem to have been a little timid."[1] They were attacking breastworks then, out at the Church Road crossing! But this is perhaps a fling at the Army of the Potomac in the soft places of "Grant's Campaign," in which they lost more men than Lee had in his entire army, and saved the other quarter by now and then entrenching when put momentarily on the defensive. Ayres does not relish this remark, whether intended for excuse or sarcasm. He answers that his troops, most of them, had fought at Gettysburg, and through the Wilderness, Spottsylvania, Cold Harbor, Petersburg, and the Weldon Railroad, and none of them had ever but once fought behind breastworks.[2]

The unsteadiness of Ayres' skirmishers was

[1] Testimony, *Warren Court Records*, p. 254. [2] *Ibid*, p 450.

no vital matter. It was a trifling circumstance, hardly relevant to the charge of indifference and incompetency on Warren's part, and did not warrant the launching of thunderbolts at the whole Fifth Corps. At the worst, the commander of the skirmish line might have been reprimanded and "relieved," but hardly the commander of the corps.

I am pained on more accounts than one to find that General Grant in his notice of our action that afternoon, as given in his *Memoirs* (volume ii., page 443), uses the following language: "Griffin's Division, in backing to get out of the way of a severe cross-fire of the enemy, was found marching away from the fighting." He adds, however, that after a while it was "brought back" and did excellent service. This is an extraordinary statement, —or at any rate it is to be hoped it is not an ordinary one in writing history,—to put down authoritatively as the record of our conduct and spirit that day.

"Backing to get out of the way of fire"? Griffin's Division? At what point in their history? "Backing from a cross-fire" here? The fire first followed was that of Munford's cavalry on their front and right while advancing according to orders; and "backing" from this would have thrown them directly on the celebrated "angle," where indeed they did arrive most timely, and on purpose to meet a "cross-fire," which they did not back out of. "Away from the fighting"? Let Ayres, and Ransom, and Wallace, and Wood, and Sheridan answer. "Found"? By whom? "Brought back"? By what? They were found at the "angle," and brought themselves there ahead of the finders. Saul, the seeker of old, got more lost than the domestic wanderers he was after: they were in their place before he was; but the seeker found a kingdom, and doubtless forgave himself and the animals whose society he missed.

But this is a very serious charge against Griffin's Division, and in time of active service would warrant a court of inquiry. And even now the statement of one so revered cannot but be injurious to its reputation and its honor.

To have stated this as fact without being sure of it is so unlike the truthfulness and magnanimity of that great character, that we are forced to believe he has here fallen before his only weakness,—that of trusting too implicitly to those whom he liked. If General Grant was to honor us by his notice at all, we should suppose he would acquaint himself with the facts. He seems, however, on so comparatively unimportant a topic, to have innocently absorbed the impression made upon him by parties interested in justifying an arbitrary act of authority. If General Grant could have looked into the case, he would have seen that this statement was not only unjust, but the very reverse of truth. The pressing sense of his approaching end compelled General Grant to finish his book in haste. However painful it may be to review words written under circumstances so affecting, it is but just to inquire into the grounds of the accusation.

Griffin's orders were to follow Crawford, but the spirit of his position was that of a reserve; and this is held in hand ready to go in at a critical moment when and where most needed. All the facts necessary to adduce are that this division strictly, and with painstaking fidelity,—not in stupid quiescence,—followed its orders, until a moment came when it promptly acted in accordance with the spirit of its orders and of the whole plan of battle. It was "reserved" for that very kind of thing. And no one can say it fell short of its duty or the standard of its ancient honor.

The evidence is explicit and ample that the head of this division was at the angle of the works with Ayres and helped him to carry it. This is directly testified to by commanding officers of the "Maryland Brigade" on Ayres' right, and of the 4th Delaware on Gwyn's right, who say that Griffin's troops were on the flank and rear of the rebel line at the angle before they attacked it in front.[1] This is confirmed by officers of the highest character in Ransom's Brigade on the left of the angle.[2] Gen-

[1] Colonel Stanton, who succeeded Bowerman in command of Ayres' Second Brigade, says the enemy were struck on their left and rear and forced in confusion on his front at the angle. Captain Buckingham, commanding the 4th Delaware, the extreme right of Ayres' Division, says our troops had struck the enemy's works from the north at the time he reached them in front, facing west

[2] Captain Faucette, 56th North Carolina, Ransom's Brigade, fully confirms this; and Honorable Thomas R. Roulac, 49th North Carolina, says that when the angle was carried, his troops had been attacked from the north and west, as well as on their proper front, and this by troops he saw moving down on them from the north, and that it was a "hand to hand" fight, "with clubbed muskets." See also *North Carolina Regiments, 1861–65*, vol. iii., p 143.

eral Ayres says substantially the same in his testimony before the Warren Court.[1] General Sheridan himself admits this.[2] It is evident, however, that in recounting his impression of the fight at the angle he failed to give prominence to the fact—of no consequence to him, or to the general result, as to the particular troops engaged; and moreover, if acknowledged, making against his charge that Warren did not bring in his other divisions to support Ayres—that Griffin's troops quite as much as Ayres' took part in carrying that angle. Indeed, he most probably regarded the troops of Griffin whom he met here as part of Ayres' command. For this would explain most of the discrepancies in his statements compared with established and admitted facts.

But in truth the fight was by no means over when the angle was carried. Although tactically the result was a foregone conclusion when this was done, and although the fighting there was for a few minutes sharp, yet the hard fighting was in the whole field where the enemy made their successive stands with such courage and desperation. Griffin's part in this, and even Crawford's, cannot be ignored.

But it is insisted that Crawford's Division marched out of the fight. What is true is that it did not swing in promptly on Ayres' when he

[1] Ayres says Chamberlain's troops at the angle were somewhat in advance of his at the critical moment. *Warren Court Records*, p. 267 and p 1080

[2] Testimony, *Records Warren Court*, p. 123.

changed front to the left. That was an error, and an inexcusable departure from positive orders, not being warranted by the developments of the battle. But something is to be said about its cause, and its practical results. The diagram indicated to Crawford that his division would strike the enemy first at the "angle." Encountering serious resistance on crossing the White Oak Road, and naturally drawn towards it, he kept on, expecting perhaps that he was shortly to encounter the main force of the enemy in their works, and not observing the more severe attack which fell on Ayres' left,—where, indeed, the general orders for the battle should have prepared him to understand it, and take accordant action. In such case, Griffin would have taken in hand what was opposing Crawford. But the enemy before him led him to a wider sweep, in the course of which he confronted not only the two thousand dismounted cavalry, but at length large bodies of the infantry broken from their first hold and trying to make a stand on the Ford Road. He had fighting all the way around. Calling our fight at the angle, on our extreme left, "the front," and saying that General Warren was not "in the fight," while it might be pardoned as an excited ejaculation in the heat of battle, will not stand as sober truth, or as the premise for so violent a conclusion. And all those people who ring changes on the "obliquing off" of Crawford and Griffin from the center of action, "marching away from the fighting," or "drifting out of" what they call (by a familiar figure of speech) "the fight," do not tell us that this appearance was because Ayres was suddenly compelled to make a square change of front, and those who did not instantly conform and follow might seem to be obliquing to the right, when in fact they were "swinging to the left" according to orders,—unfortunately by too wide a sweep, having a very active enemy in their front. In this concern, some minds are unduly affected by that very natural notion that *the* fight is where they are; although in the case of General Sheridan it must be admitted that "the point was well taken." Crawford's wide movement was undoubtedly an error, and a costly one for Warren; but the simple fact that Crawford lost more men in the battle than both the other divisions together —more indeed than all the rest, cavalry and infantry together—goes to show that some of the fight was where he was.

These accusations against the conduct of each of Warren's divisions, while susceptible of being magnified and manipulated so as to produce a certain forensic effect, are of no substantial weight. Even if true in the sharpest sense, they would be overstrained and uncalled for considering how the battle ended, and by whom it was mainly fought.

But the case against Warren seems to be labored. Small matters are accentuated and accumulated as if to make weight for some special conclusion.

First there is the accusation of a manner of indifference on Warren's part previous to the action. As to this, opinions would vary. There is no doubt this feeling on General Sheridan's part was very deep and disturbing. That must be considered. Those who knew Warren best saw no indifference. He was not in his usual spirits,—and we cannot wonder at it,—but he was intense rather than expressive. He knew what was depending, and what was called for, and put his energies into the case more mentally than muscularly. His subordinates understood his earnestness.

The broad ground of reason—and a valid one if substantiated by fact—for dissatisfaction with General Warren's conduct in the battle, and for his removal from command in consequence, would be that he was not in proper position during the battle to command his whole corps, and did not effectually command it. That at a sharp and critical point he was not present where General Sheridan wanted him is another matter, which does not in itself support the former conclusion.

In a military and highly proper sense, General Warren was responsible for the conduct of his corps, and ultimately for that of each of his divisions. There are two ways in which such control might be exercised: by prevention, or by correction. It was Crawford's duty to keep his vital connection with Ayres, and if in any way it should be broken, to be on the alert to see and to act. Warren should hold him responsible for that. And if he could not at the start rouse Crawford, whose peculiarities he knew, to a vivid conception of the anatomy and physiology of the case, he should have had a staff officer charged with the duty of keeping Crawford closed on Ayres, while he himself at the point where he could keep in touch with his whole corps should hold Griffin under his hand as the ready and trusted reserve prepared for the unexpected.

It may be questioned, perhaps, whether it was wise to give Crawford that front line and wheeling flank in a movement of such importance, and make him a guide for Griffin. It would have been better (as Griffin and Ayres said later in the day) to put Griffin on Ayres' right, in the order in which, curiously enough, Griffin's brigades put themselves as if by some spiritual attraction, or possibly only common sense.

But it may be justly said that, whatever errors the development of the battle disclosed, Warren should have made his troops conform to the state of facts. He did. We can well understand how exasperating it must have been to General Sheridan when Ayres was so suddenly, and it seems unexpectedly, struck on the left flank, to find the largest division of the corps not turning with him, but drawing away from the tactical focus and the close envelopment of it intended, and getting into the place on the wheeling flank which was assigned to Mackenzie's cavalry, and crowding Mackenzie "out of the fight." Griffin, when the exigencies on the left disclosed this error, hastened to put in his rear brigade,—the nearest,—now become the leading one. Warren with the same intent, passing him, pushed on for Crawford with feverish effort not short of agony. Indeed he did more than could be legally required. He performed acts of "supererogation,"—voluntary works and above the commandments,—which certainly should have saved him from perdition. He undertook the duties of staff officer for Crawford. He got hold of Kellogg's Brigade and posted it as a "marker" in the midst of the Sydnor woods, while he went off to find the rest of Crawford, and make him execute the grand left wheel; when one of Sheridan's staff coming along, astonished at this dumbshow, a brigade stationary, "marking time" at such a crisis, orders the marker into the "fight"; which the gallant commander begins right there, but ends soon after with a more exacting antagonist and with equal glory.

Meantime finding Crawford disporting himself on the tangent of a two-mile curve, Warren stuck to him like a tutor, leading him in on a quick radius to the supposed center,—which, be it borne in mind, we were all the time shifting off to the westward, making his route exhibit all the marvels of the hyperbola. His guide had gone into the vortex, and all he could do, in coming back with Crawford's recovered men, was to follow the fire, which we were battering off to the Forks. The cyclone had become a cycloid. So that Crawford was constantly obstructed by fugitives from the fight crowding him worse and worse all the way around; and when at last he struck the enemy's works, it was by no fault of Warren's that he struck them at their western end, near the Gilliam field, instead of at the left and center through the Sydnor fields. Things being as they were, Warren got his corps into the "fight" as quickly and effectively as he or anybody else possibly could.

But it is charged that the failure to close quickly on Ayres imperiled the result of the whole battle.[1] Recalling the fact that Griffin did not fail to close very promptly on Ayres, striking the "return" before Ayres struck the "angle," and the fact that the battle went on in the general way intended only by a wider sweep and more complete envelopment, we should give attention to this remark, made in a manner so forcible. General Sheridan's judgment as a tactician can hardly be questioned; nor can his deliberate statement of it. But as we are now on the line of hypothesis, we may be entitled to consider what would have been the result in case Ayres had been withstood, or even repulsed, in his first attack. In the assertion before us, no account is made of Griffin's troops. Is it assumed that they were a flock of stray sheep, engaged in backing out of fire? What they would do may be judged from what they did. And can anyone suppose the enemy would consider themselves in a very triumphant position between three bodies of our troops:—Ayres in front; the cavalry in rear; and two divisions of the Fifth Corps on their left flank as they would then front? How long does anyone believe it would be, at such a signal, before the whole Fifth Corps and our cavalry also would whirl in, and catch the enemy

[1] General Sheridan says: "If Ayres had been defeated, Crawford would have been captured: the battle would have been lost." Testimony, *Warren Court Records*, p 125.

in a maelstrom of destruction? What did happen, as it was, would have happened quicker had Ayres fared harder.

Or suppose Ayres was not so fortunately struck from the extended outwork, and had marched past the left of the enemy's entrenched line two hundred and fifty yards away, as he says he was doing.[1] Being on Griffin's left, he must have struck the left flank of the "return," and soon the rear of the enemy's main line on the White Oak Road. Griffin would then have been in immediate connection and would have swung with him. It would have taken a little longer; but the enemy would have been enveloped all the same. Sheridan's brilliant tactics would have been triumphant. Only Warren would have shared the glory.

Another consideration. Take things exactly as they were said to be,—Ayres at the "angle"; Griffin and Crawford out. What if those three Confederate brigades, ordered out of the Claiborne entrenchments that afternoon to fall on the flank of the Fifth Corps attacking at Five Forks, had come straight down, and not gone a long round-about way as they did, striking too late and too far away for any good or harm,—what would have been the effect in such case had not these two divisions of the Fifth Corps been out there to stop them?

But suppose, again, all had gone as ordered and

[1] Testimony, *Warren Court Records*, p. 255. Major Benyaurd, Corps of Engineers, says Ayres' left passed the "Bass" house to our right of it. *Warren Court Records*, p. 160.

intended, and Crawford and Griffin had swung in on the rear of the lines on the White Oak Road. Would it not have been awkward to have these five thousand fresh men[1] come down on the backs of our infantry, while having its hands full in front? What could Mackenzie have done with these men and Fitzhugh Lee's cavalry together? Lucky was it for us, in either case, that these five thousand infantrymen did not get down there. Lucky would it have been in such case, that Crawford and Griffin should happen to be out as flankers.

It is a very remarkable circumstance that neither of the three chief Confederate commanders was actually present on the field during the progress of the battle. They had been on the ground earlier it seems on retiring from Dinwiddie; but for one reason or another they had one by one retired across Hatcher's Run,—looking after their "communications" very likely.[2] Pickett returned to the field only after we had all gained the Ford Road at about 6 P.M., but Fitzhugh Lee and Rosser not at all. Pickett narrowly escaped the shots of our men as he attempted to pass them to reach his broken lines towards the White Oak Road.

It is also remarkable that General Robert E. Lee, although himself alert, was not kept informed by

[1] General Hunton, before the Warren Court, placed the numbers of these three brigades, when they attacked us the day before, first at seven thousand five hundred, but was induced by the effect of cross examination afterwards to reduce this to five thousand. *Records*, pp. 629 and 630.

[2] Private correspondence of Confederate officers present gives some curious details as to a shad dinner on the north side of Hatcher's Run.

Fitzhugh Lee or Pickett of the movements of the Fifth Corps in relation to Five Forks, and that Lee was led by a word from Pickett to suppose that Fitzhugh Lee's and Rosser's cavalry were both close in support of Pickett's left flank at Five Forks.[1] This was not the truth. Fitzhugh Lee's cavalry under Munford was over a thousand yards east of Pickett's left at the beginning and during the day was pressed around his rear so as to reach his troops after their lines had all been broken. And as for Rosser's cavalry they were at no time on the field. We know now that General Lee afterwards wrote General Wade Hampton in these words: "Had you been at Five Forks with your cavalry the disaster would not have befallen my army." Nor does it appear that General Anderson, commanding General Lee's reserves in this quarter, knew anything of the pressing need of them at Five Forks until all was over.

So there are some other generals beside Warren who helped Sheridan to his fame at Five Forks.

So much for the tactics of that battle. In spite of errors it was a great victory. It was Sheridan's battle. The glory of it is his. With his cavalry there was no error nor failure. Their action was not less than magnificent; the central thought carried into every brilliant act;—a picture to satisfy any point of view, idealist or impressionist.

As to the strategic merits of the battle, a few reflections may be permitted. Undoubtedly, as things were, it was an important battle. But our

[1] *Rebellion Records*, serial 95, p. 1264.

isolated position there invited fresh attack; and we only escaped it by the blundering or over-cautious course of the forces sent out by Lee from the Claiborne front that afternoon, and which in Sheridan's solicitude we were pushed out to meet that night. Then, too, we were much farther off from the Petersburg front, and the opportunity for concerted action with the other corps in the line for general assault. And finally, we were in no more advantageous position now than we should have been if we had turned the Claiborne flank of the enemy's entrenchments, and cut the Southside Road at Sutherland's the day before.[1] Indeed, the very first thing we did the next morning after Five Forks was to move back to turn this same flank on the Claiborne Road and gain possession of Sutherland's. But Miles had taken care of this, as we might have done before him. Only Lee had now got a day's start of us, the head of his column well out on its retreat, necessitated not by Five Forks alone but by gallant work along our whole confronting line,—which might have been done the day before, and saved the long task of racing day and night, of toils and tribulations and losses recorded and unrecorded, which brought fame to Appomattox, and the end of deeds rewarded and unrewarded.

A study of this battle shows vexing provocations,

[1] The right of the enemy's entrenchments on the Claiborne Road after they were driven in on the afternoon of March 31st was by no means strongly held. Testimony of General Hunton, *Warren Court Records*, p. 629.

but does not show satisfactory reasons for the removal of General Warren from command of the Fifth Corps. The fact is that much of the dissatisfaction with him was of longer standing. We recall the incident that General Sheridan did not wish to have the Fifth Corps with him at the start[1]; also the suggestion by General Grant that Sheridan might have occasion to remove him, and the authority to do so[2]; then the keen disappointments of the Dinwiddie overture the day before, and the exasperation at Warren's not reporting to Sheridan that night.[3] We recall General Griffin's remark in the morning that something like this would happen before the day was through.[4] We recur also to the complaints earlier noticed.[5] There was an unfavorable judgment of Warren's manner of handling a corps; an uncomfortable sense of certain intellectual peculiarities of his; a dislike of his self-centered manner and temperament and habit generally, and his rather injudicious way of expressing his opinion on tender topics. There was a variety of antagonism towards General Warren stored up and accumulating in General Sheridan's mind, and the tension of a heated moment brought the catastrophe.

No one can doubt General Sheridan's "right" to remove Warren; but whether he was right in doing so is another question, and one involving many elements. It is necessary that a chief com-

[1] See paper on the White Oak Road, vol. i., of this series, p. 230.
[2] *Idem*, p. 246.
[3] *Idem*, pp 244-45.
[4] *Ante.*
[5] *Ante*, note.

mander, who is under grave responsibilities, should have the power to control and even displace the subordinates on whom he depends for the execution of his plans. Nor is it to be expected that he can properly be held to give strict account of action so taken, or be called upon to analyze his motives and justify himself by reasons to be passed upon by others. In this case, there are many subjective reasons—influences acting on the mind of General Sheridan himself and not easily made known to others, impressions from accounts of previous action, the appearance of things at the moment, and his state of mind in consequence—which go to strengthen the favorable presumption accorded to his act. But as to the essential equity of it, the moral justification of it, opinions will be governed by knowledge of facts, and these extending beyond the incidents or accidents of this field.

The simple transfer of a corps commander is not a disgrace, nor necessarily an injury. General Warren had no vested right to the command of the Fifth Corps. And if Sheridan expected to have this corps with him in this campaign, in which he held assurances of a conspicuous and perhaps preeminent part, and General Warren was to him a *persona non grata*, we cannot wonder that he should wish to remove him. He had already objected to having this corps with him; but after trial he did not send back the corps, but its commander. It was the time, place, and manner of this removal, the implications involved in it, and the vague reasons given for it, which made the grievance for General Warren. He was immediately assigned to another command, but even if Grant had restored him to the Fifth Corps, this would not wipe out that record, which stood against his honor. It is highly probable that a court-martial would not have found him guilty of misconduct warranting such a punishment as dismissal from his command. There was not then, as there is not now, any tribunal with power to change the conclusion so summarily given by Sheridan, or to annul or mitigate the material effects of it. But such reasons as were given for this affected Warren's honor, and hence he persistently invoked a court of inquiry. All that he could hope for from such a court was the opportunity thus given for the facts and measurably the motives and feelings affecting the case to be brought out and placed upon the public records.

The posture of the parties before that court was peculiar. The members of the court were general officers of the active army. The applicant was then a lieutenant-colonel of engineers. The respondent—virtually the defendant—was lieutenant-general of the armies of the United States, —the superior of course, and the commander, of every member of the court, as also of most of the witnesses before it, then in the military service. The "next friend" and chief witness—called by the applicant, but necessarily for the respondent—was General Grant, ex-President of the United States, who still carried an immense prestige and influence. The traditions of the whole War Department were for sustaining military authority. We could not expect this court to bring in a verdict of censure on General Sheridan, or anything that would amount to that. We can only wonder at the courage of all who gave Warren any favorable endorsement or explanation, and especially of the court which found so little to censure in the conduct of General Warren as commander of the Fifth Corps in those last three days. The court sustained General Sheridan in his right, but General Warren felt that the revelation of the facts was of the nature of vindication. It came too late to save much of his life; it may have saved what was dearer.

I am by no means sure but that injustice must be taken by a military officer as a necessary part of his risks, of the conditions and chances of his service, to be suffered in the same way as wounds and sicknesses, in patience and humility. But when one feels that his honor and the truth itself are impugned, then that larger personality is concerned wherein one belongs to others and his worth is somehow theirs. Then he does not satisfy himself with regret,—that strange complex feeling that something is right which is now impossible,—and even the truth made known becomes a consolation.

The battle of Five Forks was also the battle of the White Oak Road, on an extended front, in an accidental and isolated position, and at a delayed hour. It was successful, owing to the character of the troops, and the skill and vigor of the commander. Appomattox was a glorious result of strong pushing and hard marching. But both could have been forestalled, and all that fighting, together with that at Sailor's Creek, High Bridge, and Farmville have been concentrated in one grand assault, of which the sharp-edged line along the White Oak Road would have been one blade of the shears, and Ord and Wright and Parke on the main line the other, and the hard and costly ten days' chase and struggle would have been spared so many noble men. Lee would not have got a day's start of us in the desperate race. Sheridan cutting the enemy's communications and rolling up their scattering fugitives would have shown his great qualities, and won conspicuous, though not supreme honors. Warren would have shared the glories of his corps. Humphreys and Wright with their veterans of the Second and Sixth, whose superb action compelled the first flag of truce contemplating Lee's surrender, would not have stood idly around the headquarters' flag of the Army of the Potomac, with Longstreet's right wing brought to bay before them, waiting till Lee's final answer to Grant should come through Sheridan to the Fifth Corps front, where Ord, of the Army of the James, commanded. And Meade, the high-born gentleman and high-born soldier, would have been spared the slight of being held back with the main body of his army, while the laurels were bestowed by chance or choice, which had been so fairly won by that old army in long years of heroic patience in well-doing and suffering;—might have been spared the after humiliation of experiencing in his own person how fortune and favor preside in the final distribution of honors in a country's recognition.

The Fifth Corps had an eventful history. Two passages of it made a remarkable coincidence. It was its misfortune to lose two of its commanders—the first and the last in the field of action—by measures so questionable as to call for a court of review, by which, long after, both were substantially vindicated: Fitz-John Porter, accounted the most accomplished corps commander on the Peninsula, and "heir apparent" to the command of the army, and Warren, whom Grant says he had looked upon for commander of the army in case anything should take from the field the sterling Meade.[1] Who from such beginning could have foretold the end! And Meade,—he, too, went from the Fifth Corps to the command of the army, and found there a troubled eminence and an uncrowned end.

Shakespeare tells us, poetizing fate or faith:

> There's a Divinity that shapes our ends,
> Rough-hew them how we will.

To our common eyes it often seems a dark divinity that rules; and the schoolmaster might interchange the verbs.

[1] Grant's *Memoirs*, vol ii, p. 216.

CHAPTER V

THE WEEK OF FLYING FIGHTS

THE victory at Five Forks had swept away a flying buttress of the enemy's stronghold. We had broken down the guard of a tactical movement to hold their threatened communications and cover their entrenched lines. We may be said to have virtually turned the right of the defenses of Petersburg and broken the Confederate hold upon Virginia. It was, indeed, a brilliant overture, giving courage to our hearts and stimulus to our energies.

Immediately on learning of Sheridan's victory at Five Forks, Grant reissued the suspended order directing an assault on the long-confronted defenses of Petersburg, which was executed by our Sixth and Ninth Corps with the assistance of the Army of the James with splendid valor and decisive effects. But he felt anxious about our isolated position at Five Forks, and ordered Humphreys to make vigorous demonstrations to find a vulnerable spot in the enemy's entrenched line in his front, and if he could not carry any portion of this, to send Miles' Division up the White Oak Road to Sheridan that night. To intensify the diversion, our whole army in that quarter was to keep up a roar of cannonading all night long.

We now have to chronicle movements of extraordinary vacillation and complexity. It will be remembered that on the night of the battle most of our corps was moved out towards the Claiborne on the White Oak Road, and that part of Griffin's Division now commanded by Bartlett remained on the field with a guard at the Ford of Hatcher's Run, and a picket encompassing that storied and now haunted ground. We hardly know what General Grant can be desiring to establish when he says (*Memoirs*, ii., p. 446) that Sheridan, "appreciating the importance of the situation, sent the Fifth Corps that night across Hatcher's Run to just south west of Petersburg, and faced them towards it." If he had done so, there would have been a "diversion" on our end of the line as well as elsewhere, and with music and dancing; for this would have called us to disprove one of the very doubtful axioms of physics, that "two bodies cannot occupy the same space at the same time," with such pyrotechnic celebration as two clouds charged with opposite electricities exhibit when driven to bivouac together in the same field of the heavens. We should have camped inside the rebel lines, and a bedlam of a bivouac that would have been.

After their defeat at Five Forks, the cavalry of both the Lees joined Rosser at the Ford crossing of Hatcher's Run, and then drew back on that road to the Southside Railroad crossing. There were gathered also the fugitives from Pickett's and Johnson's Divisions, covered by the remainder of those divisions that had not been in the fight, —Hunton's Brigade of Pickett's Division, and Wise's, Gracie's (commanded by Colonel Sanford), and Fulton's of Johnson's Division, all under command of General R. H. Anderson. Their ultimate destination was to cover the enemy's right flank at Sutherland's Station. These would have been unpleasant fellows to camp with on the night of April 1st.

Humphreys, finding the entrenchments in his front impregnable, at about midnight sent Miles up the White Oak Road to Sheridan. But at daylight Sheridan faced him right about, and with two divisions of the Fifth Corps following, pushed back down the White Oak Road to attack the Claiborne flank,—where we had left it on the night of the thirty-first. Meantime, this morning of April 2d saw the splendid and triumphant assault of our army upon the outer Petersburg defenses. Humphreys, learning of this at about nine o'clock, attacked the works in his own front along the eastern end of the White Oak Road, defended by McGowan's, MacRay's, Scales', and Cook's Brigades of Hill's Corps commanded by Heth, and forced them out of their works by their right flank towards the Claiborne Road. Humphreys followed them up with his two divisions, and receiving word from Miles that he was returning towards him, ordered the whole Second Corps to pursue the enemy along the Claiborne Road towards Sutherland's Station with a view to cutting off the retreat of the fugitives from Wright's and Ord's attacks, and closing in on Petersburg. Sheridan, arriving at the Claiborne Road and learning this, thereupon faces about the Fifth Corps, after having, strangely enough, given Miles permission to attack the enemy there, and marches his men back over the White Oak Road to Five Forks, and pushes on by the Ford Road up to Hatcher's Run. What lost labor for Miles and the Fifth Corps, running empty express up and down the White Oak Road! The shuttlecock was flying again. In the meantime Humphreys advancing with the two divisions to join Miles for the contemplated movement on the Claiborne flank and Sutherland's, having apprised General Meade of his intention, finds his action disapproved by his superiors, and receives orders to leave Miles and move his two other divisions off by the Boydton Road towards Petersburg and form on the left of the Sixth Corps. This, of course, left Miles to Sheridan, and Sheridan had now left Miles.

As these apparently absurd performances involve again the action and honor of the Fifth Corps, it is proper to bring them under examination. The accounts of the affair of Miles at Sutherland's Station given by General Badeau, General Grant, General Sheridan, and General Humphreys involve irreconcilable differences; and it is necessary to form our judgments on the subject by taking into account the means of knowledge, and probable motives of action and of utterance, which go to establish the credibility of witnesses.

First we are prone to wonder how it could be that such a man as General Sheridan,—who does not reconsider his determinations,—when within less than two miles of the intended point of attack, should suddenly retire with his whole command, and leave Miles to fight the battle alone. It seems equally strange that General Humphreys should nearly at the same time turn and march off in the opposite direction, towards Petersburg. It is certainly a curious conjuncture that both Meade and Sheridan should be pulling away from Miles' high-toned division and the very respectable company of Confederates about Sutherland's as if they were not fit for their seeing.

Sheridan gives for his action a reason which appears sufficient, and adds an opinion which is significant. He says: "On the north side of Hatcher's Run, I overtook Miles, who was anxious to attack, and had a very fine and spirited division. I gave him permission; but about this time General Humphreys came up, and receiving notice from General Meade that he would take command of Miles' Division, I relinquished it at once, and faced the Fifth Corps to the rear. I afterwards regretted giving up this division, as I believe the enemy could at the time have been crushed at Sutherland's depot. I returned to Five Forks, and marched out the Ford Road towards Hatcher's Run."

Two things are to be noted here: the reason why

Sheridan did not join the attack here, but released himself from the fight and Miles from his jurisdiction; and also his belief that this was the place at which to crush the enemy. Some of the rest of us had thought the same way on the 31st of March. This testimony is also confirmed by the opinion of the modest Humphreys, who cannot help saying that if the Second Corps could have been permitted to continue its march in the morning, "the whole force of the enemy there would probably have been captured." This cumulative testimony shows what was lost by the antipathy of polarities, in the presence of Miles, the mysterious repellant.

In reflecting on the probabilities of Meade's motive in ordering Humphreys away from Miles' Division when Sheridan was approaching it with the intention of making an important fight there, it appears more than likely that Meade had a strong intimation that Sheridan must have undisturbed control of the entire operations on the extreme left. To this effect we have the direct, although perhaps unintentional, testimony of a most competent witness. General Badeau, Grant's military secretary, in his *Military History of U. S. Grant*, vol. iii., p. 624, says: "Grant, however, intended to leave Sheridan in command of Miles, and indeed in full control of all the operations in this quarter of the field; and supposing his views to have been carried out, it was at this juncture that he ordered Humphreys to be faced to the right and moved towards Petersburg." This appears to settle that part of the question, and takes the burden entirely from Meade's shoulders, which he never seems to have had the heart to roll off for himself. Sheridan's motive, too, is readily seen by the same light. When he thought Miles had been ordered to resume relations with his own corps commander, Sheridan wished to have nothing to do with the fight, although in his estimation this was the supreme opportunity for "crushing the enemy."

It is a little confusing to try to reconcile this testimony and explanation, with General Grant's statement in his offiical report, that learning the condition of things on the morning of April 2d, Sheridan "returned Miles to his proper command." If so, why did Sheridan give Miles permission to attack at Sutherland's? And why, if the smashing up of the rebel right flank was so easy to achieve here, did he turn his back on Miles on the very edge of battle, and leave to him the solitary honor and peril of confronting there Heth's, and what of Johnson's and Pickett's Divisions and Fitzhugh Lee's cavalry, falling back that afternoon before the Fifth Corps advance, should get into his front? Certainly there were no other of the enemy west of this point at that hour worth Sheridan's marching the Fifth Corps ten miles round to hunt after.

It is a striking coincidence that Sheridan with the Fifth Corps should have come so near to Miles and the enemy,—two miles on the south of them,—in the morning, at the moment when Humphreys was first coming up with his two divisions for the fight he anticipated, and then again, after the middle of the afternoon, have come within two miles of Sutherland's and of Miles fighting, on the Cox Road west of them, and also just at the time when Humphreys was "returning" from the direction of Petersburg with his division ordered by Grant to go up to Miles' relief. The play of attraction and repulsion is something deep-lying in the "law" of forces.

An effort has also been made to give the impression that these two appearances of Sheridan, on the right and on the left of Miles at Sutherland's, were moments of one and the same action,—parts of one undivided movement. Whereas they were separated by a wider detour, possibly imperiling quite as much as the eventful one of Crawford at Five Forks, where Warren was the chief victim.

There are so many curious jumbles of coincidence and dislocation in the accounts of Sheridan's movements that day,—if we may not say in the movements themselves,—that readers who are not on the alert to keep things clear in their minds are liable to lose their bearings. Badeau "bothers" matters very much; as when he says (vol. iii., p. 520), "At noon the left wing under Sheridan was still unheard from." It would seem that the delirium of writing history had reached the stupor symptom somewhere. Grant must have known that Sheridan had dropped Miles and gone back to start for a longer run. We have Grant's statement in his official report that he got worried about Miles after a while, left as he was alone when he ordered Humphreys away from him, and Sheridan had abandoned him. He adds, in terms implying censure of Humphreys: "I directed Humphreys to send a division back to his relief. He went himself." It required considerable boldness in Humphreys to "go himself" with one of his divisions. Warren had tried that, and it took him so far he never got back. Whatever the much buffeted Humphreys could have done, in obeying orders, he would have been left with only one of his divisions somewhere, and we cannot blame him for trying to get where he had a chance of getting his eye in range of two of them, when a mixed fight was going on. And Grant ordering Humphrey's divisions makes us wonder where Meade was, supposed to command the corps of his army. Though raised to functions of a higher power, the ratio seems the same as that of Warren and Humphreys to their commands,—the instinctive dignity and abnormal solicitude of the hen with one chicken. When Humphreys got to Miles, that gallant officer had beaten the enemy from their last stand; but the most of them had got off between Meade and Sheridan.

General Grant, with the sincere kindness of his prepossessions, makes a special effort to have General Sheridan appear as a direct participator in the victory at Sutherland's. He allows Badeau to speak to this effect. And he himself says in his *Memoirs* (vol. ii., p. 451), "Sheridan then took the enemy at Sutherland's Station, on the reverse side from where Miles was, and the two together captured the place, with a large number of prisoners and some pieces of artillery, and put the remainder, portions of three Confederate corps, to flight. Sheridan followed, and drove them until night, when further pursuit was stopped. Miles bivouacked for the night on the ground which he with Sheridan had so handsomely carried by assault." It was sometime before noon when Miles made his first attack, and quite as late as 3 P.M. when he made his last and completely successful one. At this time the Fifth Corps, the head of Sheridan's column, had got around as far as Cox's Station on the Southside Railroad, within two miles of Sutherland's, and was tearing up the rails there. Our column was not near enough to Miles's fight to take part in the actual assault, although no doubt its rapid and close advance on the enemy's right had some influence on the victory. But we never thought of claiming part of the glory that belonged to Miles,—except that he was not long ago a Fifth Corps boy.

The truth is that after all the pains to secure for Sheridan the glory of whatever was achieved on the left, or as Badeau says, "in that quarter of the field," when all came to the very field where by unanimous consent the enemy's main force could have been "crushed," and in fact was broken away with less complete results by Miles' gallant fight, Sheridan came perilously near—so near in truth that the difference is inappreciable by the human mind—to being found "not in the fight," by reason of the far-reaching effect of his recoil from the suddenly appearing Humphreys, who rose upon him at the crowning moment when he gave

Miles permission to open the "crushing" fight. Shakespeare puts it:

> Ay, now, I see 'tis true;
> For the blood-boltcrèd Banquo smiles upon me,
> And points at them for his

It is a relief to resume the plain account of our pursuit of tangible beings evading Five Forks. It seems like passing from war to peace. Early on the morning of the 2d our cavalry drew off northwesterly from the Ford Road crossing of Hatcher's Run to cut off some rebel cavalry reported to have made a push in that direction. Sheridan having returned from the Claiborne Road with the rest of the Fifth Corps, at about noon our column moved out, my own command in the advance, down the Ford Road. At Hatcher's Run a vigorous demonstration of the enemy's skirmishers to prevent our crossing was soon dislodged by a gallant attack by Colonel Sniper with the 185th New York. Throwing forward a strong skirmish line, in command of Colonel Cunningham of the 32d Massachusetts, we pressed on for the Southside Railroad. Hearing the noise of an approaching train from the direction of Petersburg, I pushed forward our skirmishers to catch it. A wild, shriek of the steam-whistle brought our main line up at the double-quick. There we find the train held up, Cunningham mounted on the engine pulling the whistle-valve wide open to announce the arrival at a premature station of the last train that tried to run the gauntlet out of Petersburg under the Confederate flag. This train was crowded with quite a mixed company as to color, character, and capacity, but united in the single aim of forming a personally-conducted southern tour. The officers and soldiers we were obliged to regard as prisoners of war: the rest we let go in peace, if they could find it. It was now about one o'clock. It is to be noted that this train appears to have had no difficulty in getting by Sutherland's at that hour.

I was now directed to advance and, if possible, get possession of the Cox Road. This we found to be well defended. A force of about ten thousand men formed a strong line in front of us, but with that "light order" of disposition and movement which betokens a rear-guard. As this is sometimes, however, the mask for formidable resistance, I prepared to carry the position whatever it might prove to be. Accordingly, I threw forward the 185th New York in extended but compact order, covering the enemy's front, brought the two battalions of the 198th Pennsylvania into line of battle in support, placed the 189th New York, Lieut.-Colonel Townsend commanding, in a large tract of woods on the right with orders to move left in front, ready to face outwards and protect that flank which looked toward Sutherland's, and advanced briskly upon the opposing lines. They proved to be Fitzhugh Lee's Division of cavalry dismounted, which from character and experience had acquired a habit of conservative demeanor. But a strong dash broke them up, and we pressed them slowly before us along the Cox Road. Anticipating the burden of the retreat from the direction of Petersburg to fall this way, I prepared to hold this road against all comers, in the meantime pushing forward to the bank of a branch of Hatcher's Run a mile short of Sutherland's. Here my command was held in line and on the alert while the rest of the Fifth Corps were engaged in tearing up the Southside Railroad between us and Cox's Station in our rear. We were on the flank and rear of the enemy fighting Miles, but the stress of that fire died away as we approached. Miles had utterly routed the enemy. No doubt our advancing along the Cox Road towards this point, and also our preventing Fitzhugh Lee's cavalry from joining the resistance to Miles, had some considerable effect on the minds of the enemy, as well as in determining the direction of their retreat, and in so far helped Miles win his victory; but this could hardly be construed as part of the action.

Our cavalry shortly afterwards coming up in our rear, Sheridan with them pursued the fugitives along their retreat, now northwesterly, our rear division, Crawford's, joining in a skirmish at about dusk. We turned off the Cox Road to the Namozine, and moving out about two miles, bivouacked at the junction of this road with the River Road, which here turns north, leading to the Appomattox.

This was a hard day for my command. Being in the advance and in contact with the enemy, we had to move as nearly as possible in line of battle, taking a wide breadth of that broken country, through brush and tangle, swamp and mire. Eight hours of this right upon such severe experience the two days and nights before left the men utterly exhausted. But they gathered the sticks for their little fires, and unrolled their slender haversacks, disclosing treasures that were mostly remnants, whether pork or sugar, biscuit or blankets—things provided for their earthly sustenance while they were contending for ideals to come true for them only in some other life, or far-away form. *Sic vos non vobis*—not you for yourselves—says Virgil to his bees and birds building nests and storing up food, mostly for others. Strange shadows fall across the glamour of glory. The law of sharing for the most of mankind seems to be that each shall give his best according to some inner commandment, and receive according to the decree of some far divinity, whose face is of a stranger, and whose heart is alien to the motives and sympathies that animate his own.

At daylight on the 3d we moved out on the River Road on the south side of the Appomattox, with the purpose of cutting off the enemy's retreat from Petersburg. This day was remarkable in the fact that then, for once, we had somebody "ahead" of the Fifth Corps except the enemy. The cavalry were ahead this time, and that incident did not add to the comfort of marching in the mud, which in its nature, and without previous preparation, was a sufficient test for human powers, physical and moral. We had, however, the stimulus of hearing in exultant and wildly exaggerated phrase of the flight of the Confederate government from Richmond, the full retreat of Lee's army from Virginia, and the downfall of the Confederacy. The plain facts were enough for us: Lee's army was in retreat for Danville, the Richmond government broken up, and the Confederacy at least mounted on its last legs. The splendid work of the right wing of our army on the 2d had set this in motion, and we still thought our restless behavior on the extreme left had at least induced Lee to notify Davis on the evening of that day that he should be obliged to abandon his lines during the night and would endeavor to reach Danville, North Carolina. Davis anticipated him with military promptitude, and succeeded in getting off with his personal effects and the Confederate archives by the Danville Road.

Grant had ordered a general assault on the interior lines of Petersburg and Richmond early on this morning of the 3d, but it was then discovered that they had been evacuated during the night. These places were immediately occupied by our troops, and General Warren was assigned to the command of the forces in and around Petersburg and City Point. The order given by Lee for the general retreat had been put into execution early in the evening of the 2d; Longstreet and the troops that had been in our main front, including also Gordon's Corps, had crossed to the north side of the Appomattox, directing their course towards Amelia Court House on the Danville Railroad about equidistant from Richmond and Petersburg. Those with whom we had been principally engaged, Pickett's and Bushrod Johnson's Divisions, with Fitzhugh Lee's cavalry, moved up the south side of the Appomattox, closely followed by us. The cavalry ahead were pressing on the enemy's rear all day, and just at dusk of the evening came upon a strong line of Lee's cavalry with Hunton's and Wise's infantry brigades boldly confronting us at the crossing of Deep Creek. The cavalry had forced them away in a sharp engagement before we got up to share in it. We could not help admiring the courage and pluck of these poor fellows, now so broken and hopeless, both for their cause and for themselves. A long and hard road was before them, whatever fate should be at the end of it. We had a certain pride in their manliness, and a strong "fellow-feeling," however determined we were to destroy the political pretension which they had accepted as their cause. Before morning of the 4th General Sheridan, learning that Lee was trying to assemble his army near Amelia Court House, ordered the Fifth Corps to make all dispatch for Jetersville, a point about eight miles south of that place, to intercept Lee's communications by the Danville Road, while a column of our cavalry was sent around to strike that road still south of us and then move up to join us at Jetersville. Here, after a brisk march,—thirty-five miles, Sheridan says,—we arrived late in the day, and before midnight the Fifth Corps was in line of battle across the Danville Railroad, strongly entrenched, effectually cutting Lee's plans and therefore in a position where we were pretty sure to be ourselves attacked with desperation in the morning, by Lee's whole army. This expectation held us at high tension on the morning of the 5th, waiting for the Army of the Potomac to come up and secretly hoping in our interior confessionals that Lee would also wait for them.

We had all expected a great battle at Jetersville. A sonorous name is not necessary for a famous field. And there was a little French flavor about this name that might have brought livelier associations than "jetsam," of which also there was plenty before the week was over. Sheridan thought Lee missed his great opportunity in not attacking us here before any reinforcements got up. We shall not censure Lee. If he had doubts about the issue of a fight with the Fifth Corps we willingly accord him the benefit of his doubt. It appears, however, that Lee being informed by "Rooney" Lee, his son, that Sheridan had a heavy force of infantry here, gave up the attack and turned his columns off by a more northerly route, sending his trains by the best protected roads towards the Danville communications. So narrow was our chance of being confronted by Lee's whole army. And so great was our satisfaction at Lee's opinion of the Fifth Corps.

Our Second and Sixth Corps had been trying to follow the Fifth all the morning of the 4th, but had been stopped a long way back by one of those common, and therefore presumably necessary, but unspeakably vexatious, incidents of a forced march,—somebody else cutting in on the road, claiming to have the right of way. The cavalry had come in on them from one of the river-crossings where they had been heading off Lee from his nearest road to Amelia Court House, and precedence being given the cavalry in order, our infantry corps had to mass up and wait till they could get the road. The fields were in such condition that troops could not march over them, and the roads were not much better for the rear of a column, with all its artillery and wagons. These delayed corps were not allowed to get the rheumatism by resting on the damp ground, but were favored with the well-proved prophylactic of lively work corduroying roads, so that they could have something substantial to set foot on. At half-past two in the afternoon of the 5th, the advance of the Second Corps began to arrive in rear of our anxious, expectant, front-faced lines, and form in upon our left, soon followed by our Sixth Corps, which in like manner formed upon our right. It needs not be told what kind of a greeting we gave each other there. These corps, what had they not done since they parted on the old lines a week before! That Army of the Potomac together once again, at that turning, burning point dividing the storied past from the swift-coming end of its history.

At one o'clock that afternoon my command was suddenly called out to support the cavalry, which returning from a heavy reconnoissance had struck one of the enemy's trains moving off on our left flank, and having captured 180 wagons and five pieces of artillery, and destroyed the wagons, was bringing in the artillery and a large number of prisoners, and was severely attacked by a strong body of cavalry and infantry, not far out from our lines. This had made things lively for a time. We had not much to do, however, when we got up to them. Or perhaps that prolific and redundant principle of anticipation, by which a thing seems so much better when you want it than when you get it, and, *vice versa*, so much worse when you fear it than when you front it, may have availed here. The so-called moral effect of seeing and knowing that our plodding infantry had covered their tracks was perhaps stronger than we could have made good if we had been more severely tested in the flying fight. But our cavalry was a queer sight. Before they had destroyed the wagons, they had apparently had a custom-house inspection, and confiscated many, various, and marvelous "goods,"—contraband, and some of them contradictory, of war. It looked as if not only the grocers and tinsmiths, but also the jewelers and possibly the milliners, of Petersburg and Richmond had been disappointed in a venture they had hopefully consigned to southern ports. It was almost provocative of levity,—quite "to the prejudice of good order and military discipline,"—to see our grave cavalry forming their flowing lines of battle with silver coffee-pots and sugar-bowls thumping at their saddle-straps, and when they rallied in return to see their front fluttering with domestic symbols, and even "favors" of the boudoir, as if a company of troubadours had dismounted a squadron of crusaders between Joppa and Jerusalem. But it was with a joy deeper far than merriment that I came in touch with our splendid old First Maine Cavalry, famed for manhood and soldierhood then and ever since, with Smith at their head straight and solid and luminous as a lighthouse.

Sheridan, however, wished to move up and attack Lee, even before the other corps got up to us. Meade, having arrived in person in advance of even the Second Corps, was unwilling to move out without the other corps to attack Lee with forty thousand men in hand and in position,—if the reports which Sheridan relied upon were true. This decision of Meade, Badeau says, was "much to Sheridan's mortification." Still all he could do about it was to "tell his father." He sent a messenger to Grant saying that it was of utmost importance that Grant should come to him in person. Meade had been very ill for the last two days,—we cannot much wonder at that,—and had asked Sheridan to put the Second Corps and also the Sixth into position as he might desire, while he retired for a little rest. Grant, coming promptly up in the course of the night, held a conference with Sheridan on the situation, and especially, it now appears, on Meade's supposed or imputed plan "of moving out to his right flank," whatever that might be conjectured to mean, "and giving Lee the coveted opportunity of escaping us, and putting us in rear of him." Grant and Sheridan then went, after midnight, to see Meade, when General Grant says he "explained to Meade that we did not want to follow the enemy, but to get ahead of him, and that his (Meade's) orders would allow the enemy to escape." It seems incredible that an officer of the position, experience, and responsibility of General Meade could have listened patiently to this imputation of ignorance and stupidity. A movement to Meade's "right flank," as his army was faced, would have carried him back to our old entrenched lines. It is absurd to imagine Meade ever intended this undertaking. And it may be questioned whether the movement we did make under Sheridan's direction and Grant's authority and orders for Meade to execute did not immediately "put us in rear of Lee's army" and keep us there until the long, hard circuit to Appomattox Court House was run.

This kind of history makes it proper to look at matters a little in detail. And for the first thing as to the state of mind and purpose of General Meade, against whom such belittling reference has been made.

The last week's experiences had worked together to make Meade in truth seriously ill. Still he held up in spirit and body like a martyr. When Sheridan with the Fifth Corps at Jetersville on the 5th sent word to Meade asking for the other corps of his army, Meade, lying on his rude couch scarcely able to move, shows no lack of soldierly spirit or indeed of magnanimity. He dispatches Grant: "I have ordered Humphreys to move out at all hazards at 3 A.M.; but if the rations can be issued to them prior to that, to march as soon as issued; or if the temper of the men, on hearing the dispatch of General Sheridan communicated to them, leads to the belief that they will march with spirit, then to push on at once, as soon as they can be got under arms." In his order then issued Meade says: "The troops will be put in motion regardless of every consideration but the one of ending the war. . . . The Major-General commanding feels that he has but to recall to the Army of the Potomac the glorious record of its repeated and gallant contests with the Army of Northern Virginia, and when he assures the army that in the opinion of so distinguished an officer as Major-General Sheridan, it only requires these sacrifices to bring this long and desperate contest to a triumphant issue, the men of this army will show that they are as willing to die of fatigue and of starvation as they have ever shown themselves ready to fall by the bullets of the enemy."

This may not carry all the incitements of persuasive eloquence; but whatever concentric or eccentric meanings it may bear, it is the testimony of a high and heroic soul. He was the senior of Sheridan in rank and service and in command, and had now begun to comprehend the plans for Sheridan in the coming campaign beyond the part of commander of the cavalry forces. But he sends him this word: "The Second and Sixth Corps shall be with you as soon as possible. In the meantime your wishes or suggestions as to any movement other than the simple one of overtaking you will be promptly acceded to by me, regardless of any other consideration than the vital one of destroying the Army of Northern Virginia." Deep-drawn is this simple language: deeplier significant the more one ponders it. We have the high authority of General Adam Badeau that "this is the stuff of which commanders are made." That is,—self-effacement and renunciation at the behest of a rival! We are not so sure about this definition of the proper "stuff" for the composition of commanders; but certainly this message is an almost sublime utterance of a gentleman and a patriot,—an unselfish and magnanimous man. To my mind, it seems like the last words of an Algernon Sidney or a Montrose: "The noblest place where man can die is where he dies for man."

In this same spirit he rises from his couch of suffering and passing his troops upon the road, finds his Fifth Corps in advance of Sheridan's cavalry, square across the Danville Railroad, faced towards Lee's then approaching army, and asks Sheridan to place the rest of the Army of the Potomac, as it comes up, in such order of battle as Sheridan may think proper, and trusting that all will be done in the spirit that has animated his whole movement thus far, asking only that this overmarched advance shall not be hurled against Lee's whole entrenched army before our main body is all up, Meade sinks down to his couch for a respite at least of mental suffering. Here he is visited by Grant and Sheridan with the very distinct intimation that his plans are weak and silly, and that Sheridan's plans would now be put into execution. Then, to sleep, we may suppose. And in that sleep what dreams might come, those who watched his troubled rest spoke not what they divined. For it needed not vision nor prophet, nor Urim nor Thummim to read through the palpitating air that another sun had arisen. Samuel had already anointed David and Saul could get no answer from the Lord. It needed no far-sighted glasses to see that Meade was no longer in reality commander of the Army of the Potomac but only the vanishing simulacrum of it. Was he dreaming perchance of the affront offered him by the false charge of an intended "right flank" movement which would lead him past the enemy's rear? Or lamenting in helpless agony the lost opportunity of striking a decisive blow at Lee's last vital stand had he not been sent off by Grant and Sheridan to Amelia Court House whence Lee had already fled? For it was well known to some whose business it was to know, that Meade had planned to move in a very different direction and on shorter lines on the morning of April 6th, and strike Longstreet at Rice's Station on the Lynchburg Road where there is every reason to believe he would have brought about the beginning of the end. Alas for Meade! He never saw his army together again,—not even in the grand review at Washington,—from which time too he sunk from sight.

To return to our story it will be borne in mind

that the Fifth Corps and the cavalry held Jetersville from the afternoon of the 4th of April to the afternoon of the 5th, in the face of Lee's whole army. But as things were before morning Sheridan returns the Fifth Corps to the command of Meade, an act which he states he "afterwards regretted" —a conciliatory phrase which had become habitual. Assured by him that Lee's army is at Amelia Court House, Grant orders Meade to move out in that direction in the order of battle in which his corps were already formed, to attack the enemy in position there, while Sheridan with the cavalry should take the direction Meade had intended for his army,—towards the Danville and Lynchburg road-crossings. We had moved in this way five miles of the eight, when Griffin learns that Lee's army is not at Amelia Court House, having left there on the evening before, and being now well on its way around our left flank. Humphreys caught sight of some of Lee's rear columns moving on a road about four miles northwest of us, and immediately sent out a detachment to cut them in two. It was no part of Lee's plan to wait to be attacked by our whole army, and on learning of our gathering at Jetersville he began his retiring movement at eight o'clock in the evening, sending his several corps by all the roads leading in the desired direction, either for Danville or for Lynchburg. So Meade was actually sent out with the foregone certainty of doing what he had no thought of doing, but was charged with having contemplated,—letting Lee pass him, and putting us in his rear.

Meade at once faces his army about and directs his several corps by different roads to follow, outmarch, and intercept Lee's flying army. Griffin is sent by the most northerly and roundabout way, through Painevillc (well-named), Ligontown, and Sailor's Creek,—in doing this, observe, moved from the extreme left to the extreme right of the army. Humphreys moves on the left of the Fifth Corps to Deatonsville, and thence towards Sailor's Creek, while the Sixth Corps under Wright moves from Jetersville by the shortest roads to the same rendezvous. Now began the terrible race and running fights, swift, bold, and hard; both armies about equally tasked and tried, and both driven to the prayer: "Give us this day our daily bread."

We could not well understand our being moved by so roundabout a way to reach our destination. It is explained, however, by a passage in General Grant's *Memoirs* (vol. ii., p. 473), which considering the pressure upon time and strength and generous resolution falling upon our men, is remarkable as showing what motives sometimes control military movements. It is remarkable also in showing what part General Meade had in commanding his army corps. The passage reads: "When the move towards Amelia Court House had commenced that morning, I ordered Wright's Corps, which was on the extreme right, to be moved to the left, past the whole army, to take the place of Griffin's, and ordered the latter at the same time to move by, and place itself on the right. The object of this movement was," proceeds this naive narration, "to get the Sixth Corps, Wright's, next to the cavalry, with which they had formerly served so harmoniously and so efficiently in the valley of Virginia."

The Sixth Corps now remained with the cavalry and under Sheridan's direct command, until after the surrender.

This is in truth a gracious reference to the work of the Sixth Corps before the onset of Early when Wright had already made a stand and was turning the tide backward as Sheridan came riding "from Winchester twenty miles away." But the last remark will provoke a smile. The wish was father to the thought, no doubt; but the fact was a "bar sinister." The Sixth Corps was under Sheridan's direct command only in the one fight at Sailor's Creek, and Sheridan did not get sight of it again,—not even in the grand review at the disbandment of the armies. Moreover, for that one fight, Sheridan complains that although Wright obeyed his orders, he refused to make his report to him until positively ordered to do so by the Lieutenant-General himself.

Lee had got ahead of us; we were mortified at that. But he found his way a "hard road to travel." His hope was now to get to the Danville junction at Burkesville, where he expected rations, and possibly a clear road to Danville or Lynchburg. So he pushes the heads of his flying columns along the roads running between the Southside and the Appomattox, a path traversed by many and difficult streams, only to find at every crossing some hot vanguard of Sheridan or Humphreys or Wright or Griffin, or at last of Ord; and each time, too, after fighting more or less severe to be beaten off with ever new disaster, wasting powers, and spreading demoralization. Yet stretching on with ever increasing desperation. . . . As one has seen some poor worm upon the forestick, girdled with fire, again and again attempt to cross the deadly edge and recoil writhing from the touch; wearing out his life in the frantic effort to save it; his struggles the more frenzied and wild the less his chances are—so now for these brave spirits who held together for manhood's sake in the name of what they already felt to be a doomed Confederacy. Virginia was but a prison-pen; the Southside Railroad was the dead-line; the river the Lethean stream. There was blood at every bridge and ford. Yet higher and higher up road and river stretched the two armies; one with the frenzy of a forlorn hope; the other with the energy of fierce resolve.

Our privilege was to push things; and there was no default of that. Our advanced infantry corps were operating with cavalry; which means doing cavalry-work marching and infantry-work fighting. And the example of the cavalry was superb.

For all our haste, we moved with caution; skirmishers and flankers well out; every moment looking for some hard-pressed rear-guard to turn and give battle, to gain time for their crowding columns ahead to pass some obstacle, or reach some favorable ground for respite or defense. For the most part the road of our pursuit was hard and smooth and clean; with no particular marks of disorder save here and there a dead man by the wayside, or an empty haversack which want had made superfluous, or a musket which haste and hopelessness had made too heavy.

Now we come to low ground where the ruts are axle deep and the road strewn with wreckage: broken-down forage trains, empty but unwieldy; abandoned cannon and battery-wagons stuck fast in the mire,—the trembling mules still harnessed to the wreck; horses starved and overtasked, but still saddled or packed, turned loose by their masters, whose future interests so outweighed the present that they couldn't stop to ride; queer Virginia farm-carts, as queerly freighted, with which some ignorant citizen was bearing off his household gods, and goddesses as well, fleeing before the Yankees with the full persuasion that they were after them with hoofs and horns in the likeness of their master, the evil one.[1]

Now we come to the deep creek, where the fugitives have destroyed the bridge behind them to check our oncoming, but checking more effectually their own followers; strewn, the stream, with sunken and floating remnants of almost every kind that man strives to put together and fate is busy to take to pieces; betokening how many, soldier and civilian, have reached the stream too late for the bridge, and have attempted the dangerous ford; while crowding on the banks are still

[1] *Of R R.* xlvi , pp. 733–1102, Serial 97.

stranger vehicles and convoys; wild-looking men in homespun gray, standing sulkily by, or speaking only to insist that they are civilians and not soldiers,—what they know of prison-pens not being attractive, as compared with starving in the open barrens; sometimes white men, or what seem to be, declaring they are not white, but colored;—a claim not often set up in that section of the Republic, though there might be some truth in it for all that; for there was in those days a whimsical variance between law and fact,—between being actually white and legally white,—as indeed under all climes and constitutions one may be found physically one color and morally the other.

But sometimes there was no mistake. For here we have come upon a waif of the deluge,—a token of the dispersion of peoples, the survival of the fittest, the stock and cradle of a race. Mounted on a pile of worldly goods that might have been blown together by the four winds, or rolled up by the waves of as many lost civilizations, crowded into a vehicle till it was a vehicle no longer, as it could neither carry nor go, sat supreme the irrepressible "man and brother" himself, surrounded by his ebony tokens of the earth's replenishment,—proof and promise of plenty,—cheerful, hopeful, imperturbable, all of them alike, trusting to luck as ever, for all it seemed rather against them just then; bound for the promised land, and piously waiting a special dispensation from heaven in their behalf, some Moses hand that cleft the Red Sea before the chosen.

Obstacles like these give check to the pursuit. A bridge must be built that the ammunition wagons may pass dry. Loiterers and impatient voyagers are alike impressed for service. The pioneers search shores and woods and hamlets for timber and planks. The stalled forage wagons are dragged in to form the temporary piers. The mounted officers dash about to find a safe ford for the men. The most intrepid of them follow breast-deep, cartridge-boxes and haversacks borne upon the bayonets high above their heads, to keep both kinds of ammunition dry. Some enterprising surgeon or meandering chaplain, thinking to do better than the hard-headed pioneers or adventurous orderlies for the men's welfare, shouts from the middle of the stream above or below that he has found the ford, and in the midst of his jubilation suddenly sinks into an unforeseen hole, whence after stirring variations from plain song to rapid minor and staccato, and splurges of diminuendo and crescendo, he returns to the hither shore in dismal cadence and saturated conviction.

Some men here, too, have their daintinesses as well as those who are delicately apparelled and live in kings' houses. It is hard to march in gurgling shoes after wading neck-deep. They wish to take off wet garments, assume the nethermost Highland costume, or even to emulate the Sandwich Island fellow-citizen in church array, and then stop to dry and dress again on the other side. But this dandyism cannot be indulged. Time is an essential element of this contract. Not a moment must the pursuit lose its semblance of forwardness if we mean to catch Lee's army. So each superior takes his own style of persuasion according to his conception of personal and official dignity. The higher the rank, the loftier the style. The corporals and sergeants coax; the captains command; the colonels scold; the generals scowl;—and several who appear to have conscientious scruples against affirming, freely avail themselves of that other alternative which the laws so charitably provide.

But fairly over at last, instead of halting anywhere the column is pushed on at the "double quick," to make up for lost time. We climb the way, the narrow cut scarce wide enough for a single track, here again choked with abandoned artillery and entangled mules, whose strength succumbed after passing purgatory. The way is strewn with new tokens of the painful ascent for our leaders. Among these some quite unwelcome waifs, such as loaded percussion shells jolted out of the galloping chests, which for aught we know the blow of a horse's hoof might explode in our faces; gun-carriages and caissons set on fire by the desperate fugitives, and when we pass them the flames already within a foot of the fuses and powder-bags. There is not much loitering about that sort of a camp-fire. Better crunch the earth with wet shoes for a good, dead pull than take the chance of being hung up to dry on a clay bank, or aired on a tree-top.

Now we reach a spot where Sheridan had burst

across the flying column and left a black and withered track behind him like the lightning's path. Our orders are to destroy all military equipage we capture or overtake. The war had not ended then, and military necessity was both lawful and expedient rule. Such masses of war-material must not be left unspoiled behind us, for aught we can foresee or foreordain by some chance of battle or of movement to fall into the enemy's hands and serve them against us again. War is destruction,—word and deed. So we make wild bonfires of wagon heaps and munitions, throw into the swamps and streams what we dare not risk ourselves to add to the lesser piles of ammunition capping the fire-stacks, and chop and slash the wheel-spokes of the gun carriages we cannot stop to burn.

Forward again! On a fresh track. Suddenly the rattling musketry of the skirmishers ahead tells that we have struck the enemy's rear-guard. A bold battery of flying artillery runs up out of a cross-road on a hillside half a mile away, and opens back on the head of our column with case-shot and shell. This offers variety, which is said to be the spice of life, if spice is what we need. A regiment is thrown forward into line at the double quick; a brigade follows in column of support. There comes a blast of canister, the answering swell of musketry; this for a few minutes; then a wild shout goes up into the rolling smoke; the battery manages to limber up and is off at a gallop, or sinks into sudden silence with all around. We reach the spot, and find our gallant fellows resting on their line, with a goodly half-glad company of prisoners in hand, and a patient group of the wounded of both parties for the ambulances which come galloping to the front, and alas, not without some brave men, our brothers, born near or far, to be buried here by the lonely wayside, lost but unforgotten!

We will look at these things with a more military eye, and something more of detail. When Meade had been sent off to Amelia Court House on the morning of the 6th, Sheridan sent his cavalry in the opposite direction,—the way Meade had intended to go with his army,—towards Farmville, where we had learned from intercepted dispatches Lee expected to find rations for his famishing troops. The cavalry soon got on the flank of Lee's trains; however, they were well guarded, and our forces were unable to inflict more injury than to hold the enemy in check until the Second and Sixth Corps, faced about and sent back by Meade, should come up, to take their accustomed and decisive share in the work. Barlow's Division of the Second had been turned off to the right of the road taken by his corps, towards that on which the Fifth Corps was moving, and where the enemy was expected to be encountered. But the enemy's columns on this road had already passed in the night, so that Barlow and the Fifth Corps had their hard and eager march with no material effect upon the enemy but that of capturing prisoners and destroying overtaken material of war. The other two divisions of the Second Corps took the road for

Deatonsville towards Sailor's Creek and the Appomattox, and soon found themselves in a running fight with Gordon's Corps, which held the costly honor of forming the rear-guard of Lee's main army. Our troops had a very difficult country to overcome,—broken, tangled, and full of swamps. They had to cross streams by wading armpit deep, and then push on to strike the flank or rear of the sullen ranks. Meanwhile a portion of our men were building bridges after Humphreys's rapid fashion, for the passage of our artillery and ambulances. Thus we succeeded in keeping the artillery up to the skirmish lines, and in carrying the strong positions which the well-handled enemy had managed to entrench in their own rear-guard style and efficiency. In this way Humphreys pushed them for more than sixteen miles, the road much of the way strewn with wagons, camp equipage, battery-forges, and limbers—a stream of wreckage. At Perkinson's Mills, near the mouth of Sailor's Creek, Gordon made a definite stand, with a well-placed line of battle. But Humphreys' splendid handling of his plucky men inspired them to their best, and a sharp fight left the Second Corps masters of the field, and of large numbers of the enemy. This cost the corps 311 men killed and wounded. The loss of the enemy was still greater. The captures of the corps were thirteen battle-flags, four cannon, and seventeen hundred prisoners. After this defeat, Gordon pushed his retreat to High Bridge, a crossing of the Appomattox five miles below Farmville.

Meantime Ewell and Anderson had been brought to a stand by our cavalry higher up Sailor's Creek, three miles on Humphreys's left. It was our Sixth Corps that now came upon them; the sharp issue soon joined. This corps fought with all its old hardihood, and our cavalry surpassed itself, riding over the enemy's works, saber to bayonet. This splendid courage and soldiership won commensurate results. General Ewell was compelled to surrender, and nearly all of his command, over six thousand men, fell into our hands. Among these were many distinguished generals, both of his corps, and of Pickett's Division.

These were most brilliant victories for the Second and Sixth Corps, and we of the Fifth were proud of them, for they were our own. We expected this of Sheridan and the cavalry, but were glad the old Army of the Potomac infantry came in for an undeniable share of the solid work as well as of the glory.

There was some unaccountably poor generalship that day in the Confederate army. Longstreet held his troops all day at Rice's Station waiting for Anderson and Ewell and Gordon to come up, who had been held back to cover the trains. But for all that, Lee lost his trains, and by reason of this effort to save his trains he lost also a large part of his army and his main chance of escape. General Humphreys in his admirable review of this day's business, noting the fact that "Ewell's whole force was lost, together with nearly half of Anderson's and a large part of Gordon's, all in a useless effort to save the trains," goes on to say in effect that if Lee had abandoned all surplus artillery and camp equipage and retained only his ammunition and hospital wagons, and established temporary depots of supplies at important railroad stations, he might have been able to move rapidly enough to make a successful junction with Johnson at Danville, or at least, to reach the mountains of Lynchburg.

What would this have availed to the main issue? Already the shadow of doom drew over the drifting Confederacy. The hour of deliverance and dispersion was almost welcomed by its armies. And it was reserved for Lee to be confronted by a man as magnanimous as himself, and guided by a better star. He had to go down, honored and beloved indeed for the man he was, but the more lamented for the unhappy choice he made when he cast in his lot with those who forsook the old flag for a new one, which did not recognize the fact that old things had become new,—that even constitutions move with the march of man, with wider interpretations and to their appointed goals, and that the old flag borne forward by farther-seeing men held its potency not only in the history of the past but for the story of the future.

General Ord with the Army of the James by hard marches after splendid fighting in the old lines had reached Burkesville on the evening of the 5th, and on the morning of the 6th was directed to destroy the High Bridge and all other bridges which might be used by Lee in the direction of

Danville or Lynchburg. This Ord proceeded to do with promptitude and vigor. But not aware of the proximity of the head of Lee's column, he sent out only a small party for this purpose, which after heroic and desperate fighting with Rosser's and Munford's cavalry, and the loss of the gallant General Reed and Colonel Washburn and many of their command, were forced to surrender what remained.

As for the Fifth Corps, we had made a day of it, marching thirty-two miles, burning and destroying, and bivouacked after dark in the vicinity of Sailor's Creek on the Appomattox. We had encountered only cavalry rear-guards and scouts, and had captured much material of war and over three hundred prisoners. We had many delays, bridge-building and burning; but our step was quickened by the roar of the Second and Sixth Corps battling on our left, and by sight of the dense black smoke that rose from the piles where our cavalry were burning the wagon-trains they captured on the roads to Farmville. Marvelous stories borne through the air, of our cavalry darting everywhere across the pathway of the fugitives, made good cheer around the camp-fires when we cooked frugal portions of precious coffee with cautious admixtures of turbid and possibly more deeply stained waters that came down to us from the ensanguined banks of Sailor's Creek.

As soon as it was dark on the night of the 6th, Longstreet pushed forward to Farmville, where his men at last got a supply of rations. For two or three days past they had been living on parched corn,—if they could stop to make a fire to parch it. Longstreet did not tarry here; but on the morning of the 7th he crossed the river, burning the bridges behind him and moving out on the road to Lynchburg. Gordon, with Johnson's and Mahone's Divisions following, crossed to the north side of the Appomattox at High Bridge, five miles below Farmville. Our Second Corps closely followed, reaching the river just as the fugitives had blown up the bridge-heads forming its southern defense, and had set fire to the wagon bridge near by. Barlow hurrying forward saved it, and thus secured the passage of the Second Corps. Thereupon in the belief that Longstreet was moving toward Danville, he was sent up the river towards Farmville, and had a sharp engagement with some of Gordon's rear-guard on that road—while Humphreys with the rest of his corps, pushing closely out on the Lynchburg road, came suddenly on the enemy, who had turned to give battle, and who opened on him with sixteen pieces of artillery. He at once informs General Meade that he has the whole of Lee's remaining army in front of him, and asks that our Sixth Corps shall attack from the Farmville side while he takes the enemy in his front.

In the meantime the Fifth Corps had moved from Sailor's Creek at daylight, and at 9.50 had arrived at High Bridge. A singular movement is now put into effect, the purpose of which to ordinary minds seems inscrutable. From the extreme right where Grant had so carefully placed us in order that the Sixth Corps might be next to Sheridan, the Fifth Corps is now marched past the rear of the Second and Sixth,—needing help as Humphreys did,—and ordered to the "extreme left" again,—which begins to seem our natural place after the manner of the "opposition" in the French Assembly. The queer thing about this is, that it puts us again into immediate contiguity with Sheridan and his cavalry, where General Grant had led us to fear we were not "harmonious," as the good Sixth Corps was. But we were not such bad fellows after all. Having the last three days proved our prowess in marching, we were assigned the honor of making a cavalry-sweep around the left flank and front of Lee's rushing army while our Second and Sixth Corps did all they could to drive them beyond us. So by 7.30 that night we bivouacked at Prince Edward's Court House, as far south of the rest of our army as we had been north of it the day before.

Meantime Grant, now at Farmville, sends word to Humphreys confronting Longstreet and Gordon on the opposite side of the river, between High Bridge and Farmville, that the Sixth and Twenty-fourth Corps are at hand, and that "the enemy cannot cross the river,"—for what purpose it is difficult to divine, as he had already crossed to the north side and destroyed the bridges behind him, and could not be suspected of cherishing a desire to get back to the other side again at this juncture of affairs. Crook's cavalry managed to wade the river and make a bold attack, but was repulsed with loss, the gallant General Irvin Gregg being rash enough to get into the enemy's lines, where he was held as prisoner.

But it was the Sixth and Twenty-fourth Corps that "could not cross," and so Humphreys stood up there before Lee's army in a very perilous position. It was like the situation of our First Division sent across the Potomac at Shepardstown Ford after the battle of Antietam,—Lee's army in front of them, and a river behind them, perfectly surrounded by the enemy. Had Lee but understood Humphreys's situation, he might have destroyed the Second Corps, if he struck quickly, before the Fifth could have got over the river at High Bridge, and the Sixth and Twenty-fourth could have come around from Farmville by that long route.

Meade, indeed, had promptly ordered the Sixth and also the Twenty-fourth Corps—the latter being now by its proximity subject to his orders—to cross and attack as Humphreys had requested, on the enemy's right flank. Nobody at either headquarters seems to have been aware that the bridges at Farmville had been destroyed. So Humphreys, hearing the firing from Crook's attack, and believing it was that of these two infantry corps, made a bold stand and a bluff fight (almost in the slang sense of that term) all along the salient points of the line, which had the important effect of causing Lee to lose a day, which he could but ill afford. For in the meantime the cavalry and the Fifth Corps with Ord's advance were driving with all their might to get across Lee's track.

Could our army that morning in easy reach of High Bridge have been rapidly concentrated according to Humphreys's earnest suggestion, and Meade's intention, and a little more "dash" and skillful engineering been put into exercise in the crossing at Farmville, there can be no question but that the Army of the Potomac would have "ended matters there, before they went back."

But perhaps Grant thought there had been bloodshed enough, for that evening he writes a note to Lee making this thought the basis for asking the surrender of Lee's army. At half-past eight, this letter is sent by General Humphreys through his picket line. An hour's truce was given at this time to enable the enemy to gather up their wounded lying between the lines, which were only a few hundred yards apart. Lee's answer comes back within an hour, not offering to surrender but asking the terms that would be given in such case. In the course of the night, as might have been anticipated, Lee retires, making all possible dispatch for Lynchburg, the Second Corps by daylight in close pursuit, followed by the Sixth. We, of course, knew nothing of this at the time; but only of what was going on in the road to Appomattox.

For our part, on the morning of the 8th the Fifth Corps moved out at six o'clock, pressing with all our powers to outflank Lee's march. This morning I received a wholesome lesson of the results of inattention. In crossing Buffalo River, my horse had a pardonable desire to take a drink. I let him advance half his length into the water, knee-deep or more,—which I thought enough; but with that unaccountable instinct of a drinking horse (or other fellow) to get further in, to "take another," my horse kept creeping forward, and I was stupid enough to let him—until suddenly stepping over a steep bank of the channel his whole body was forced to follow, as also his master, —or who should have been. Decidedly all was not over,—mostly the reverse; two emergent heads absurdly trying to look dignified marking the vital center. We made for the nearest bank; but could not effect a landing on account of the extreme tendency of the earth and water there to resume prehistoric conditions. The horse, not being a saurian, could neither walk nor swim in that mire. I had to act the part of a "lighter" and the horse and I assumed more than original relations,—I being now the leader and something like the bearer. I got out first,—having only two feet to hold me fast. Then the dispensation of grace took the place of natural law, and two or three of my self-renouncing, now nearly sanctified, men went to the rescue of the crestfallen but still admired Charlemagne. What they had to do for us both afterwards, official dignity prevents explaining.

This driving pursuit, this relentless "forward," was altogether new experience for our much-enduring, much-abused old Army of the Potomac, —so taunted with not moving,—urged "on to

Richmond" with the spur, but held to cover Washington with the curb, hitherto forced by something in the rear to stand still after our victories, and by something we did not understand to draw back from some of our best-fought fields. Yet it had been so managed that at the worst the enemy seldom got sight of our backs. For our part, we had come off in good order from Bull Run and Fredericksburg in '62, and equally well from Chancellorsville in '63, and from all the long series of terrible drawn battles from the Rapidan to the James in '64. And we had many times seen the rebel army retiring in good order from great disaster; for Lee showed his best generalship in the defensive, his best manhood and humanity in orderly retreat. But we had never seen anything like this. Now we realized the effects of Grant's permission to "push things,"—some of these things being ourselves. But the manifest results on others helped our spirits to sustain the wear and tear of body. The constantly diminishing ratio of the strength of Lee's army compared with ours made it clear that we should soon overcome that resistance and relieve Virginia of the burden of being the head of the Confederacy, and from that must follow the downfall of the Confederacy itself.

In this race, the 8th of April found the Fifth Corps at Prospect Station on the Southside Railroad, nearly abreast of Lee's hurrying column, ten miles north of us at New Store, across the Appomattox,—Meade with his two corps close upon his rear. We had been now a week in hot pursuit, fighting and marching by sharp turns, on a long road. At noon of this day we halted to give opportunity for General Ord of the Army of the James to have the advance of us upon the road. He had come across from his successful assault on the center of the enemy's entrenchments before Petersburg to join our force and had with him the Twenty-fourth Corps under General Gibbon and Birney's Division of the Twenty-fifth Colored troops,—whom we had not seen in the field before. The Fifth Corps was under Sheridan's immediate orders but General Ord being the senior officer present was by army regulations commander of our whole flanking column. He was very courteous to us all and we greeted him heartily. The preference of his corps to ours on the road was but natural considering his rank, and I am sure no one thought of taking offense at it. But we could not resist the thought that it was for some reasons other than military that General Ord's command instead of being directed upon Lee's rear by the shortest course should be sent around to the extreme left to co-operate with Sheridan, while the Army of the Potomac was dismembered and divided right and left,—thus as we thought entailing much needless hard marching when time and human strength were prime elements of our problem; with the reflection also that the breaking up of familiar companionship was not good economy for a fighting force. However, our duty was to obey orders and keep our thoughts to ourselves.

These men of the Army of the James had been doing splendid work,—especially in getting up to us. But the hard march to overtake us had pretty nearly used them up. A marching column under such circumstances cannot help stretching. This was the case before us now. When we pulled out to follow their column we found it dragging and lagging before us, the rear moving at a rate ever slower than the head. This made it very hard on our men. We had managed hitherto to keep in pretty close touch with the cavalry; but this constant checking up was a far worse trial. It fretted our men almost to mutiny. Men who were really "the best fellows in the world," as many a girl had told them on fairer evenings, and who wholly respected their officers and loved them, would greet the luckless officers believed to be leading the column with very insubordinate and wholly impracticable advice as to the merits of this march, and the duty of treating our men with some sense. The head of our column seemed more like a mob than our patient well-disciplined soldiers. The headquarters wagons and pack mules which made the bulk of that real rabble ahead got unceremoniously helped along. Whoever blocked the way was served with a writ of ejectment in quite primitive fashion. After dark the belated artillery obstructing the way was treated without much reverence. Even the much suffering horses were held responsible, and prodded and belabored by men who wanted to put two legs in the place of four. The drivers defended their poor beasts by directing their whips against the assailants, whose "high primed parry" with their muskets and bayonets availed little against the lithe and cutting lash. As little did the replications and rejoinders settle the issue of justice in the all too "pending case." We tried to drown the tumult, if we could not pacify the spirits of our exasperated men, by bringing the bands to the head of the column to administer the unction of the "Girl I left behind me " However, this seemed to make them want to "get there" all the more.

Commanding officers could not exercise "discretion" about moving. We could not bring our men to a halt when there was this kind of obstacle before us, impassable as if it were a wall or a bog, and let them rest until the way could be cleared, as would have been reasonable. For some roving staff officer would happen along just then, and without inquiring into the case, would report to headquarters that such an officer was not moving according to orders, but was absolutely halting on the road. Then back would come an unjust reprimand, or perhaps the stultification of an "arrest,"—of which there was quite too much already. So officers had to seem like incapables, and the men, poor fellows, had to keep on their feet, creeping at a snail's pace, or standing like tripods, on two legs and a musket-butt; weighed down with burdens of "heavy-marching order," which the mere momentum of marching, the changing play of muscles, would have helped to bear; all knowing full well that they would have to make up for this weary work by running themselves fever-wild for hours at the end.

We of the Fifth Corps had a good right to be tired, too. We had had a brisk week's work of it since the White Oak Road and Five Forks—rushing and pushing night and day, fighting a little now and then for the sake of that variety which is the spice of life. Many of our big-hearted fellows lost patience whose only disobedience of orders was that they refused to die of fatigue and starvation, as Meade had promised Sheridan they were ready to do.

At last our lingering predecessors turn off. We have the road and the mood to make the most of it. We did not know that Grant had sent orders for the Fifth Corps to march all night without halting; but it was not necessary for us to know it. After twenty-nine miles of this kind of marching, at the blackest hour of night, human nature called a halt. Dropping by the roadside, right and left, wet and dry, down went the men as in a swoon. Officers slid out of saddle, loosened the girth, slipped an arm through a loop of bridle-rein, and sank to sleep. Horses stood with drooping heads just above their masters' faces. All dreaming,—one knows not what, of past or coming, possible or fated.

CHAPTER VI

APPOMATTOX

THE darkest hours before the dawn of April 9, 1865, shrouded the Fifth Corps sunk in feverish sleep by the roadside six miles away from Appomattox Station on the Southside Road. Scarcely is the first broken dream begun when a cavalryman comes splashing down the road and vigorously dismounts, pulling from his jacket-front a crumpled note. The sentinel standing watch by his commander, worn in body but alert in every sense, touches your shoulder. "Orders, sir, I think." You rise on elbow, strike a match, and with smarting, streaming eyes read the brief, thrilling note, sent back by Sheridan to us infantry commanders. Like this, as I remember: "I have cut across the enemy at Appomattox Station, and captured three of his trains. If you can possibly push your infantry up here to-night, we will have great results in the morning." Ah, sleep no more. The startling bugle notes ring out "The General"—"To the march." Word is sent for the men to take a bite of such as they have for food: the promised rations will not be up till noon, and by that time we shall be perhaps too far away for such greeting. A few try to eat, no matter what. Meanwhile, almost with one foot in the stirrup, you take from the hands of the black boy a tin plate of nondescript food and a dipper of miscalled coffee;—all equally black, like the night around. You eat and drink at a swallow; mount, and away to get to the head of the column before you sound the "Forward." They are there—the men: shivering to their senses as if risen out of the earth, but something in them not of it. Now sounds the "Forward," for the last time in our long-drawn strife. And they move—these men—sleepless, supperless, breakfastless, sore-footed, stiff-jointed, sense-benumbed, but with flushed faces pressing for the front.

By sunrise we have reached Appomattox Station, where Sheridan has left the captured trains. A staff officer is here to turn us square to the right, to the Appomattox River, cutting across Lee's retreat. Already we hear the sharp ring of the horse-artillery, answered ever and anon by heavier field guns; and drawing nearer, the crack of cavalry carbines; and unmistakably, too, the graver roll of musketry of opposing infantry. There is no mistake. Sheridan is square across the enemy's front, and with that glorious cavalry alone is holding at bay all that is left of the proudest army of the Confederacy. It has come at last,—the supreme hour. No thought of human wants or weakness now: all for the front; all for the flag, for the final stroke to make its meaning real—these men of the Potomac and the James, side by side, at the double in time and column, now one and now the other in the road or the fields beside. One striking feature I can never forget,—Birney's black men abreast with us, pressing forward to save the white man's country.

We did not know exactly what was going on. We did know that our cavalry had been doing splendid work all night, and in fact now was holding at bay Lee's whole remaining army. I was proud to learn that Smith's Brigade—our First Maine Cavalry in the van—had waged the most critical part of the glorious fight.

Ord's troops were in lead, pushing for the roar of the guns to bring relief to our cavalry before Lee's anxious infantry should break through. The storm-center was now on the Lynchburg Pike, a mile or so beyond Appomattox Court House. The Fifth Corps followed, Ayres' Division ahead; then our old Third Brigade of the First Division,—once mine, since Bartlett's; next, my command, my own brigade and Gregory's; at the rear of the column Crawford's fine division, but somehow unaccountably slow in its movements and march.

I was therefore in about the middle of our Fifth Corps column. The boom of the battle thickened ahead of us. We were intent for the front. Suddenly I am accosted by a cavalry staff officer dashing out of a rough wood road leading off to our right. "General, you command this column?"—"Two brigades of it, sir; about half the First Division, Fifth Corps."—"Sir, General Sheridan wishes you to break off from this column and come to his support. The rebel infantry is pressing him hard. Our men are falling back. Don't wait for orders through the regular channels, but act on this at once."

Of course I obey, without question. Sending word forward to Griffin, in command of our Fifth Corps, that he may understand and instruct Crawford to follow the main column and not me, I turn off my brigade and Gregory's and guided by the staff officer, push out to see if we can do as well on a cavalry front as we had at their heels. My guide informed me of the situation. Ord's troops were holding Gordon's hard on the Lynchburg Pike; this latter command was now a formidable force, having taken in the heart of Stonewall Jackson's and A. P. Hill's corps, and what was left of Anderson's. But the rear of this column pressing on had made a demonstration indicating that they were now about to try a final forlorn hope to cut through near the Court House while the head of their column was engaging Ord. General Sheridan, to thwart this attempt, had taken Devins's Cavalry Division back to meet them, at least until our infantry could be brought up. The barrier of cavalry alone could not withstand the desperate Confederate veterans essaying their last hope, and in fact was slowly receding. This explained the reason of our summons.

Sharp work now. Pushing through the woods at cavalry speed, we come out right upon Sheridan's battle flag gleaming amidst the smoke of his batteries in the edge of the open field. Weird-looking flag it is: fork-tailed, red and white, the two bands that composed it each charged with a star of the contrasting color; two eyes sternly glaring through the cannon-cloud. Beneath it, that storm-center spirit, that form of condensed energies, mounted on the grim charger, Rienzi, that turned the battle of the Shenandoah,—both, rider and steed, of an unearthly shade of darkness, terrible to look upon, as if masking some unknown powers.

Right before us, our cavalry, Devins' division, gallantly stemming the surges of the old Stonewall brigade, desperate to beat its way through. I ride straight to Sheridan. A dark smile and impetuous gesture are my only orders. Forward into double lines of battle, past Sheridan, his guns, his cavalry, and on for the quivering crest! For a moment it is a glorious sight: every arm of the service in full play,—cavalry, artillery, infantry; then a sudden shifting scene as the cavalry, disengaged by successive squadrons, rally under their bugle-calls with beautiful precision and promptitude, and sweep like a storm-cloud beyond our right to close in on the enemy's left and complete the fateful envelopment.

Ord's troops are now square across the Lynchburg Pike. Ayres and Bartlett have joined them on their right, and all are in for it sharp. In this new front we take up the battle. Gregory follows in on my left. It is a formidable front we make. The scene darkens. In a few minutes the tide is turned; the incoming wave is at flood; the barrier recedes. In truth, the Stonewall men hardly show their well-proved mettle. They seem astonished to see before them these familiar flags of their old antagonists, not having thought it possible that we could match our cavalry and march around and across their pressing columns.

Their last hope is gone,—to break through our cavalry before our infantry can get up. Neither to Danville nor to Lynchburg can they cut their way; and close upon their rear, five miles away, are pressing the Second and Sixth Corps of the Army of the Potomac. It is the end! They are now giving way, but keep good front, by force of old habit. Halfway up the slope they make a stand, with what perhaps they think a good omen,—behind a stone wall. I try a little artillery on them, which directs their thoughts towards the crest behind them, and stiffen my lines for a rush, anxious for that crest myself. My intensity may have seemed like excitement. For Griffin comes up, quizzing me in his queer way of hitting off our weak points when we get a little too serious; accusing me of mistaking a blooming peach tree for a rebel flag, where I was dropping a few shells into a rallying crowd. I apologize—I was a little near-sighted, and hadn't been experienced in long-range fighting. But as for peaches, I was going to get some if the pits didn't sit too hard on our stomachs.

In a few minutes Griffin rides up again, in quite a different mood. "General," he says, "I want you to go back and bring up Crawford's Division. He is acting in the same old fashion that got Warren into trouble at Five Forks. He should have been up here long ago. We need him desperately. He deserves to be relieved of his command." —"General, do you mean to relieve me of mine, and make me a staff officer? It can't come to that."—"I mean to put you in command of that division," he answers; "I will publish an order to that effect."—"General, pardon me, but you must not do that. It would make trouble for everybody, and I do not desire the position. It would make great disturbance among Crawford's friends, and if you will pardon the suggestion they may have influence enough at Washington to block your confirmation as Major-General. Besides, I think General Baxter of the Third Division is my senior; that must settle it."

This is a singular episode for such a moment. But it may be cited as showing the variety of commotions that occupied our minds.

But now comes up Ord with a positive order: "Don't expose your lines on that crest. The enemy have massed their guns to give it a raking fire the moment you set foot there." I thought I saw a qualifying look as he turned away. But left alone, youth struggled with prudence. My troops were in a bad position down here. I did not like to be "the under dog." It was much better to be on top and at least know what there was beyond. So I thought of Grant and his permission to "push things" when we got them going; and of Sheridan and his last words as he rode away with his cavalry, smiting his hands together—"Now smash 'em,

I tell you; smash 'em!" So we took this for orders, and on the crest we stood. One booming cannon-shot passed close along our front, and in the next moment all was still.

We had done it,—had "exposed ourselves to the view of the enemy." But it was an exposure that worked two ways. For there burst upon our vision a mighty scene, fit cadence of the story of tumultuous years. Encompassed by the cordon of steel that crowned the heights about the Court House, on the slopes of the valley formed by the sources of the Appomattox, lay the remnants of that far-famed counterpart and companion of our own in momentous history,—the Army of Northern Virginia—Lee's army!

In the meantime Crawford's troops have begun to arrive, and form in between Gregory and Bartlett on our left.

It was hilly, broken ground, in effect a vast amphitheater, stretching a mile perhaps from crest to crest. On the several confronting slopes before us dusky masses of infantry suddenly resting in place; blocks of artillery, standing fast in column or mechanically swung into park; clouds of cavalry small and great, slowly moving, in simple restlessness;—all without apparent attempt at offense or defense, or even military order.

In the hollow is the Appomattox,—which we had made the dead-line for our baffled foe, for its whole length, a hundred miles; here but a rivulet that might almost be stepped over dry-shod, and at the road crossing not thought worth while to bridge.

Around its edges, now trodden to mire, swarms an indescribable crowd. worn-out soldier struggling to the front; demoralized citizen and denizen, white, black, and all shades between,—following Lee's army, or flying before these suddenly confronted terrible Yankees pictured to them as demon-shaped and bent; animals, too, of all forms and grades; vehicles of every description and non-description,—public and domestic, four-wheeled, or two, or one,—heading and moving in every direction, a swarming mass of chaotic confusion.

All this within sight of every eye on our bristling crest. Had one the heart to strike at beings so helpless, the Appomattox would quickly become a surpassing Red Sea horror. But the very spectacle brings every foot to an instinctive halt. We seem the possession of a dream. We are lost in a vision of human tragedy. But our light-twelve Napoleon guns come rattling up behind us to go into battery; we catch the glitter of the cavalry blades and brasses beneath the oak groves away to our right, and the ominous closing in on the fated foe.

So with a fervor of devout joy,—as when, perhaps, the old crusaders first caught sight of the holy city of their quest,—with an up-going of the heart that was half pæan, half prayer, we dash forward to the consummation. A solitary fieldpiece in the edge of the town gives an angry but expiring defiance. We press down a little slope, through a swamp, over a bright swift stream. Our advance is already in the town,—only the narrow street between the opposing lines, and hardly that. There is wild work, that looks like fighting; but not much killing, nor even hurting. The disheartened enemy take it easy; our men take them easier. It is a wild, mild fusing,—earnest, but not deadly earnest.

A young orderly of mine, unable to contain himself, begs permission to go forward, and dashes in, sword-flourishing as if he were a terrible fellow, —and soon comes back, hugging four sabers to his breast, speechless at his achievement.

We were advancing, tactically fighting, and I was somewhat uncertain as to how much more of the strenuous should be required or expected. But I could not give over to this weak mood.

My right was "in the air," advanced, unsupported, towards the enemy's general line, exposed to flank attack by troops I could see in the distance across the stream. I held myself on that extreme flank, where I could see the cavalry which we had relieved, now forming in column of squadrons ready for a dash to the front, and I was anxiously hoping it would save us from the flank attack. Watching intently, my eye was caught by the figure of a horseman riding out between those lines, soon joined by another, and taking a direction across the cavalry front towards our position. They were nearly a mile away, and I curiously watched them till lost from sight in the nearer broken ground and copses between.

Suddenly rose to sight another form, close in our own front,—a soldierly young figure, a Confederate staff officer undoubtedly. Now I see the white flag earnestly borne, and its possible purport sweeps before my inner vision like a wraith of morning mist. He comes steadily on, the mysterious form in gray, my mood so whimsically sensitive that I could even smile at the material of the flag,—wondering where in either army was found a towel, and one so white. But it bore a mighty message,—that simple emblem of homely service, wafted hitherward above the dark and crimsoned streams that never can wash themselves away.

The messenger draws near, dismounts; with graceful salutation and hardly suppressed emotion delivers his message· "Sir, I am from General Gordon. General Lee desires a cessation of hostilities until he can hear from General Grant as to the proposed surrender."

What word is this! so long so dearly fought for, so feverishly dreamed, but ever snatched away, held hidden and aloof; now smiting the senses with a dizzy flash! "Surrender"? We had no rumor of this from the messages that had been passing between Grant and Lee, for now these two days, behind us. "Surrender"? It takes a moment to gather one's speech. "Sir," I answer, "that matter exceeds my authority. I will send to my superior. General Lee is right. He can do no more." All this with a forced calmness, covering a tumult of heart and brain. I bid him wait a while, and the message goes up to my corps commander, General Griffin, leaving me mazed at the boding change.

Now from the right come foaming up in cavalry fashion the two forms I had watched from away beyond. A white flag again, held strong aloft, making straight for the little group beneath our battle-flag, high borne also,—the red Maltese cross on a field of white, that had thrilled hearts long ago. I see now that it is one of our cavalry staff in lead,—indeed I recognize him, Colonel Whitaker of Custer's staff; and, hardly keeping pace with him, a Confederate staff officer. Without dismounting, without salutation, the cavalryman shouts: "This is unconditional surrender! This is the end!" Then he hastily introduces his companion, and adds: "I am just from Gordon and Longstreet. Gordon says 'For God's sake, stop this infantry, or hell will be to pay!' I'll go to Sheridan," he adds, and dashes away with the white flag, leaving Longstreet's aide with me.[1]

I was doubtful of my duty. The flag of truce was in, but I had no right to act upon it without orders. There was still some firing from various quarters, lulling a little where the white flag passed near. But I did not press things quite so hard. Just then a last cannon-shot from the edge of the

[1] The various accounts that have been since given of the reception of the flag of truce on this occasion might lead to the impression upon readers of history that we were all under great agitation of mind and that our memories were somewhat confused or possibly our habit of truth telling But those who were acquainted with the facts will not be disturbed in their inferences or judgments In accordance with Lee's instructions several flags were sent out at important points along his own line, and several came in on our Appomattox front. The flag-bearers I refer to were Capt P. M Jones, now U. S. District Judge in Alabama, and Capt. Brown of Georgia.

town plunges through the breast of a gallant and dear young officer in my front line,—Lieutenant Clark, of the 185th New York,—the last man killed in the Army of the Potomac, if not the last in the Appomattox lines.[1] Not a strange thing for war,—this swift stroke of the mortal; but coming after the truce was in, it seemed a cruel fate for one so deserving to share his country's joy, and a sad peace-offering for us all.

Shortly comes the order, in due form, to cease firing and to halt. There was not much firing to cease from; but "halt," then and there? It is beyond human power to stop the men, whose one word and thought and action through crimsoned years had been but forward. They had seen the flag of truce, and could divine its outcome. But the habit was too strong; they cared not for points of direction, it was forward still,—forward to the end; forward to the new beginning; forward to the Nation's second birth!

But it struck them also in a quite human way. The more the captains cry, "Halt! the rebels want to surrender," the more the men want to be there and see it. Still to the front, where the real fun is! And the forward movement takes an upward turn. For when we do succeed in stopping

[1] It has been claimed that the last man killed in the Appomattox lines belonged to the Army of the James. That may possibly be so, as the reception of flags began on our right, and probably did not reach the extreme left where the Army of the James was until some time after. So there may have been some firing and casualties after the truce had been received on our right. The honor of this last death is not a proper subject of quarrel

their advance we cannot keep their arms and legs from flying. To the top of fences, and haystacks, and chimneys they clamber, to toss their old caps higher in the air, and leave the earth as far below them as they can.

Dear old General Gregory gallops up to inquire the meaning of this strange departure from accustomed discipline. "Only that Lee wants time to surrender," I answer with stage solemnity. "Glory to God!" roars the grave and brave old General, dashing upon me with an impetuosity that nearly unhorsed us both, to grasp and wring my hand, which had not yet had time to lower the sword. "Yes, and on earth peace, good will towards men," I answered, bringing the thanksgiving from heavenward, manward.

"Your legs have done it, my men," shouts the gallant, gray-haired Ord, galloping up cap in hand, generously forgiving our disobedience of orders, and rash "exposure" on the dubious crest. True enough, their legs had done it,—had "matched the cavalry" as Grant admitted, had cut around Lee's best doings, and commanded the grand halt. But other things too had "done it"; the blood was still fresh upon the Quaker Road, the White Oak Ridge, Five Forks, Farmville, High Bridge, and Sailor's Creek; and we take somewhat gravely this compliment of our new commander, of the Army of the James. At last, after "pardoning something to the spirit of liberty," we get things "quiet along the lines."

A truce is agreed upon until one o'clock—it is

now ten. A conference is to be held, or rather colloquy, for no one here is authorized to say anything about the terms of surrender. Six or eight officers from each side meet between the lines, near the Court House, waiting Lee's answer to Grant's summons to surrender. There is lively chat here on this unaccustomed opportunity for exchange of notes and queries.

The first greetings are not all so dramatic as might be thought, for so grave an occasion. "Well Billy, old boy, how goes it?" asks one loyal West Pointer of a classmate he had been fighting for four years. "Bad, bad, Charlie, bad I tell you; but have you got any whisky?" was the response,—not poetic, not idealistic, but historic; founded on fact as to the strength of the demand, but without evidence of the questionable maxim that the demand creates the supply. More of the economic truth was manifest that scarcity enhances value.

Everybody seems acquiescent and for the moment cheerful,—except Sheridan. He does not like the cessation of hostilities, and does not conceal his opinion. His natural disposition was not sweetened by the circumstance that he was fired on by some of the Confederates as he was coming up to the meeting under the truce. He is for unconditional surrender, and thinks we should have banged right on and settled all questions without asking them He strongly intimates that some of the free-thinking rebel cavalry might take advantage of the truce to get away from us. But the Confederate officers, one and all, Gordon,

Wilcox, Heth, "Rooney" Lee, and all the rest, assure him of their good faith, and that the game is up for them.

But suddenly a sharp firing cuts the air about our ears—musketry and artillery—out beyond us on the Lynchburg pike, where it seems Sheridan had sent Gregg's command to stop any free-riding pranks that might be played. Gordon springs up from his pile of rails with an air of astonishment and vexation, declaring that for his part he had sent out in good faith orders to hold things as they are. And he glances more than inquiringly at Sheridan. "Oh, never mind!" says Sheridan, "I know about it. Let 'em fight!" with two simple words added, which, literally taken, are supposed to express a condemnatory judgment, but in Sheridan's rhetoric convey his appreciation of highly satisfactory qualities of his men,—especially just now.

One o'clock comes; no answer from Lee. Nothing for us but to shake hands and take arms to resume hostilities. As I turned to go, General Griffin said to me in a low voice, "Prepare to make, or receive, an attack in ten minutes!" It was a sudden change of tone in our relations, and brought a queer sensation. Where my troops had halted, the opposing lines were in close proximity. The men had stacked arms and were resting in place. It did not seem like war we were to recommence, but wilful murder. But the order was only to "prepare," and that we did. Our troops were in good position, my advanced line across the road, and we stood fast intensely waiting. I had mounted, and sat looking at the scene before me, thinking of all that was impending and depending, when I felt coming in upon me a strange sense of some presence invisible but powerful—like those unearthly visitants told of in ancient story, charged with supernal message. Disquieted, I turned about, and there behind me, riding in between my two lines, appeared a commanding form, superbly mounted, richly accoutred, of imposing bearing, noble countenance, with expression of deep sadness overmastered by deeper strength. It is no other than Robert E. Lee! And seen by me for the first time within my own lines. I sat immovable, with a certain awe and admiration. He was coming, with a single staff officer,[1] for the great appointed meeting which was to determine momentous issues.

Not long after, by another inleading road, appeared another form, plain, unassuming, simple, and familiar to our eyes, but to the thought as much inspiring awe as Lee in his splendor and his sadness. It is Grant! He, too, comes with a single aide, a staff officer of Sheridan's who had come out to meet him.[2] Slouched hat without cord; common soldier's blouse, unbuttoned, on which, however, the four stars; high boots, mud-splashed to the top; trousers tucked inside; no sword, but the sword-hand deep in the pocket; sitting his saddle with the ease of a born master, taking no notice of anything, all his faculties gathered into intense thought and mighty calm.

[1] Colonel Marshall, chief of staff.

[2] Colonel Newhall.

He seemed greater than I had ever seen him,—a look as of another world about him. No wonder I forgot altogether to salute him. Anything like that would have been too little.

He rode on to meet Lee at the Court House. What momentous issues had these two souls to declare! Neither of them, in truth, free, nor held in individual bounds alone; no longer testing each other's powers and resources, no longer weighing the chances of daring or desperate conflict. Instruments of God's hands, they were now to record His decree!

But the final word is not long coming now. Staff officers are flying, crying "Lee surrenders!" Ah, there was some kind of strength left among those worn and famished men belting the hills around the springs of the Appomattox, who rent the air with shouting and uproar, as if earth and sea had joined the song! Our men did what they thought their share, and then went to sleep, as they had need to do; but in the opposite camp they acted as if they had got hold of something too good to keep, and gave it to the stars.

Besides, they had a supper that night, which was something of a novelty. For we had divided rations with our old antagonists now that they were by our side as suffering brothers. In truth, Longstreet had come over to our camp that evening with an unwonted moisture on his martial cheek and compressed words on his lips: "Gentlemen, I must speak plainly; we are starving over there. For God's sake! can you send us something?"

We were men, and we acted like men, knowing we should suffer for it ourselves. We were too short-rationed also, and had been for days, and must be for days to come. But we forgot Andersonville and Belle Isle that night, and sent over to that starving camp share and share alike for all there; nor thinking the merits of the case diminished by the circumstance that part of these provisions was what Sheridan had captured from their trains the night before.

Generals Gibbon, Griffin, and Merritt were appointed commissioners to arrange the details of the surrender, and orders were issued in both armies that all officers and men should remain within the limits of their encampment.

Late that night I was summoned to headquarters, where General Griffin informed me that I was to command the parade on the occasion of the formal surrender of the arms and colors of Lee's army. He said the Confederates had begged hard to be allowed to stack their arms on the ground where they were, and let us go and pick them up after they had gone; but that Grant did not think this quite respectful enough to anybody, including the United States of America; and while he would have all private property respected, and would permit officers to retain their side-arms, he insisted that the surrendering army as such should march out in due order, and lay down all tokens of Confederate authority and organized hostility to the United States, in immediate presence of some representative portion of the Union Army. Griffin added in a significant tone that Grant wished the ceremony to be as simple as possible, and that nothing should be done to humiliate the manhood of the Southern soldiers.

I appreciated the honor of this appointment, although I did not take it much to myself. There were other things to think of. I only asked General Griffin to give me again my old Third Brigade, which I had commanded after Gettysburg, and with which I had been closely associated in the great battles of the first two years. Not for private reasons, however, was this request made, but because this was to be a crowning incident of history, and I thought these veterans deserved this recognition I was therefore transferred from the First Brigade, of which I had been so proud, to the Third, representing the veterans of the Fifth Corps. The soul-drawing bugle-call "Lights Out!" did not mean darkness and silence that momentous evening; far into the night gleamed some irrepressible camp fire and echoed the irrepressible cheer in which men voiced their deepest thought,—how different for each, no other knows!

At last we sleep—those who can. And so ended that 9th of April, 1865—Palm Sunday,—in that obscure little Virginia village now blazoned for immortal fame. Graver destinies were determined on that humble field than on many of classic and poetic fame. And though the issue brought bitterness to some, yet the heart of humanity the world over thrilled at the tidings. To us, I know, who there fell asleep that night, amidst memories of things that never can be told, it came like that Palm Sunday of old, when the rejoicing multitude met the meekly riding King, and cried: "Peace in Heaven; glory in the highest."

Morning dawned; and then, in spite of all attempts to restrain it, came the visiting and sight-seeing. Our camp was full of callers before we were up. They stood over our very heads now,—the men whose movements we used to study through field-glasses, or see close at hand framed in fire. We woke, and by force of habit started at the vision. But our resolute and much-enduring old antagonists were quick to change their mood when touched by appealing sentiment; they used their first vacation to come over and see what we were really made of, and what we had left for trade. Food was what was most needed; but was precisely what we also most lacked. Such as we parted with was not for sale, or barter; this went for "old times"—old comradeship across the lines. But tobacco, pipes, knives, money—or symbols of it,—shoes,—more precious still; and among the staff, even saddles, now and then, and other more trivial things that might serve as souvenirs, made an exchange about as brisk as the bullets had done a few days ago. The inundation of visitors grew so that it looked like a country fair, including the cattle-show. This exhibit broke up the order of the camp; and the authorities in charge had to interpose and forbid all visiting. All this day and part of the next our commissioners were busy arranging for the reception and transportation of surrendered property and the preparation of parole lists for the surrendering men. It was agreed that officers should sign paroles for their commands. But it took work and time to get the muster rolls in shape, not for "red tape" reasons, but for clear and explicit personal and public record. On our part most of us had time to think,—looking backward, and also forward.

Most of all, we missed our companions of the Second and Sixth Corps. They were only three miles away and were under orders to move back at once to Burkeville. It seemed strange to us that these two corps should not be allowed that little three-mile march more, to be participants of this consummation to which they perhaps more than any had contributed. Many a longer detour had they made for less cause and less good.

But whatever of honor or privilege came to us of the Fifth Corps was accepted not as for any preeminent work or worth of ours, but in the name of the whole noble Army of the Potomac; with loving remembrance of every man, whether on horse or foot or cannon-caisson, whether with shoulder-strap of office or with knapsack,—of every man, whether his heart beat high with the joy of this hour, or was long since stilled in the shallow trenches that furrow the red earth from the Antietam to the Appomattox!

It may help to a connected understanding of these closing scenes, if we glance at the movements of that close-pressing column for a day or two before. On the evening of the 7th, General Grant had written General Lee a letter from Farmville, and sent it through General Humphreys' lines, asking Lee to surrender his army. Lee answered at once declining to surrender, but asking the terms Grant would offer. The pursuit being resumed on the morning of the 8th, Grant wrote to Lee a second letter, delivered through Humphreys' skirmish line and Fitzhugh Lee's rear-guard, proposing to meet him for the purpose of arranging terms of surrender. To this Lee replied that he had not intended to propose actual surrender, but to negotiate for peace, and to ask General Grant what terms he would offer on that basis; proposing a meeting at 10 o'clock on the morning of the 9th between the picket lines, for discussion of this question. Grant answered declining the appointment for this purpose, saying in effect that the only way to secure peace is for the South to lay down their arms.

General Grant must have felt that the end was fast coming, even without negotiations; and he seems quite earnest to impress this upon General Lee. For, after all the solicitude about sparing further bloodshed, he in no wise permits his pursuing columns to remit their activity. The natural result of this must be a battle, a destructive and decisive one. Indeed, in the present situation of our Second and Sixth Corps, this battle is imminent. Still, at this very juncture,—Lee being now in his immediate presence, so to speak, close upon Humphreys' skirmish line,—for reasons which he has not made fully apparent but which we of the White

Oak Road could without difficulty surmise, General Grant deems it proper to transfer his own personal presence, as he says, "to the head of the column," or, as Badeau puts it, "to join Sheridan's column." This was now fighting Gordon's command and Lee's cavalry at Appomattox Court House. Accordingly, General Grant, having sent this suggestive answer to General Lee, took a road leading south from a point a mile west of New Store, for a good twenty-mile ride over to Sheridan, leaving great responsibility on Humphreys and Wright. Lee was repeatedly sending word to Humphreys asking for a truce pending consideration of proposals for surrender. Humphreys answered that he had no authority to consent to this, but, on the contrary, must press him to the utmost; and at last, in answer to Lee's urgency, he even had to warn General Lee that he must retire from a position he was occupying somewhat too trustingly on the road not a hundred yards from the head of the Second Corps column. Lee's reason undoubtedly was that he was expecting the meeting with Grant which he had asked for between the skirmish lines at ten o'clock. Half an hour after the incident, and half a mile beyond this place, the Second Corps came up to Longstreet's entrenched lines three miles northeast of Appomattox Court House; and the Sixth Corps closely following, dispositions were made for instant attack. At this moment General Meade arrives on the ground, and the attack is suspended. For Lee in the meantime has sent a further letter through Humphreys to Grant, asking an interview on the basis of Grant's last letter, and Meade reading this, at once grants a truce of an hour on his own lines, awaiting the response from Grant. But Grant had already left that front. Had he been here, matters could have been quickly settled. A staff officer is sent to overtake General Grant, and at noon, half-way on his journey, the General sends back answer to Lee that he is pushing forward "to the front" for the purpose of meeting him, with the very queer advice that word may be sent to him on the road he is now on, at what point General Lee wishes the meeting to be—that is, by a messenger out-galloping Grant. There is not much choice for Lee now. Grant being on so long a road and at such distance from both of the two "columns," communication with him is for a time impracticable. In consequence of this necessary delay, Lee sent a flag of truce both to Meade in his rear and to Sheridan in his front, to ask for a suspension of hostilities until he could somewhere meet General Grant, and himself took the shortest road for Appomattox Court House.

To resume my point of time and place, I was most of this day and the next adjusting relations in my changing commands, and with a part of my men, in picking up abandoned guns and munitions of value along the track of the Confederate march. I also had some thoughts which, as this is a personal narrative, it may be permitted to recall. For those who choose, the passage may be passed by. Some people have naturally asked me if I knew why I was designated to command the parade at the formal surrender. The same query came to my mind during the reflections of this day. I did not know or presume to ask those who perhaps would not have told me. Taking the assignment as I would any other, my feeling about it was more for the honor of the Fifth Corps and the Army of the Potomac than for myself. In lineal rank the junior general on the field, I never thought of claiming any special merit, nor tried to attract attention in any way, and believed myself to be socially unpopular among the "high boys." I had never indulged in loose talk, had minded my own business, did not curry favor with newspaper reporters, did not hang around superior headquarters, and in general had disciplined myself in self-control and the practice of patience, which virtue was not prominent among my natural endowments.

Some of my chief superiors had taken notice of this latter peculiarity apparently, as, when the recommendations for my promotion to brigadier-general after Gettysburg were ignored by the "delegation" at Washington, I found myself very soon assigned to command of a brigade. When, after the sharp tests of the Bristoe and Culpeper campaign, I was sent disabled to hospital from Rappahannock Station, and found on returning to duty that General Bartlett, of the Sixth Corps, sent over to relieve the dearth of generals in the Fifth, had chosen to take my brigade, I cheerfully returned to my regiment. Having in the meantime been applied for to command the Regular Brigade in Ayres' Division, I declined the offer at the request of General Griffin, who desired me to remain with the First Division. So remaining, I was often put in charge of peculiarly trying ventures, advance and rear-guard fights, involving command of several regiments, from Spottsylvania to Cold Harbor. Immediately after this, being still Colonel of the 20th Maine, I was assigned in special orders by General Warren to the command of a brigade of six Pennsylvania regiments, made up of veterans of the First Corps, who had distinguished themselves at Gettysburg by their heroism and their losses, with a fine new regiment of full ranks,—mostly veterans also. I devoted my best energies to the perfecting of this command during the campaign before Richmond and the opening assaults on Petersburg, but in the first battle here was severely wounded leading a charge, after rather presumptuously advising against it. Here General Grant promoted me on the field to Brigadier-General in terms referring to previous history. Returning to the front after months in Annapolis Naval School Hospital, I found my splendid brigade broken up and scattered, and its place filled by two new regiments, one from New York and one from Pennsylvania, both of finest material and personnel, but my command was reduced from the largest brigade in the corps to the very smallest. Although offered other highly desirable positions, I quietly took up this little brigade and with no complaints and no petitions for advancement went forward in my duty with the best that was in me. The noble behavior of these troops was the occasion of the brevet of Major-General, and no doubt in consideration of meekness in small things General Griffin placed under my orders for all the active engagements of this campaign, the fine Second Brigade of the division,—thus giving me a command equal to my former one, or any other in the corps.

So I had reason to believe that General Griffin had something to do with General Grant's kind remembrance, and negative merits appeared to stand for something. *Tout vient à point pour qui sait attendre*—"Everything comes in good time to him who knows how to wait."

On the morning of the 11th our division had been moved over to relieve Turner's of the Twenty-fourth Corps, Army of the James, near the Court House, where they had been receiving some of the surrendered arms, especially of the artillery on their front, while Mackenzie's cavalry had received the surrendered sabers of W. H. F. Lee's command.

Praises of General Grant were on every tongue for his magnanimity in allowing the horses of the artillery and cavalry that were the property of the men and not of the Confederacy, to be retained by the men for service in restoring and working their little plantations, and also in requesting the managers of transportation companies in all that region to facilitate in every way the return of these men to their homes.

At noon of the 11th the troops of the Army of the James took up the march to Lynchburg, to make sure of that yet doubtful point of advantage. Lee and Grant had both left: Lee for Richmond, to see his dying wife; Grant for Washington, only that once more to see again Lincoln living. The business transactions had been settled, the parole papers made out; all was ready for the last turn,—the dissolving-view of the Army of Northern Virginia.

It was now the morning of the 12th of April. I had been ordered to have my lines formed for the ceremony at sunrise. It was a chill gray morning, depressing to the senses. But our hearts made warmth. Great memories uprose; great thoughts went forward. We formed along the principal street, from the bluff bank of the stream to near the Court House on the left,—to face the last line of battle, and receive the last remnant of the arms and colors of that great army which ours had been created to confront for all that death can do for life. We were remnants also: Massachusetts, Maine, Michigan, Maryland, Pennsylvania, New York; veterans, and replaced veterans; cut to pieces, cut down, consolidated, divisions into brigades, regiments into one, gathered by State origin; this little line, quintessence or metempsychosis of Porter's old corps of Gaines' Mill and Malvern Hill; men of near blood born, made nearer by blood shed. Those facing us—now, thank God! the same.

As for me, I was once more with my old command.

But this was not all I needed. I had taken leave of my little First Brigade so endeared to me, and the end of the fighting had released the Second from all orders from me. But these deserved to share with me now as they had so faithfully done in the sterner passages of the campaign. I got permission from General Griffin to have them also in the parade. I placed the First Brigade in line a little to our rear, and the Second on the opposite side of the street facing us and leaving ample space for the movements of the coming ceremony. Thus the whole division was out, and under my direction for the occasion, although I was not the division commander. I thought this troubled General Bartlett a little, but he was a manly and soldierly man and made no comment. He contented himself by mounting his whole staff and with the division flag riding around our lines and conversing as he found opportunity with the Confederate officers. This in no manner disturbed me; my place and part were definite and clear.

Our earnest eyes scan the busy groups on the opposite slopes, breaking camp for the last time, taking down their little shelter-tents and folding them carefully as precious things, then slowly forming ranks as for unwelcome duty. And now they move. The dusky swarms forge forward into gray columns of march. On they come, with the old swinging route step and swaying battle-flags. In the van, the proud Confederate ensign—the great field of white with canton of star-strewn cross of blue on a field of red, the regimental battle-flags with the same escutcheon following on, crowded so thick, by thinning out of men, that the whole column seemed crowned with red. At the right of our line our little group mounted beneath our flags, the red Maltese cross on a field of white, erewhile so bravely borne through many a field more crimson than itself, its mystic meaning now ruling all.

The momentous meaning of this occasion impressed me deeply. I resolved to mark it by some token of recognition, which could be no other than a salute of arms. Well aware of the responsibility assumed, and of the criticisms that would follow, as the sequel proved, nothing of that kind could move me in the least. The act could be defended, if needful, by the suggestion that such a salute was not to the cause for which the flag of the Confederacy stood, but to its going down before the flag of the Union. My main reason, however, was one for which I sought no authority nor asked forgiveness. Before us in proud humiliation stood the embodiment of manhood: men whom neither toils and sufferings, nor the fact of death, nor disaster, nor hopelessness could bend from their resolve; standing before us now, thin, worn, and famished, but erect, and with eyes looking level into ours, waking memories that bound us together as no other bond;—was not such manhood to be welcomed back into a Union so tested and assured?

Instructions had been given; and when the head of each division column comes opposite our group, our bugle sounds the signal and instantly our whole line from right to left, regiment by regiment in succession, gives the soldier's salutation, from the "order arms" to the old "carry"—the marching salute. Gordon at the head of the column, riding with heavy spirit and downcast face, catches the sound of shifting arms, looks up, and, taking the meaning, wheels superbly, making with himself and his horse one uplifted figure, with profound salutation as he drops the point of his sword to the boot toe; then facing to his own command, gives word for his successive brigades to pass us with the same position of the manual,—honor answering honor. On our part not a sound of trumpet more, nor roll of drum; not a cheer, nor word nor whisper of vain-glorying, nor motion of man standing again at the order, but an awed stillness rather, and breath-holding, as if it were the passing of the dead!

As each successive division masks our own, it halts, the men face inward towards us across the road, twelve feet away; then carefully "dress" their line, each captain taking pains for the good appearance of his company, worn and half starved as they were. The field and staff take their positions in the intervals of regiments; generals in rear of their commands. They fix bayonets, stack arms; then, hesitatingly, remove cartridge-boxes and lay them down. Lastly,—reluctantly, with agony of expression,—they tenderly fold their flags, battle-worn and torn, blood-stained, heart-holding colors, and lay them down; some frenziedly rushing from the ranks, kneeling over them, clinging to them, pressing them to their lips with burning tears. And only the Flag of the Union greets the sky!

What visions thronged as we looked into each other's eyes! Here pass the men of Antietam, the Bloody Lane, the Sunken Road, the Cornfield, the Burnside-Bridge; the men whom Stonewall Jackson on the second night at Fredericksburg begged Lee to let him take and crush the two corps of the Army of the Potomac huddled in the streets in darkness and confusion; the men who swept away the Eleventh Corps at Chancellorsville; who left six thousand of their companions around the bases of Culp's and Cemetery Hills at Gettysburg; these survivors of the terrible Wilderness, the Bloody-Angle at Spottsylvania, the slaughter pen of Cold Harbor, the whirlpool of Bethesda Church!

Here comes Cobb's Georgia Legion, which held the stone wall on Marye's Heights at Fredericksburg, close before which we piled our dead for breastworks so that the living might stay and live.

Here too come Gordon's Georgians and Hoke's North Carolinians, who stood before the terrific mine explosion at Petersburg, and advancing retook the smoking crater and the dismal heaps of dead—ours more than theirs—huddled in the ghastly chasm.

Here are the men of McGowan, Hunton, and Scales, who broke the Fifth Corps lines on the White Oak Road, and were so desperately driven back on that forlorn night of March 31st by my thrice-decimated brigade.

Now comes Anderson's Fourth Corps, only Bushrod Johnson's Division left, and this the remnant of those we fought so fiercely on the Quaker Road two weeks ago, with Wise's Legion, too fierce for its own good.

Here passes the proud remnant of Ransom's North Carolinians which we swept through Five Forks ten days ago,—and all the little that was left of this division in the sharp passages at Sailor's Creek five days thereafter.

Now makes its last front A. P. Hill's old Corps, Heth now at the head, since Hill had gone too far forward ever to return: the men who poured destruction into our division at Shepardstown Ford, Antietam, in 1862, when Hill reported the Potomac running blue with our bodies; the men who opened the desperate first day's fight at Gettysburg, where withstanding them so stubbornly our Robinson's Brigades lost 1185 men, and the Iron Brigade alone 1153,—these men of Heth's Division here too losing 2850 men, companions of these now looking into our faces so differently.

What is this but the remnant of Mahone's Division, last seen by us at the North Anna? its thinned ranks of worn, bright-eyed men recalling scenes of costly valor and ever-remembered history.

Now the sad great pageant—Longstreet and his men! What shall we give them for greeting that has not already been spoken in volleys of thunder and written in lines of fire on all the river-banks of Virginia? Shall we go back to Gaines' Mill and Malvern Hill? Or to the Antietam of

Maryland, or Gettysburg of Pennsylvania?—deepest graven of all. For here is what remains of Kershaw's Division, which left 40 per cent. of its men at Antietam, and at Gettysburg with Barksdale's and Semmes' Brigades tore through the Peach Orchard, rolling up the right of our gallant Third Corps, sweeping over the proud batteries of Massachusetts—Bigelow and Philips,—where under the smoke we saw the earth brown and blue with prostrate bodies of horses and men, and the tongues of overturned cannon and caissons pointing grim and stark in the air.

Then in the Wilderness, at Spottsylvania and thereafter, Kershaw's Division again, in deeds of awful glory, held their name and fame, until fate met them at Sailor's Creek, where Kershaw himself, and Ewell, and so many more, gave up their arms and hopes,—all, indeed, but manhood's honor.

With what strange emotion I look into these faces before which in the mad assault on Rives' Salient, June 18, 1864, I was left for dead under their eyes! It is by miracles we have lived to see this day,—any of us standing here.

Now comes the sinewy remnant of fierce Hood's Division, which at Gettysburg we saw pouring through the Devil's Den, and the Plum Run gorge; turning again by the left our stubborn Third Corps, then swarming up the rocky bastions of Round Top, to be met there by equal valor, which changed Lee's whole plan of battle and perhaps the story of Gettysburg.

Ah, is this Pickett's Division?—this little group left of those who on the lurid last day of Gettysburg breasted level cross-fire and thunderbolts of storm, to be strewn back drifting wrecks, where after that awful, futile, pitiful charge we buried them in graves a furlong wide, with names unknown!

Met again in the terrible cyclone-sweep over the breastworks at Five Forks; met now, so thin, so pale, purged of the mortal,—as if knowing pain or joy no more. How could we help falling on our knees, all of us together, and praying God to pity and forgive us all!

Thus, all day long, division after division comes and goes, surrendered arms being removed by our wagons in the intervals, the cartridge-boxes emptied in the street when the ammunition was found unserviceable, our men meanwhile resting in place.

Meantime many men had been coming in late in the day, complaining that they had been abandoned by their officers and declaring that they preferred to give their parole in surrender, rather than encounter all the difficulties and hardships of an attempt to escape.

There are incidents of that scene which may be worth repeating. There was opportunity for converse with several Confederate generals. Their bearing was, of course, serious, their spirits sad. What various misgivings mingled in their mood we could not but conjecture. Levying war against the United States was serious business. But one certain impression was received from them all; they were ready to accept for themselves and for the Confederacy any fate our Government should dictate. Lincoln's magnanimity, as Grant's thoughtfulness, had already impressed them much. They spoke like brave men who mean to stand upon their honor and accept the situation. "General," says one of them at the head of his corps, "this is deeply humiliating; but I console myself with the thought that the whole country will rejoice at this day's business." "You astonish us," says another of equally high rank, "by your honorable and generous conduct. I fear we should not have done the same by you had the case been reversed." "I will go home," says a gallant officer from North Carolina, "and tell Joe Johnston we can't fight such men as you. I will advise him to surrender." "I went into that cause" says yet another of well-known name, "and I meant it. We had our choice of weapons and of ground, and we have lost. Now that is my flag (pointing to the flag of the Union), and I will prove myself as worthy as any of you."

In fact that was the whole drift of the talk, and there is no reason to doubt that it was sincere. Equally so but quite different was the strain of another. I saw him moving restlessly about, scolding his men and being answered back by them instead of ordering them. He seemed so disturbed in mind that I rode down the line to see if I could not give him a word of cheer. With a respectful salutation, calling his attention to the bearing of the men on both sides, "This promises well for our coming good-will," said I; "brave men may become good friends." "You're mistaken, sir," he turned and said. "You may forgive us but we won't be forgiven. There is a rancor in our hearts [here came in an anatomical gesture] which you little dream of. We hate you, sir." "Oh, we don't mind much about dreams, nor about hates either. Those two lines of business are closed," was the quiet reply. Then as if a little sorry for his opening, fixing his gaze on two ungainly looking holes in the breast of my coat and a much-abused sleeve, he exclaimed in a milder tone: "Those were ugly shots, General. Where did you get these?" Unfortunately I had to admit that this happened on the first day of the campaign in an afternoon I had the honor of spending with him and his party on the Quaker Road, where there were plenty of quakers and shakers also, and some few runners who left me a parting souvenir. "I suppose you think you did great things there," he burst in. "I was ordered to attack you and check your advance; and I did it too with a vim, till I found I was fighting three army corps, when I thought it prudent to retire." I was really sorry to have to reassure him that there was no more than the third part of one corps present on our side. "I know better," he cries; "I saw the flags myself." I think that he did stop to count three before he left us, leaving his cap behind. But I could not resist saying: "You saw the flags of three regiments; steady eyes could see no more." One of his staff officers corroborates this, and for a moment he subsides. Then he breaks out again:

"It's a pity you have no lawyers in your army,"—I did not know what was coming now, unless he wanted to make his will,—"you don't know how to make out paroles. Who ever heard of paroles being signed by any but the parties paroled?" I tried to explain to him that this was a matter of mercy and humanity, for if we should keep all their men there till every individual could sign his parole, half of them would be dead of starvation before their turn came. "Nonsense," he rejoins; "all that is *spargere voces;* every lawyer knows such a parole as this is a mere *brutum fulmen.*" "Sir," I answer, "if by brute thunderbolts you mean a pledged word to keep the peace accepted and adopted by the recipient of the favor, I don't believe your people need any lawyer to instruct them as to the word of honor." I was about to turn away; he catches the suggestion of the motion and issues a parting order. "You go home," he cries, "you take these fellows home. That's what will end the war." "Don't worry about the end of the war," I answer. "We are going home pretty soon, but not till we see you home." "Home!" he snatches up the word. "We haven't any. You have destroyed them. You have invaded Virginia, and ruined her. Her curse is on you." "You shouldn't have invited us down here then," was the obvious reply. "We expected somebody was going to get hurt when we took up your challenge. Didn't you? People who don't want to get hurt, General, had better not force a fight on unwilling Yankees."

By this time the thing grew comic. The staff officers both in blue and gray laughed outright; and even his men looked around from their somber service and smiled as if they enjoyed the joke. He turned away also to launch his "brute thunderbolts," not waiting to receive my thanks for instruction in Law and Latin. "The wise man foreseeth the evil and hideth himself, but the foolish pass on and are punished, says the old proverb." If there are no exceptions to this rule, then this gentleman was not rightly named.

With this comedy ends, in classic fashion, the stern drama of the Appomattox. A strange and somber shadow rose up ghost-like from the haunts of memory or habit, and rested down over the final parting scene. How strong are these ties of habit! How strange the undertone of sadness even at the release from prison and from pain! It seems as if we had put some precious part of ourselves there which we are loath to leave.

When all is over, in the dusk of evening, the long lines of scattered cartridges are set on fire, and the lurid flames wreathing the blackness of earthly shadows give an unearthly border to our parting.

Then, stripped of every token of enmity or instrument of power to hurt, they march off to give their word of honor never to lift arms against the old flag again till its holders release them from their promise. Then, their ranks broken, the bonds that bound them fused away by forces stronger than fire, they are free at last to go where they will; to find their homes, now most likely stricken, despoiled by war.

Twenty-seven thousand men paroled; seventeen thousand stand of arms laid down or gathered up; a hundred battle-flags. But regiments and brigades—or what is left of them—have scarce a score of arms to surrender; having thrown them away by road and riverside in weariness of flight or hopelessness of heart, disdaining to carry them longer but to disaster. And many a bare staff was there laid down, from which the ensign had been torn in the passion and struggle of emotions, and divided piece by piece; a blurred or shrunken star, a rag of smoke-stained blue from the war-worn cross, a shred of deepened dye from the rent field of red, to be treasured for precious keepsakes of manhood's test and heirlooms for their children.

Nor blame them too much for this, nor us for not blaming them more. Although, as we believed, fatally wrong in striking at the old flag, misreading its deeper meaning and the innermost law of the people's life, blind to the signs of the times in the march of man, they fought as they were taught, true to such ideals as they saw, and put into their cause their best. For us they were fellow-soldiers as well, suffering the fate of arms. We could not look into those brave, bronzed faces, and those battered flags we had met on so many fields where glorious manhood lent a glory to the earth that bore it, and think of personal hate and mean revenge. Whoever had misled these men, we had not. We had led them back, home. Whoever had made that quarrel, we had not. It was a remnant of the inherited curse for sin. We had purged it away, with blood-offerings. We were all of us together factors of that high will which, working often through illusions of the human, and following ideals that lead through storms, evolves the enfranchisement of man.

Forgive us, therefore, if from stern, steadfast faces eyes dimmed with tears gazed at each other across that pile of storied relics so dearly there laid down, and brothers' hands were fain to reach across that rushing tide of memories which divided us, yet made us forever one.

It was our glory only that the victory we had won was for country, for the well-being of others, of these men before us as well as for ourselves and ours. Our joy was a deep, far, unspoken satisfaction,—the approval, as it were, of some voiceless and veiled divinity like the appointed "Angel of the Nation" of which the old scriptures tell—leading and looking far, yet mindful of sorrows; standing above all human strife and fierce passages of trial; not marking faults nor seeking blame; transmuting into factors of the final good corrected errors and forgiven sins; assuring of immortal inheritance all pure purpose and noble endeavor, humblest service and costliest sacrifice, unconscious and even mistaken martyrdoms offered and suffered for the sake of man.

Now on the morrow, over all the hillsides in the peaceful sunshine, are clouds of men on foot or horse, singly or in groups, making their earnest way as by the instinct of the ant, each with his own little burden, each for his own little home. And we are left alone, and lonesome. We miss our spirited antagonists in the game, and we lose interest. The weight is taken out of the opposite scale, and we go down. Never are we less gay. And when we took up the long, round-about march homeward, it was dull to plod along looking only at the muddy road, without scouts and skirmishers ahead, and reckless of our flanks. It was tame to think we could ride up to any thicket of woods we pleased, without starting at the chirrup of those little bluebirds whose cadence was so familiar to our ears, and made so deep a lodgment in our bosoms too, sometimes. It was dreary to lie down and sleep at night and think there was no vigilant picket out on the dubious-looking crests around to keep faithful watch and ward. And it seems sheer waste of opportunity and mark of military incapacity, when we emerge from some deep wood or defile and no battery belches destruction upon us from so advantageous a position as the commanding heights beyond.

But slowly these lingering images of memory or habit are lost in the currents of a deeper mood; we wonder at that mysterious dispensation whereby the pathway of the kingdom of Love on earth must needs be cut through by the sword, and why it must be that by such things as we had seen and done and suffered, and lost and won, a step is taken in the homeward march of man.

CHAPTER VII

THE RETURN OF THE ARMY

ALTHOUGH fraught with deepest interest and filled with occupations of great variety, our sojourn at Appomattox Court House was a hard experience. We had raced to that point in lightest marching order; there was no superfluity of equipage. The packs were slender; overcoats and blankets had proved too heavy for those thirty-mile marches. The shelter-tent cloths had to serve for these, and for towels also, which they most resembled. The rations reduced to sediment in the haversacks smelt of lead and gunpowder. To be sure, a few supply wagons had managed to get up to us, and our cavalry had captured some trains at Appomattox Station; but all we had we shared with our surrendering competitors, technically called "the enemy,"—now become our sympathizing guests. For a day or two past all hands had to forage for a living, and many a ten-mile tramp resulted only in armfuls of corn on the cob, which needed a good deal of soaking to yield to our practised jaws. It got it. For when on Saturday morning we took up the march for Burkeville and had got well stretched out on the road, we were overtaken by a pouring rain, which made mulch of everything. Seeking the center of the earth by a force of gravity we could fully sympathize with, it soon formed a junction in the roads and fields to the extent of four or five inches of "half and half," denominated in the Low-German dialect "mudde"; but later circumstances inclined certain travelers to transpose the superfluous final "d" and put it to use as the initial prefix of a deeply descriptive adjective. Drenched, hungry, draggled in mire, that long, lank body presented an image not unlike that reported by Daniel on the king's dream,—the head gold, the belly brass, the legs iron, and the feet clay,—but the proportions were not so well observed. We were informed in animated tones that we were to draw rations that night,—but what kind of a "draw" it was to be we were by no means assured. We noticed that the goal was fixed a long stretch ahead; it suggested to us what we had seen offered a team of cattle tolled on by a show of forage fastened well forward of the yoke or pole.

Near Evergreen Station we struck the Southside Railroad, and hoping to save the men's strength, I told the colonel of the leading regiment to have his men take the railroad track and keep out of the heavy mud. They tried it for a while, but soon I saw them jumping back into the mire ankle deep; and, wondering at this, I felt rebuked for my simplicity, when informed that the men found it much more wearing to watch the varying distance of the cross-ties spaced anywhere from eighteen inches to two feet, and measure every step accordingly, than to take the road as it was, and be free to put their feet down wherever they could get them out again. So dear is liberty.

Long after dark we were led to a place designated for a camp. To reach this we were countermarched or turned off on a tangent for quite a space, and halted on a flat-pine land, some cubit lower and knee deeper than the road. I heard no orders given the regiments to "break ranks," the effort of the officers was to get their men together, that they might be looked after, and possibly, though a whimsical suggestion, to draw rations. But no commissary could find us in that dark and drench, even if the wagons could worry through the muddle. Fire would be of no use; the thought of trying to make one would do more good, for it would raise our spirits to join "the mighty laughter of the vernal floods." It was interesting to hear the men—poor fellows—making their beds, some on the rugged roots of the pines, or cradled between two broken branches to lift them from softer pillows, or securing the shelter of a big bough, which ever and anon swaying under accumulated weight, bent down to envelop them in unwelcome "sheets." Now some one seeking the open,—less covering the best,—reckless of all things, now that they had returned to "chaos and old night." One bright, belated fellow, seeking to share some luckier sleeper's cot, was heard muttering with "wakeful" reminiscence, "Sure, a Yank wud shleep uf the divil sat at his hid!" To us, in so-called headquarters—though quarters were not perfectly distinguished that night amidst such mingling of the elements—a kind of ichthyosaurian sleep came at last—dreaming that the whole earth was about this way once, and fully sympathizing with the Hebrew description of it as 'Tohoo vaw Vohoo," if not exactly "without form and void."

In the morning the men sighted the few places where they could get splinters enough to make a fire to cook their last "ration" of pickled pork and gunpowder. Then pulling out at 6 A.M. under chilly rain and lowering clouds, we took the road for Farmville. It was Sunday afternoon when we reached its vicinity, and were welcomed by a sky clear and serene, overlooking the town. The trains were there, and so a breakfast—in literal terms, though belated fact. The clouds had rolled away and field and camp were flooded with sunshine. All the domestic arts were soon in evidence, —largely that of washing-day;—as if we had not had enough in the previous twenty-four hours. Gradually a Sabbath peace stole over the scene. All were at rest, mind and body, and the very heart of nature breathed soft airs and mellow light.

Headquarters had been taken in the ample front yard of an old mansion of the ancient régime. Here at about four o'clock the fine German Band of my old First Brigade came over to reciprocate the smiles of heaven by choice music, ministering also to our spiritual upgoings. They were in the midst of a bright and joyous strain when there came galloping up the old familiar figure—the mud-splashed, grave-faced, keen-eyed cavalryman,—the message-bearer. It was no uncommon thing to receive a military telegram in those days; but something in the manner and look of this messenger took my attention. He rode up in front of the sentinel and the colors, and dismounted. My chief of staff went out to meet him. "I think the General would wish to treat this as personal," he said. I beckoned him to the rear of our group, and he handed me a yellow tissue-paper telegram. It read as I remember it,—the original was kept by somebody as a memento:

"WASHINGTON, April 15, 1865.

"The President died this morning. Wilkes Booth the assassin. Secretary Seward dangerously wounded. The rest of the Cabinet, General Grant, and other high officers of the Government included in the plot of destruction."

I should have been paralyzed by the shock, had not the sense of responsibility overborne all other thoughts. If treachery had overturned the Government, and had possession of the Capitol, there was work for us to do. But the first thought was of the effect of this upon our soldiers. They, for every reason, must be held in hand. "Put a double guard on the whole camp immediately. Tell the regimental commanders to get all their men in, and allow no one to leave,"—was the first word sent out. "Then tell the gentlemen I would like to see them here." I stepped back and with especial pains to be calm and courteous I thanked and dismissed the band, and they quietly withdrew. All eyes were on me, but not until my officers came up did I disclose to any one this appalling news. I enjoined upon them absolute reticence until we had made all secure. Against what? and whom? Our men. They could be trusted well to bear any blow but this. Their love for the President was something marvelous. Their great loving hearts of sterling manhood seemed to have gathered him in. After each success and especially after each great reverse, he had been accustomed to come out to see them. That honest, homely face, showing how heavily pressed the terrible burden that had come upon him,—of settling the "irrepressible conflict" which had been growing for a century; that look of an infinite sadness in the eyes that rested with such trust and such solicitude on these men, the only instruments with which to fulfill his task! Heart-wrung by the sacrifice, he had taken deep hold on the soldier's heart, stirring its many chords. Now the cowardly, brutal blow, when his words of gentleness to all were still warm as the breath of the returning spring, must stir their yet unfathomed depths. It might take but little to rouse them to a frenzy of blind revenge. And right before them lay a city, one of the nerve-centers of the rebellion, and an easy and inviting prey to vengeance. Large quantities of goods, military and merchandise, had been stored there, it was said; many citizens had gathered there for safety against the marauders of a demoralized army; a young ladies' seminary, we were told, serving especially as a sort of sanctuary for the tender and sensitive, which they thought would be respected even in those turbulent times.

How could we be sure that change of century had made men different from what they were when Tilly at Magdeburg, Cromwell at Wexford, or Wellington at San Sebastian had been powerless to restrain dire passions, excited by far less cause? How could we be sure that lessons and thoughts of home, the habit of well formed character, and the discipline of the field would be sufficient to hold within the bounds of patience men who saw that most innocent and noble-hearted man, their best-beloved, the stricken victim of infernal outrage? I knew my men thoroughly, high-minded and self-controlled; but what if now this blackest crime should fire their hearts to reckless and implacable vengeance?

But a heavier responsibility, perhaps, awaited us. Strange forebodings pressed upon the mind. It seemed as if the darkest things might be yet to come; as if, now that men of honor had given up the fight, it had fallen to baser hands; as if victory, magnanimity, and charity, accepted by those who had lost in the manly appeal to arms, were all to avail nothing against the sullen treacheries that lurked in the shadows of the capital.

As I was pacing the ground, wrapped in anxious thoughts, the lady of the house—there were never any men at home in those days—came out to ask what had happened that disturbed us so deeply.

"It is bad news for the South," said I. "Is it Lee or Davis?" she asked, a look of pain pinching her features. "I must tell you, madam, with a warning," I replied. "I have put your house under a strict guard. It is Lincoln."

I was sorry to see her face brighten with an expression of relief. "The South has lost its best friend, madam," was the only thing to say.

All being now secure in camp, with the assurance that the news should be prudently broken to the men, instinct and habit turned to the superior officers. Even the companionship of these experienced men would be some relief; and perhaps there might be counsel to be taken now, as in so many a dark and boding hour before. Leaving General Gregory at my quarters with instructions, I mounted my horse. My thought was anticipated. Scarcely had I got beyond the limits of our camp when I saw a figure often welcome to many eyes,—Charles Griffin riding up,—our corps commander now, and never more prized than at this hour. "I was coming to see you," he says; "now let us get Ayres." Finding Ayres—soldier born, and tried and true,—we discussed possible tactics on an unknown field. We did not pretend to be men of influence in statecraft; but we well knew we were likely, if anything was to be done, to be men of action. So we had reason and right to forecast events. All we knew as yet of the condition of things at Washington was what the brief telegram had told. But that looked dark enough. It was a daring attempt, and, as it was told to us, must have had reserved force to support it, as well as reckless impulse to carry it out. Lee's army had been broken up; many able and honorable officers, and perhaps thirty thousand of their best men had given their parole; but Davis and officers of his Government had got away, and there were other armies and other men, whom the shock of the surrender and remoteness from the controlling influence had made desperate rather than discouraged.

Our little conference was soon concluded. "Now let us go up and see Meade," said Griffin. We found him sad—very sad. He had only two corps with him, the Second and Fifth; the Sixth had been sent in another direction. And the course of dealings in this last campaign led to gloomy forebodings as to his own treatment when we should arrive at Washington. We well knew what his mood and meditations were—like St. Paul's: "I go bound in spirit up to Jerusalem, not knowing the things that shall befall me there." But this supreme exigency roused all the patriot and soldier in him.

The upshot of this conference was expressed in words I well remember: "The plan is to destroy the Government by assassination. They probably have means to get possession of the capital before anybody can stop them. There is nothing for it but to push the army to Washington, and make Grant military dictator until we can restore constitutional government." This may be smiled at now, as the habit is after the peril has passed, especially on the part of those who never realized it. But in the situation of things then, there was little to laugh at. The spirit of that evening conference showed one reliance to be counted on in case the need had come.

We returned at evening to our several stations, ready for anything. But no worse news came from the capital. Our soldiers, like our people, wonderfully patient in severest stress, kept their self-command even now. So the march was resumed calmly and orderly as before, and more so, now that we had free course and a fair road. In the meantime I had been assigned to the command of the First Division of the Fifth Corps, General Bartlett having been transferred to the Ninth Corps at Alexandria. Two days' additional rations were issued at daylight on the 17th, and we marched out for Burkeville. Near here we were by some blunder switched off on the Danville Road, and encamped near Liberty Church by the Little Sandy River. The erroneous move being now discovered, we resumed our march early the next morning, almost retracing our steps, and finally encamped near Burkeville. On the nineteenth, the day appointed for the funeral of the President at Washington, an order came from the War Department for us to halt the march and hold all still while the funeral was passing at the capital. Then we thought, why not for us a funeral? For the shadow of one reverenced and beloved was to pass before our souls that day, and we would review him, now.

We began by draping headquarters tents with mourning rosettes of crape; then also draping the colors and our sword-hilts, with a wreath of crape, too, on the left arms of all. At noon, the solemn boom of the minute-guns, speaking power and sorrow, hushed all the camp. I summoned the senior chaplain of the division, Father Egan, and told him we looked to him for the memorial address, cautioning him to prepare beforehand, not so much what to say, as what not to say. For I knew his Irish warmth and power of speech, and that he might, if not restrained, stir the hearts of the men too much for our control. He assured me he would be very careful. The division was formed in hollow square, facing inward. The old flags were brought to the front of their regiments, battle-torn and smoke-dimmed, draped in sorrow, but some of them blazoned with a crimson deeper than their red, touching the stars. Behind these the men stacked arms, and stood, tense and motionless, as a hushed sea. Those faces spoke depths of manliness, and reaches of deeds words do not record. The veterans of terrible campaigns, the flushed faces from Appomattox, the burning hearts turned homewards, mighty memories and quenchless love held innermost. On the open face of the square, on a little mound, we planted the red Maltese cross of the division,—itself emblem and memorial of great things suffered and done for man. Around it gathered the generals and staff:

Griffin chief, never forgetting his old division, with which he had passed through all things from the beginning, its name and soul the same, after terrible transmutations,—Griffin, graceful in figure, sincere and brave of speech, reverential and religious in cherished thought; Ayres, too, ours from the beginning, solid and sure as the iron guns he brought, holding all his powers well in hand, faced to the front; gallant, ever-ready, dashing Pearson; dear old Gregory, pure-souled as crystal, thinking never of self, calmest in death's carnival; others, younger,—how shall I name them all? Staff officers, cool, keen, and swift as sword flash, fulfilling vital trusts, even at vital cost;—of such our group. On the little platform of ammunition boxes I held myself close in reach of the chaplain ready to enforce my warning.

Catching the keynote of the last cannon-boom, strikes in the sincere, deep-feeling German Band with that wondrous "Russian Hymn" swelling with its flood of music,—deep calling unto deep:

> "God, the all-terrible; Thou who ordainest,
> Thunder Thy clarion, and lightning Thy sword."

That whelming flood of chords with the breath-stifling chromatic cadences, as if to prepare us for whatever life or death could bring.

Then, a few words—such as could be spoken—introducing the occasion and its orator. His very first words deepened the passion of the music echoing in the hearts of that stern, impressionable, loving, remembering assembly. With countenance precluding speech, in measured articulation made more impressive by its slightly foreign cast, he launches forth his thrilling text: "And she, being instructed of her mother, said, 'Give me here the head of John Baptist in a charger.'" The application went through men's minds with a thrill. But he took it up phrase by phrase. The spirit of rebellion against the country's life and honor, he said, incited its followers to murder the innocent and just. Even on its own showing, the cause of secession was narrow and trivial. The will of a section rooted in self-interest, should not outweigh the vital interests of a whole people. Lincoln had committed no crime in being constitutionally elected President of the United States. He then portrayed the character of Lincoln, his integrity, his rugged truth, his innocence of wrong, his loyalty and lofty fidelity to the people. Then having raised this figure to its highest ideal lights and most endearing attractiveness, he pictured him stricken down by dastard hand in the very midst of acts of mercy and words of great-hearted sympathy and love. Gathering up the emotions of his audience with searching, imploring glance, he reminded the soldiers of Lincoln's love for them, and theirs for him; that brotherhood of suffering that made them one in soul with him.

"And will you endure this sacrilege?" he cried. "Can heavenly charity tolerate such crime under the flag of this delivered country?" "Will you not rather sweep such a spirit out of the land forever, and cast it, root and branch, into everlasting burning?" Men's faces flushed and paled. Their muscles trembled. I saw them grasp as for their stacked muskets, instinctively, from habit, not knowing what else, or what, to do. I myself was under the spell. Well that the commander was there, to check the flaming orator. Men could not bear it. You could not, were I able to reproduce the scene. Then the speaker stopped. He stood transfixed. I seized his arm. "Father Egan, you must not stop. Turn this excitement to some good." "I will," he whispers. Then lifting his arm full height, he brought it down with a tremendous sweep, as if to gather in the whole quivering circle before him, and went on: "Better so. Better to die glorious, than to live infamous. Better to be buried beneath a nation's tears, than to walk the earth guilty of a nation's blood. Better, thousandfold, forever better, Lincoln dead, than Davis living."

Then admonished of the passion he was again arousing, he passed to an exhortation that rose into a prayer, then to a pæan of victory, and with an oath of new consecration to the undying cause of freedom and right, he gave us back to ourselves, better soldiers, and better men. Who that heard those burning words can ever forget them? And who that saw, can ever forget that congregation in the field? Meekly returning from their glories at Appomattox, and sternly sharing—for it was of theirs also—the sacrifice at Washington. Steadfast and noble in every test, unto the end. God bless them beyond, likewise!

That evening came the orders for the corps to stretch itself out for permanent duty along the railroad between Burkeville and Petersburg, and the next morning we moved for the new field. Ayres' Division took ground from Burkeville to Nottaway Court House, his headquarters being at the latter place, which was also headquarters of the corps. From this Crawford's Division extended six miles farther to the station called "Blacks and Whites," where he made his headquarters. His jurisdiction also reached to Wilson's Station. Here my division, the First, took up the line from Wilson's Station to Petersburg, headquarters being at Wilson's. The distance from here to Petersburg being twenty-seven miles, made for me a disproportionate responsibility, and an order from army headquarters terminated my jurisdiction at Sutherland's Station, ten miles out.

Our assigned duty was to guard the railroads and the adjacent territory. But there were many other duties necessitated by the condition of the country and of the inhabitants. This region had been overrun successively by the two hostile armies for the last two years, hence it was now a scene of desolation. This was exemplified within the limits of my own command. My First Brigade, commanded by Colonel Sniper, had its headquarters at Wilson's, which was in the vicinity of our conflicts on the White Oak Road; my Second Brigade, under General Gregory, made headquarters at Ford's Station, its jurisdiction covering the battlefields of Five Forks, Dinwiddie, and the White Oak Road;

and the Third, the Veteran Brigade, of nine regiments—lately my own—commanded now by Colonel Edmunds of the 32 Massachusetts, was placed at Sutherland's Station, which covered the fields of the Quaker Road, Armstrong's Mill, Hatcher's Run, and of many minor fights on the left of our old entrenched lines. It was familiar ground. It was painful to be brought into contact with the ruin, waste, and desolation that had been wrought upon proud old Virginia, and her once prosperous homes. Well were they reluctant to declare themselves foes of the American Union; dearly had they paid for the distinction when the Confederacy demanded that its defiance to the Union should be enforced under their prestige and entrenched upon their soil.

Settling into our new position we soon found that obeying orders was not the whole of our duty. To be sure the war was not yet over by official recognition; but these suffering people were our own,—citizens of our common country we had fought to preserve. Had they not been so, humanity and honor would have commanded our aid. Peace indeed there was on all the face of the country,—the desolation that has been called a "Roman peace." But the inhabitants we had to defend against lawlessness and violence, and save them from starvation and despair. Since the breaking up of the rebel lines, three weeks before, the whole region had been a scene of marauding upon the defenseless citizens, who were unable to remove to any other place than this, which they had still to call their home. The depraved and soulless take advantage of others' misery, and make the day of calamity their holiday. Such had been the case at Richmond but a few weeks before, when, freed from the control of Lee's army, it was pillaged and fired by the base hidden within its limits, and it was humane conquerors who restored order and repaired hurt and harm. We found the negroes especially unruly. All restraints which had hitherto held them in check were set loose by the sudden collapse of the rebel armies. The flood-gates were opened to the rush of animal instinct. The only notion of freedom apparently entertained by these bewildered people was to do as they pleased. That was what they had reason to suppose white men did. To act according to each one's nature was liberty, contrasted with slavery. Numbers gave them a kind of frenzy. Without accustomed support, without food, or opportunity to work, they not unnaturally banded together; and without any serious organization and probably without much deliberate plotting of evil, they still spread terror over the country. They swarmed through houses and homes demanding food, seizing all goods they could lay their hands on, abusing the weak, terrifying women, and threatening to burn and destroy. This was an evil that had to be met promptly, and we construed our orders to protect the country liberally. So the First Brigade under Colonel Sniper was sent out charged with the duty of protecting the homes of the people, and the peace of the community, more especially against the depredations of the lawless negro bands, of whom there were about a thousand within my jurisdiction. For our lines were extensive in depth as well as length, somewhat to the confusion of ordinary geometry. A constant reconnoissance was going on to break up, drive off, or hold at bay the hordes that were hovering about the towns and farm-houses. In cases of personal violence or outrage, my orders were sharp, and the process more summary than that authorized by courts. There was no other way.

Meantime the condition of the citizens of that region had excited the attention of our authorities, and much correspondence had been going on. Orders hitherto had forbidden us to furnish food for citizens unless they took the oath of allegiance to the United States. But conditions compelled us sometimes to take responsibility not strictly authorized. I had adopted some measures of a domestic character. One of them was in the commissary's and quartermaster's departments. The lack of food among the people was a condition which laid on us an imperative duty. We had seized, of course, all the commissary's supplies belonging to the Confederacy and distributed them among the citizens. I felt obliged now to take under control all the necessities of life to whomsoever belonging, both for protection and for judicial distribution. Mills, shops, and stores were also taken under control and put in operation, and the products distributed according to need. Strict accounts were kept; debits and credits carefully adjusted to the parties concerned. Abandoned vehicles, implements, and animals, chiefly Confederate property, were seized and put in the hands of those who could make use of them for livelihood.

We also had to undertake the administration of justice. There were no courts, or municipal or police officers, exercising functions in that region; in fact no semblance of authority, human or divine, except our own. We had no civil jurisdiction; we acted under the laws of war,—not of martial, but of military law, which admits of some discretion on the part of its responsible agents. It is said: "Necessity knows no law"; but it compelled us to make them. There was a great back country around us. Demoralized relics and stragglers from both the Confederate and the Union armies were coming in, and became for a time our guests, voluntary or involuntary, according to behavior. Complaints were constant from civil and military sources as to the misbehavior of some of these men. Now and then charges were brought against our own men. These cases must be disposed of. Otherwise our provost guard would be swamped with prisoners. So a division court-martial was duly organized, with General Pearson as president. This was in effect at least a tribunal of justice, and it inspired respect, as well as compelled obedience. The court, ably conducted, was very careful in its procedure and its decisions. It came to be looked upon as a legitimate if not legal authority. Citizens high and low were often the complainers, and, assuming the power to summon witnesses and cause attend-ance, we could generally discover the real culprit or delinquent, who preferred to accept our decision rather than risk himself away from our protection. The queer thing about our court was that its fame soon went abroad, and it was appealed to by many reputable citizens who could not otherwise settle their difficulties with their old servants or with each other. We did not undertake to settle questions of property, but only of conduct. The records of that court must be very amusing. I do not think they all went to the archives at Washington. Nor would I quite wish to disclose all that came within my knowledge.

But we had one constant difficulty no reconnoissance or court could settle. Our Government authorized the issue of food from our commissary stores absolutely necessary for the sustenance of citizens; but only on the condition, to be strictly enforced, that the beneficiaries should first take the oath of allegiance to the United States. Many of our clients gave this rather too promptly for the satisfaction of our solemn justiciary of the commissary department. There was a misgiving—not to indulge a pun—lest people who had been calling the Yankees all the bad names they could hit upon, were altogether too easy in accepting favors of them, and in their new kind of swearing towards the United States. For my own part, I had not this opinion. I believed there was more genuineness in this declaration of allegiance than in their real loyalty to the Confederacy. Very many felt that they had been drawn into this by a play upon their State pride and the example of great men whom they revered. In truth it was a grave responsibility they took upon themselves, these leading minds, in issues so deep-reaching and effects so disastrous to the well-being of a State honored and beloved by us all for its part in the making of the Union.

Some cases of this oath-taking drew their own peculiar meed of tender regard. One such was reported to me by our young provost marshal. A young lady of finest manners had ridden to our headquarters, followed by a servant on a mule bearing a coarse bag, which she earnestly desired to have filled with materials for food, if nothing more than potatoes. The story of her home was enough. Our provost marshal, who kept our oaths for us, told her of the requirement, and demanded this acknowledgment, asking her to kiss the book in token. To both of these suggestions she opposed a very firm determination. Indeed, considering the aspect of these two respective objects, I would not have blamed her if she preferred to reverse the directions, swear to the book and kiss the officer. Her charming and coquettish ways, indicating a habit of easy conquest, caused an æsthetic efflorescence among the emotional susceptibilities of this personage, and so melted the firm face of his official habit, that he did not consider himself wholly fit for duty, and came to me stating the case, and asking if he might bring the reluctant petitioner for a hearing before me. Of course I assented, notwithstanding his remark that she was considered the belle of Dinwiddie, and the fact that I was not then on the superannuated list myself. Her graceful bearing as she entered my tent, composed manner of address, and I must add her beauty as she adjusted herself to our courtesies, left me no doubt of her status,—whatever might be my own. My guests took two camp chairs placed at an angle from my center of about sixty degrees, which I believe is the frost angle, perhaps salutary here. I could not but be amused at their mutual bearing in stating the case in which they were presumed to be antagonist parties. It would be an infelicity in language to say my young officer was demoralized. On the contrary, all the moral emotions—that is to say, the spiritual—were at a sublime exaltation. But it was a comical sight when in their presentation of the case, they exchanged glances. Her air was that of an injured party, and he the aggressor. At every soft impeachment his color rose to the Jacqueminot. He was a handsome fellow; there were united states to which she might be ready to take the oath of allegiance, where the vitalizing function in testimony of loyal devotion would not be sustained by a book.

The captivating client stated her case with Ciceronian skill. She said it was unreasonable to require her to entertain a feeling of duty and allegiance to the "North," while her brothers and all her manly friends were in the Southern service; and that it was cruel, if not more deeply immoral, to demand the form of such a declaration when she could not give it heartily or truly; moreover, to take advantage of her distress to demand what was immoral and impossible, did not accord with her ideal of chivalrous gentlemen.

"My dear young lady, you intend to live in this country, do you not?" began the not altogether self-commanding commander, endeavoring to retain his official importance and personal composure.

"That is my present intention," was the demure reply, which allowed a little "leeway" for the possibilities now sublimating the faculties of the ingenuous youth, her duty-bound opponent.

"Then you will have to live under the authority of the United States of America," was the next link in the inexorable logic prepared to compel our young rebel into the compliance necessary for our consciences to yield to our hearts in granting whatever she should ask.

"I shall obey the laws of my State," she astutely rejoins.

"Your more immediate personal and domestic plans can be sanctioned and consummated, no doubt, under the laws of Virginia," proceeds the prosy, didactic court of final resort, "but Virginia is not at present exercising her functions as a State anywhere; and under the jurisdiction of what you will allow to be the *de facto* power of the United States, in order to enjoy its advantages and reciprocate its good will, you will be required to declare yourself its loyal citizen, and not its enemy."

"If to grant my humble and needful request," replies the indomitable Portia, "you require me to swear that I will bear true allegiance to the

United States, when by her actual power she can compel me to do so or withdraw her protection, I am ready to say, not that I do, but that I will, bear such allegiance."

"Do you say now that you will do so,—the 'will' meaning not simply in future time, but with full purpose?" interrogates the dazed General.

"I will take that oath," is the gracious concession; and the court is able to take a conscience-approving breath.

The fair conqueror, triumphant in her refutation of the slanderous pronouncement that "the woman who deliberates is lost," steps forward, bends over the book deftly covered with a fold of her soft handkerchief,—both held in the trembling hand of the young officer, who balances himself with such extremely Delsartian proneness that he does not seem to fear it if he should fall completely forward,—and the saving oath is taken. With what mental reservation, or spiritual committals, the defective records of earth do not show. There was, however, a lingering twilight of the transaction in the fact that there was immediately a daily unaccountable diminution among the finer delicacies of our private headquarters' mess-stores; and that on moonlight evenings there was as item of the report, "present but not accounted for," concerning the horse and also the material personality of our provost marshal; both of whom had undoubtedly passed into a state which science taking refuge in electrical metaphysics denominates "the fourth dimension."

We were kept very busy. Even the relief of duty from Sutherland's to Petersburg left us seventeen miles to care for, and enlarging duties. Our numbers were increasing rapidly. Not only were many men belonging to our command recalled from detached service to their regiments but eighteen hundred convalescents and recruits belonging to the Fifth Corps reported themselves at Sutherland's to be cared for there and thence distributed to their proper commands. The troops and garrisons at City Point were also assigned to the corps and finally taken up in Ayres' Division. We certainly had all the responsibility we could well exercise; and we had now a pretty solid and efficient corps, which we took pleasure in keeping up in discipline and character, and in as good spirits as possible. Near the end of the month notice came to us that we were to prepare to move and to start for Richmond on the 2d of May.

It may be a trace of that curious paradox in the human heart which makes us love those who have been a care and trouble to us, that the thought of leaving these stricken and helpless people brought as much sorrow to some of us as the thought of going home did of joy. Indeed what is home in deepest truth, but the place where by our thought and toil and tender care we are able to promote the well-being of others? Is not that satisfaction love's best support and toil's best reward? We are made and meant to care. And where we have given of our best, even if unavailing, there the heart holds a certain treasure. There was here, too, a pleasant counterpart of this sentiment when the people among whom we had exercised this autocratic power learned of our near departure. Our domination had been but for a little while but our points of contact with the people had been many and close. And we had made our rule of conduct towards each other such as was befitting those who were to live together as fellow-citizens in peace and good will.

On one of those last fair April mornings I received a formal visit from a deputation whose personal appearance, bearing, and manner wore a solemnity almost religious in suggestion, but betokening high character and sincere purpose. They announce themselves as a delegation appointed by the citizens of Dinwiddie County to tender me a public dinner in testimony of what they were pleased to characterize as judicious management and kindly spirit in dealing with the confused elements and powers of that difficult situation. While a certain incongruity between the spiritual motive and the material constituence of their proffer might be conducive to a smile, yet there were elements in its seriousness which commanded sentiments even deeper than respect. However much their approving feeling may have overpassed their material means of expression, the proffer sprang from generous and noble sentiments exercised under trying conditions and was a testimony which it was an honor to receive. Literal acceptance of the compliment, however, was not to be thought of. But all the more my response should show sincere appreciation and even more than common courtesy. "Gentlemen," I replied, "I deeply appreciate your expression of approval and good will in respect to my conduct of affairs. Your personal regard I fully reciprocate. But you must pardon me. I am aware of the conditions in your homes. Let me say then that if you have any surplus in your store of food to be disposed of, I beg you will give it to your own suffering people, and not to me. I confess to a certain pain in leaving you. I shall ever think of you with respect and affection, and not without solicitude. The preservation of this Union is for the benefit of all its citizens; and I trust will soon result in one of deeper effect in drawing our hearts together as never before."

They responded in words I shall not undertake to record.

The order of march for May 1st reversed the order of the division camps. Ayres was to start early in the morning, followed by the artillery and trains. On his reaching Black's and White's Crawford was to follow Ayres, and when the two reached my division I was to follow them, if they passed me. The corps would thus be gathering itself up as it marched. Moreover, by this order the whole corps would, so to speak, pass itself in review. It was a sort of "break from the left to march to the right." All these divisions did, however, that day was to reach my headquarters at Wilson's Station, where instead of having to break camp, I had the pleasure of receiving several honored guests, especially General Griffin.

At 5.30 on the morning of the 2d, I began to take up my troops and my part in the march; the Third Division followed mine, then the headquarters train, the Second Division, the artillery, and the ambulances and general train. By night we had reached Sutherland's, seventeen miles from my left to my right, and the whole corps was massed. At six o'clock on the 3d the corps took up its march along the Cox Road towards Petersburg. That was an interesting and picturesque march. The successive breaking of camps, all seasonably to fall into the column in due order; the tents struck regiment by regiment, the little shelter-tents at will, the pieces folded up and packed in each man's knapsack; then at a bugle-note down go the officer's tents, with the funeral rosettes still on their gable-fronts, disappearing at a breath, as the dissolving of a dream; and the column comes out, colors draped in mourning, and the crape on arm and sword-hilt. It had a certain majesty of tone,—that returning army of august memories. A solemn march it was,—past so many fields from which visions arose linking life with the immortal. First past the Five Forks not far away, at the Ford Station where a month before we had forced back Fitzhugh Lee and caught the last train out of Petersburg under Confederate auspices; then Sutherland's, ten miles farther, which we were so strangely prevented from making our own on the 31st of March, and where the gallant Miles two days afterwards made a maelstrom of the out-rushing currents of Lee's broken army; then passing the focal point where three roads crossing made a six-pointed star, behind Burgess' Mill, and the Quaker Road where my stubborn little First Brigade made the costly overture of the last campaign; then moving along that well-worn road between the Boydton Plank and the Appomattox so graven in our brain, so grave in history. All forsaken and silent now, the thundering salients and flaming crests since our Sixth and Ninth Corps and Gibbon with his men from the James burst over them in overwhelming wave. That silent, upheaved earth, those hidden covered ways,—what did they speak of gloomy patience, and hardening fortitude and costly holding,—the far-stretching, dull red crests and trenches which splendid manhood, we thought mistaken, had made a wall of adamant against us during all the long, dreary, unavailing siege; and as we look across the farther edge, the grim bastions of Fort Mahone and Fort Sedgwick,—not unfitly named in soldier speech "Fort Hell" and "Fort Damnation,"—the latter front carried a year before by the dark and desperate charge of my old veteran brigade; the forlorn Balaklava onset thereafter, and terrible repulse before the enemy's main entrenchments,—that darkest day of darkest year, 1864; and farther on, amidst the funereal pines, the spot where I was laid on boughs tearfully broken for what was thought my last bed, but where, too, Grant touched me with the accolade and woke new life.

We passed also the gloomy remnants of the great

outworks—well known to us—where our comrades of the Second, Sixth, and Ninth Corps and the Army of the James won imperishable fame by desperate valor; and farther on we passed with averted gaze the Crater of the Mine of fearful memory.

And now we enter Petersburg, filled with thoughts that fleck the sunshine; pondering the paradox of human loss which is gain,—not jubilant but firm-stepped, reverently, as treading over graves.

Warren was in the city. He had alighted here, where with corps flag in hand he had passed like a meteor infantry and cavalry and leaped the rebel breastworks down into the faces of the astonished foe, and Sheridan sent him otherwhere. He was commanding this city now,—promotion downward; but down is up for half the world. Griffin could not pass him without fitting recognition; the men of the Fifth Corps, who had seen him in their front from the beginning, could not pass him now, voiceless themselves as he. General Griffin had sent Warren word that the corps would like to give him the salute of honor as they marched through the city. He accepted, and placed himself with his wife and some members of his staff in the balcony of the Bolingbroke Hotel, while the corps passed before him in review. But the regulations for such ceremony were traversed by strange signs not written in that zodiac. Drums ruffled, bands played, colors dipped, officers saluted with their swords; but for the men it was impossible to hold the "carry," or keep the touch of elbow and the guide right. Up turned the worn, bronzed faces; up went the poor old caps; out rang the cheers from manly hearts along the Fifth Corps column;—one half the numbers, old and new together, that on this very day a year ago mustered on the banks of the Rapidan, their youthful forms resplendent as the onlooking sun. One half the corps had gone, passing the death-streams of all Virginia's rivers; two hundred miles of furrowed earth and the infinite of heaven held each their own. Warren, too, had gone in spirit, never to rise, with deeper wound than any who had gone before.

There was much to interest us in this city we had held "so near and yet so far"; long gazing or fitfully glancing at the hazard of our lives, where it lay glistening in morning light or wrapped in sunset splendor, or perchance shrouded in cannon-smoke, or lurid canopy of exploding mine, with phantasmagory human and superhuman. But we pressed through without stopping, and camped that night five or six miles out on the Richmond turnpike.

On the fourth we had a fine, smooth road before us, and marched briskly, having the right of way. We took a little nooning at Fort Darling on Drury's Bluff, and spent most of our time in admiring the strength and beauty of these works, proving the skill of the engineers, educated at our West Point, admiring still more the frankness of the strong soldier whose home was there, declaring that the appeal they had so resolutely taken was decided against them, and now there must be but one flag.

At evening we reached Manchester, a pleasant little town opposite Richmond where we closed up to be ready to pass through Richmond the next day in ceremonial order. But a heavy rain kept us rather quiet all day, except for some who with difficulty got permission to go over and visit the famed city which the newspapers had ordered us "on to" since 1861. Our camp made slender shelter, expecting but the "tarry of a night." I had my headquarters in the front yard—not the house—of a courteous Virginia gentleman of the old school, who seemed to like my name, which if braced with an aristocratic *y* in the last syllable stood high he said in that section. Much might have happened if my ancestors had not prided themselves in straight lines and in not striking below the belt. So they held to the simple iota in writing out their long name. Therefore I could not claim honors and he waived the demand, offering a fresh mint julep to settle accounts, but this exception did not prove the rule.

The Second Corps had now come by way of Amelia Court House and the Danville Road, and on the morning of the sixth we prepared to pass through Richmond. These two corps were all; the Ninth had been set loose again from our army and was sent to Alexandria; the Sixth had been sent back to the Danville Road to take care of the North Carolina communications. Our corps was formed in numerical order of divisions; this gave me the head of the column although the junior commander. The artillery followed the infantry. No other wheeled vehicles were allowed in the column o review; but they were sent by another way, to rejoin the troops outside the city on the road to Hanover. We crossed the James on the upper pontoon bridge. This gave a glimpse of Libby and Belle Isle prisons, which I had always carefully instructed my men never to allow themselves to get into, but to prefer death,—by which desperate tactics they sometimes saved their lives, cutting their way out of capture like madmen. But these buildings carried heavy thoughts to some among us, which ministered to "silence in the ranks." Orders had been given to the Twenty-fourth Corps to pay us some attention; accordingly we passed in review along the front of that corps,—General Halleck and General Meade being in their line. These troops had instructions to present arms to every general officer by regiments in succession, and afterwards to stand at "order arms." We were about as threadbare a set of fellows as was not usually seen, to use the French idiom. But we were clean and straight. We bore ourselves with greatest military precision,—that was something we could do,—mostly out of pride. Looks go for a good deal, especially when you have a previous reputation to meet somehow or other. The Twenty-fourth Corps, paraded in our honor, gave us hearty greeting; quite transcending orders and regulations. We had not met since side by side we had double-quicked up to Sheridan's hard-pressed front at Appomattox Court House; and when their manual dropped from the "present"

20

to the "order," there was a demonstration running along their line in which manly hearts took command, the contagion of which disturbed our perfect military demeanor.

It was a city of strange contrasts then; famous always for its beauty and the nobleness of its public buildings. But the incendiary had done much to mar the picture: the charred ruins our route of march could not wholly conceal telling either of desperate loyalty unwilling that so rich a trophy should fall into our hands; or else of some renegades, thinking all was lost, giving way to general disgust with all creation. The houses of Lee and of Davis received much attention,—the latter apparently already pillaged. The famous statue of Washington stood solitary in the square, seeming to rebuke somebody,—not us, we confidently believed. In the streets and dooryards all was confusion, like a grand "May moving-day"—furniture scattered and piled as if having nowhere to go or stay; papers flying loose everywhere; Confederate money cheap,—to be had almost for the asking from the ebony runners flashing their white teeth and eyes in joy of our coming. Multitudes of good citizens, however, lined the streets; while here and there some closed doors and shrouded windows showed where grief or bitterness was holding its despair.

It was rather hard for our men to be held in such strict order, and, after passing in review, to be pushed on as if still in pursuit of Lee. Yet on we pressed, out through the fortifications of Richmond, and not inward, whither we had so long striven; but now when we saw their terrible strength, we were not wholly sorry that we satisfied ourselves with the Wilderness, Spottsylvania, and Cold Harbor, and took a wide sweep to the southern flank of those entrenchments rather than "fight it out on that line all summer." Out towards the old battlefields we drew, crossing the baleful Chickahominy and the unforgotten Totopotomoy, scarcely pausing until ten o'clock at night, when we were halted, after a singularly hard march, at "Peake's Turn Out" on the Virginia Central Railroad, not far from Hanover Court House. This was familiar ground for the Fifth Corps. Here it was that our First Division in the ardor of its youth made the gallant fight three years before, and where especially our Second Maine under the chivalrous Roberts proved the quality of its soldiership and manhood.

In the darkness of establishing bivouac, I heard some mutterings, as I had seen some sour looks before, among the men, seeming to hold me responsible for the hardships of the twenty-mile forced march, because I had the head of the column and was supposed to set the pace. But they did not understand that our camps as well as our routes were strictly appointed as to time and place by orders from high headquarters. If I could have appointed the routes and hours of that homeward march, I would not have been governed so much by considerations of "the shortest distance between two points" on the earth, as of a line running tortuously and deep-chambered through soldiers' hearts, and darkly graven in all the homes of the land. We had to pass very near many storied spots; and one day more for the whole march would have allowed our men the somber satisfaction of reviewing the fields of lost battles, which have their place, also, in making up life's full account. Broken threads are sometimes well worth picking up. If this is mere sentiment, I confess to it; outlawed I dare say in scientific circles, but not therefore banished from the make-up of manhood. If discipline means bracing the heart and will as well as the body it is part of good discipline to give the soldier satisfaction for his sacrifice, if only to see the ground where he fought in darkness and blind obedience, and gave his best even though in defeat, and perhaps, by such recognition, giving him part in the continuity of great endeavor.

Other orders of being also share this halt at the bridge of life and death. I give place to a night-episode. At about midnight when the tired camp was still, the sentinel in front of my bivouac spoke nervously, saying there was something strange going on about my horse not far away in rear of us. He had been hastily tethered there amidst a little growth of scrubby pines, so near, and the place so quiet, there seemed to be no need of a guard. The boy who cared for him had dropped down near by in a swoon of sleep. I rose and went out myself; and before I reached him my foot crushed through the breast-bones of a body half buried by the fallen pine-cones and needles so long undisturbed, now gone back mostly ashes to ashes. I found that the horse, pawing the earth within the scope of his picket-rope, had rolled out two skulls and scattered the bones of bodies he had unearthed, and was gazing at the white skulls as if lost in doubt; now and then snorting to call others to solve the mystery, or swaying at his tether as if to get away himself. It was a weird, uncanny scene: the straggling, uncompanionable pines; the night brooding still and chill; black lowering clouds, now massing, now rifting, disclosing, then shutting out of sight, the white skulls mocking life. The horse was not easily pacified,—not until I had gathered up the menacing skulls and the outlying limbs too, and laid them where I saw glimmering amidst the dusky débris of the pines other bones as if adrift on a Sargasso sea, and showed him that I was not afraid.

In the morning the men got to looking around among the bodies and relics, and by initials cut into the breast-plates or other marks or tokens identified the remnants of bodies of comrades long left among the missing. As we were not to move until ten o'clock, they asked permission to gather up these mournful remnants and pack them in the empty cracker-boxes in our supply trains, to be sent to friends who would gladly cherish even such tokens of the fate of the unreturning brave. I was glad to grant this and to instruct the wagoners to take especial care of these relics on the road or in camp. And so the strange column set forth bearing in its train that burden of unlost belongings, as

Moses coming up out of Egypt through the wilderness of the Red Sea, bearing with him the bones of Joseph the well-beloved.

Ayres led that day; we had the rear of the column, with the artillery. Passing through Hanover Court House, and crossing the Pamunkey, we made twelve miles march and camped at Concord Church, not far from our battlefield of the North Anna and Jericho Mills. On the 8th, the Third Division led, the First following. We crossed the Mattapony and bivouacked at Milford, south of Bowling Green, at 5 P.M., having marched about fifteen miles. On the 9th, we moved at 7 A.M., passing through Bowling Green, which wakened for me thrilling reminiscences of a rear-guard fight, and crossing the Massaponax we encamped near Fredericksburg not far from our old battlefields of 1862. We made this long march more easily because of the fine Bowling Green Pike that served us a good part of the way. Although we had marched twenty miles, some of the men of the First Division could not resist the opportunity to visit the storied Marye's Heights, up which they had charged,—the fifth line they had seen go on to be swallowed up in flame, and cut level with the earth the moment it reached the fatal crest before the stone wall,—and holding flat to earth, were able to be drawn off only under the blackness of a rainy midnight, the last to leave the front line, to catch the last pontoon bridge below the city just as it was swung to the safe shore.

In the morning we crossed again the Rappahannock—two years and a half later; and what years, and with what changes of men!—and moved up abreast of the city, whose slopes on the morning of that other crossing we saw through misty eyes, trampled to gory mire, and so flecked with bodies of our comrades that the whole heights shone blue.

The artillery leading and we in rear of the column, —thoughts lingering too,—we passed through our old camping ground of 1862, where first we learned how little we knew how to take care of ourselves or of those committed to our care, but where we learned also under the discipline of the accomplished Ames how to behave ourselves in battle. Visions more than sad passed with us. Hooker and the Grand Divisions, and the grand reviews; the tournaments of the reorganized cavalry; the sword presentations with their afterglow; the "Ladies' Days"—Princess Salm-Salm the Valkyrie, the witching Washington belles, strange new colors flying, sweet forms grouped around tent doors, lithe in the saddle; days so bright and nights so silver toned,—*lenesque sub noctem susurri*,—where are you, forms and souls, men and women, where in these days of stern rejoicing triumph, but so forlorn? Then days of the Adversary: the Mud March; tragic Chancellorsville; and dreary return to dull Stoneman's Switch and dolorous smallpox hospital—they, too, stood for something as prelude to the Gettysburg campaign. This is the procession that passes as we pass. Pensively we crossed the Aquia Creek, old debouchure from Washington of all that food for death, and of the spectral gayeties of what is called life. Plunging now into lower levels we found a hard road to travel, and crossing the Choppawamsic and Quantico, we went down with the sun in dreary bivouac at Dumfries.

The roads were bad; pressing feet and heavy hoofs and cutting wheels had made them worse. General Humphreys, following with the Second Corps, thoughtful ever for his men, and as an accomplished engineer scorning such crude conditions, sent out two entire divisions to repair the road before he would undertake to move, and even then was forced to take another route. In our movement on this morning of the 11th of May General Griffin leading out with the artillery sent the pioneers of the Third Division following to move with the artillery and help it along, while sending the pioneers of the First and Second Divisions to attend the trains which followed. One half the ambulances followed their respective divisions, and there was sore need of them. The memory of this day and night march will last its participants a lifetime, of which I have no doubt these experiences shortened many. The roads rough and ragged; the hills steep and as it were cross-furrowed; the valleys swamps; the track a trap of mire. We toiled painfully and patiently along, testing that formula of the chiefest virtue,—the charity that "beareth all things; believeth all things; hopeth all things; endureth all things." In the middle of the afternoon a heavy rainstorm swept over us, opening with terrific summons of thunder and lightning, sky and earth meeting. I chanced to be at that moment on the summit of a very high hill, from which I could see the whole corps winding its caravan with dromedary patience. The first lightning-bolt nearly stunned me. I saw its forerunner flashing along the cannon far ahead and illuminating Crawford's column with unearthly glare; and turning quickly towards my own I could see the whole black column struggling on and Ayres a mile behind urging and cheering his men with condensed reserve energies all alive; when this ever-recurrent pulse of flame leaped along the writhing column like a river of fire. It looked to me as if the men had bayonets fixed, the points of intense light flew so sharp from the muzzles sloping above the shoulders. Suddenly an explosion like a battery of shrapnel fell right between our divisions. An orderly came galloping up to me, with word that one of the ambulances was struck, killing the horses and the driver, and stunning the poor fellows who, unable to keep up with the rushing column, had sought this friendly aid. It was a mile away from me, but I knew Ayres close following would see the right thing done till my orders came. I sent instructions for the stricken men to be cared for, and for the following forage trains to take along the disabled ambulance. We were bringing along one dead body already, besides the strange freight of rescued fragments packed in the bread-boxes. This was the body of Lieutenant Wood, of the 20th Maine, killed in his tent by a careless wagoner's unauthorized discharge of a musket some way off the day before,—such an act as some call accident; I did not treat it as such.

The storm and turmoil of the elements kept on all the afternoon; and all our company, man and beast, were drenched and sodden,—body and soul. In such plight we crossed the Occaquan, and in four hours more we "stopped for refreshments" on soggy ground and in pitchy darkness about a mile below Fairfax Station on the Orange & Alexandria Railroad. Then began the orgies of which five elements were the factors, the human, and air, earth, water, fire,—the last deemed divine in Grecian legend, but difficult to harmonize that night with Promethean will or human need.

What cannot be helped must be borne. Well-doing is not a smooth road and its rewards do not instantly appear. But good heart, nevertheless! Dear poor Tom Pinch knew all about it. "'Wher's the pudding?'" said Tom, "for he was cutting his jokes, Tom was."

Why we were marched so hard and made to suffer such discomforts on that homeward journey no one of us could understand. Thoughtless men, as is usual, laid it to their officers; and that is perhaps not unjust as their short reasoning went. It is great part of an officer's duty to take care of his men. But there is always strong motive for officers to be reasonable; those who march with their men are not likely to be cruel to them. In the saddle hour upon hour, day after day, marching is almost as wearisome for rider as for footman. The balancing mental medicine for the rider is that he can get from point to point quicker, and get over more ground in a given time. Keeping pace with obstructed and slow-moving infantry is hard for the horsemen too.

But here we were, marched as hard as if we were a forlorn hope, or a Lucknow relief, hurled in for life and death—only going to be mustered out. It was, I suppose, a measure of economy, to save the expense of maintaining an army not now actively engaged, and so far from the principal base of supplies, and to shorten the days before us for the final discharge. It seemed as if somebody was as anxious now to be rid of us as ever before to get us to the front. That is a fair inference from the orders that came to the commander of our army; and his orders were no doubt the result of this urgency. We commanders in the Fifth Corps had not so much to say about it as the men had; and what we did say is not written, and would have been of little avail for them if spoken aloud, and not calculated to put us in pleasant relations with those above us, including what Sterne would call "the recording angel."

We moved once more at 9 o'clock on the morning of the 12th, the corps in the order of its divisions, followed by the artillery and trains. At Fairfax Court House we received orders to take the Columbia Pike and passing Falls Church Station to go into permanent camp on Arlington Heights. This brought us near the ground where our First

Division, now comprising all that were left of the original Fifth Corps, had its station after the battle of Bull Run Second, and whence we started early in September for the Antietam campaign. A new procession of associations, farther reaching than those before, thronged our minds and spirits. We had not seen this ground since those earlier troubled days; and what had been given us to traverse since, and forms once with us, now taken away, all rose before us in tumultuous phantasies. Here was Lee's home, too; and we gazed at it earnestly, wondering if it was true only in poetry

> "That men may rise on stepping-stones
> Of their dead selves to higher things"

Poor, great-hearted Lee; what was his place in the regenerated country?

And for us: we were returning from our part in the redemption of the nation's life,—the vindication of its honor and authority; we were summoned to the capital to report the completion of this service and this trust; to lay down our arms and colors, emblems of costly sacrifice and great deliverance; to receive thanks, perhaps; but for best reward the consciousness that what we had lost and what we had won had passed into the nation's peace; our service into her mastery, our worth into her well-being, our life into her life.

Now the satisfied earth, returning its excess of rain heavenward in canopy of mists, overspread us with shadow, shutting us in with ourselves. But just as we reached the heights, the clouds withdrew their veil, and the broad sunlight lay upon the resplendent city; highest the dome of the delivered Capitol, and nearest, it seemed, the White House, home of Lincoln's mighty wrestle and immortal triumph. Around us some were welcoming with cheers; but for our part, weighted with thought, we went through our accustomed motions mechanically, in a great silence. The sun, transfiguring for a moment our closing ranks, went down in glorious promise for the morrow,—leaving us there to ourselves again, on the banks of the river whose name and fame we bore, flowing in darkness past us, as from dream to dream.

CHAPTER VIII

THE ENCAMPMENT

MANY circumstances tended to make our camp on Arlington Heights an ideal one. We well knew that its material existence was to be brief; but its image in thought was to hold for us the traces of momentous history and to remain the most visible token of the probation under which our personal characters had been moulded. We took therefore a certain pride in this last encampment; we looked upon this as the graduation day of our Alma Mater. The disturbing incidents which had forbidden us ever to make a perfect camp were now overpassed, and it afforded some satisfaction to show that we had kept alive a scientific knowledge and skill we had never fairly put into practice, and cherished ideals of soldierly living, which though never projected on the earthly plane, may have somehow left an indwelling impress in our characters.

There was now an abundance of camp equipage. Tents were distributed and established in accordance with ideal regulations. And the extensive preparations for final accounting and muster-out justified an extra number of great hospital tents for crowding clerical work. These were a convenience and incentive for social gatherings at hours so disposable. We had many visitors also, to whom we were glad to show civil and military courtesies.

To increase the magnitude and also the complications of this gathering, Sherman's army came up on the 20th of May and encamped on the same side of the river but lower down towards Alexandria,—a situation not so conspicuous nor otherwise desirable as ours, a circumstance which had place in some further incidents of the field in the War for the Union. These troops were not the whole of Sherman's great Army of the West. The part of it which he brought here comprised many high names and titles, as well as stalwart men: the old Army of the Tennessee (once McPherson's, later Howard's, now under Logan), composed of the Fifteenth Corps, Hazen commanding (Sherman's old corps), and the Seventeenth Corps under Blair, together with the Army of Georgia, commanded now by Slocum, composed of the Fourteenth Corps (part of Thomas' old Army of the Cumberland), now under Davis, and the Twentieth Corps under Mower,—this latter composed of the Eleventh and Twelfth Corps of the Army of the Potomac sent to Sherman after Gettysburg, with Howard and Slocum. That part of Sherman's old army known as the Army of the Ohio, now commanded by Schofield, and made up of the Twenty-third Corps under Cox and the

Tenth Corps under Terry,—of Fort Fisher fame,—was not brought to this encampment.

The fame of these men excited our curiosity and wish to know them better. Although not much interchange of visiting was allowed, we started out with very pleasant relations,—which unfortunately not being very deep-rooted soon withered. Still we admired them at a distance, and had it in our own hands to keep up that kind of a friendship. I am speaking now for our men of the rank and file, whose good nature would stand a good deal.

Within our own camp things were harmonious and more than that. The Second and Fifth Corps grew nearer and dearer to each other. One pleasing incident in my command may be worthy of record. The officers of my division desired to present to Major-General Griffin, our corps commander, a worthy token of the deep regard in which he was held in this division so honorably known as his in the last campaign, and with which he had been conspicuously associated since the heroic days of Fitz-John Porter. A Maltese cross was decided on as the basis for this memorial, and the design for it being entrusted to me by the committee in charge, was sent to Tiffany of New York for execution. It was our battle flag in miniature,—the Red Maltese cross on a white field, the colors enameled on a gold ground, the cross bordered with small diamonds, and in the center a diamond worth a thousand dollars.

Orders were now out for the grand review of our

army on the 23d of May, and we decided to hold our presentation ceremonies on the evening before this, when so many old comrades and distinguished visitors were near by to join us. It is needless to say everything was ordered on a scale worthy of such occasion. Four large hospital tents were put together cathedral-like for our service, and clusters of smaller tents were grouped around, like chapels, to serve as offices and dressing-rooms. It had not the magnificence of array and grandeur of titled personages of the Field of the Cloth of Gold, but the sentiment and soul that animated the greeting and farewell were of a fellowship more than royal. Beauty and chivalry were not lacking; nobility of soul made high presence. Soft summer airs were stirring all things to tremulous pulse. The scene without enwrapped our senses, and that within thrilled our hearts. Soon through the trembling hush the martial bugle rang out the "Assembly of Trumpeters." Then flowed forth from a symphony of trumpets that orison of the setting sun, "The Retreat," with final cadence of the "Sunset Gun," answering afar.

Now the shadows descended, and the deep stars, brooding close over the night, lent the immortal presence. Soon all the slopes glimmered with scores of thousands of lights illuminating great fields of white tents of our army and Sherman's far outspread, like the city of a dream. So atmosphered, guest-greetings lingered; new friendships grew "old"; farewells begun,—never to end. And when all the deep influences of the hour were at their fullness, we drew within the canvas cathedral for our consummation. Here circled another scene,—bright, clear, and strong,—the presence of cherished womanhood shed a glory upon the stern faces and martial forms of men long lost to dreams like these. The great assembly hushed itself to silence in expectation. General Griffin was seated in the focus of all this; it was my part to present the material memorial. I had no experience in public speaking, and felt hardly competent to express the feeling which then filled every heart of the assembly. But words like these were somehow given me:

"GENERAL GRIFFIN:

"Our hearts stir as I speak the name,—so familiar, so revered; so interwoven with experiences deep as life and death.

"The officers of your old division have desired to present you with a testimonial of their appreciation and esteem. They have selected for this purpose the badge of our division,—the Red Maltese Cross,—as the most fitting remembrance of your long association with them,—a memento of the toils and trials and desperate deeds and the sufferings you have not shunned to share with them, and a token of honorable service they are proud to share with you.

"This cross of ours is already famed in story. Now it has a new history,—a new sanctity. Not more worthily was this the chosen emblem of those who thronged to redeem the Holy Sepulchre from

Infidel hands, than of these men of yours who have rallied to rescue a nation's life from assaults the more bitter because dealt by those we had deemed as brothers. On no breasts was this ever more bravely borne in battle—on no banners more proudly emblazoned—in no cathedral arches more sacredly enshrined.

"But this is not the hour for words. The tongue cannot follow where the feet have trod, nor reach where the heart aspires.

"It remains for me, therefore, to present you with this cross, in behalf of the officers of your old division who wait to greet you. But not all. Some who were with us, and would have been of the brightest to grace this festival, greet us here no more,—hearts warmest in friendship, truest to trust, bravest in the day of battle. We know and hallow the spots where they fell, first or last, in the ranks of honor. But not one of them all,—I say it before these witnesses,—not one of those is lying in his lowly bed to-day through any fault or failure or rashness of our commander.

"In memory, then, of those, and in behalf of these,—in the name of all,—I give this cross into the hand of a soldier without reproach. It is red,—with blood more precious than its diamonds; red,—after the symbolism of sacred art,—with love more lasting than its stars.

"In this day of the country's victory and peace, in this hour of sacred associations, we meet, and we part, under this cross, emblem of the world's dearest memories and most blessed hopes. Receive it, therefore, with its legend and benediction: *In hoc signo vinces.*"

General Griffin received the badge, and holding it in his hand, responded:

"GENERAL:

"Your words have overcome me with a sense of what it is to be thus honored by men who have added honor to this symbol. You remind me of what has been the cost of this fame, and what has been the value of this service. You yourself, General, a youthful subordinate when I first took command of this division, now through so many deep experiences risen to be its tested, trusted, and beloved commander,—you are an example of what experiences of loyalty and fortitude, of change and constancy, have marked the career of this honored division. I say to you all, that you have written a deathless page on the records of your country's history, and that your character and your valor have entered into her life for all the future.

"For myself, having seen and served with you from the first, my affection for you is in the deepest places of my heart, and as often as I shall look upon this token in the coming years, I shall thank God for the manhood that has made it glorious."

As he spoke these last words, I advanced and pinned the badge over his breast, and pressing his hand upon it he turned and bowed before the assembly. Then it was as if the slumbering chords of thousands of hearts had challenged the song of the morning stars. First the low ripple of hand-clapping after common custom, but more were clasping each others' hands in emotion they knew not how to express. Strong men rose to their feet or bent their heads in sobs. But soon murmurs found voice, and this swelled to shouting until the band struck up its rhapsody, "Hail to the Chief," when all left their seats and crowded around General Griffin, who for once was not able to give command,—even to himself. Slowly we broke into friendly groups, calming ourselves down in circling cadences of farewells until at a signal we drew together in the song of *Auld Lang Syne*, after which the heart-searching bugle-call "Lights Out" calling as from some far-away home dispersed us under the stars.

CHAPTER IX

THE LAST REVIEW

IT was now the morning of May 23d, 1865, the day appointed for the final grand review of the Army of the Potomac, to extend from the Capitol to the White House along Pennsylvania Avenue in the city of Washington. It is with deep emotion that I attempt to tell the story of my last vision of that army,—the vision of its march out of momentous action into glorious dream.

This is not an essay in composition—military, historic, or artistic. I seek to hold fast the image which passed before my eyes. But this will no less be truth,—one aspect of *the* truth, which in its manifold, magnificent wholeness would take the notes and memories of thousands to portray. It will be manifest that I cannot undertake to reduce all the features of the picture to a common scale, nor to exhibit merit equitably. Some points, no doubt, are set in high light, under the emotion which atmospheres them; but it is not meant to throw others into shadow. If, in so rapid and condensed a passage, only familiar and prominent commanders can be named, it is not that I forget that in every grade and all through the ranks are men whose names deserve remembrance as immortal as their devotion was sublime. Neither can I forget, while yielding to none in my appreciation of the honor due to "the man behind the musket," that the military efficiency of such is largely affected by the instruction, discipline, and influence of those in authority and responsibility over them, and their success and fame largely due to the manner in which they are "handled." A command is likely to be what its commander is. There are crises when confidence in his ability turns the scale of battle. There are supreme moments when the sudden sweep to the front by a commanding character strikes the heart and exalts the spirit of men so that they do superhuman things. Such are the men who are to pass before us.

It is the Army of the Potomac. After years of tragic history and dear-bought glories, gathering again on the banks of the river from which it took its departure and its name; an army yet the same in name, in form, in spirit, but the deep changes in its material elements telling its unspeakable vicissitudes; having kept the faith, having fought the good fight, now standing up to receive its benediction and dismissal, and bid farewell to comradeship so strangely dear.

We were encamped on Arlington Heights, opposite the capital. As yet there were but two corps up—the Second and the Fifth. The Sixth had been sent back from Appomattox to Danville, to secure the fruits of the surrender, and stand to the front before the falling curtain of the Confederacy. They had fulfilled that duty, and on this very day were setting forth for this final station. Of those that had come up, all the detachments had been called in. My division that left Appomattox five thousand strong now mustered twice that number. The ranks stood full—what there were of the living—for one more march together, one last look and long farewell.

Troops that had been with us and part of us in days of need and days of glory, were brought with us again: the Cavalry Corps, and the Ninth Corps, with a division of the Nineteenth. The Ninth, by the circumstance of its commander outranking all other generals except Grant, although of late often with us, was not incorporated with our army until the twenty-fourth of May, 1864, when Burnside magnanimously waived his rank and with his corps became part and parcel of our army through the terrible campaign of that dark year, and until relieved at Burkeville a few days after the surrender at Appomattox. To these old companions General Meade with generous courtesy gave the post of honor and precedence. Sherman's great army had lately come up, and was encamped on the river bank at no great distance below.

A mighty spectacle this: the men from far and wide, who with heroic constancy, through toils and sufferings and sacrifices that never can be told, had broken down the Rebellion, gathered to give their arms and colors and their history to the keeping of a delivered, regenerated nation.

For our review the order of march was to be the following: headquarters of the Army of the Potomac; the cavalry corps; the provost marshal's brigade; the engineer brigade; the Ninth Corps with a division of the Nineteenth; then the Army of the Potomac, that stood here upon the earth—the Fifth Corps and the Second; the infantry and artillery, and ambulances too—great sharers of eventful service.

The Ninth Corps crossed the Potomac on the afternoon of the twenty-second and went into bivouac east of the Capitol. The engineer brigade, the provost guard, and the escort moved to bivouac near Long Bridge, to start at 3.30 in the morning for their rendezvous at the foot of the Capitol front, ready to follow the cavalry ordered to be there at 9 A.M. At 4 A.M., of the twenty-third, the Fifth Corps began its march over Long Bridge, Canal Bridge, and Maryland Avenue to First Street, East, moving "left in front," in order to draw out easily right in front, for the ceremonial column. The Second Corps, leaving camp at 7 A.M., followed the Fifth to the vicinity of the Capitol, ready to follow in review.

The movement was to be up Pennsylvania Avenue. The formation was in column by companies closed in mass, with shortened intervals between regiments, brigades, and divisions; the company fronts equalized to twenty files each, so the number of companies corresponded to the total numbers of the regiment, some having twelve or fifteen companies, so many had gathered now for the grand muster-out.

Six ambulances were to follow each brigade, moving three abreast. The artillery brigades were to accompany their respective corps. The infantry were to take "route step" and right shoulder arms until reaching the State Department building, where they take the cadenced step and the shoulder arms, later known as the "carry." Here also the "guide left" was to be taken, as the reviewing stand was in front of the President's house. He was the proper reviewing officer; but arrangements were made for the accommodation also of the Cabinet, the Foreign Diplomatic Corps, the governors of States, and other distinguished personages and high officials. In the salute, drums were to ruffle and colors dip, but only mounted officers were to salute. The bands were not to turn out in front of the reviewing officer, as is the custom in reviews. All precautions were taken to preserve relative distances, so as to avoid crowding, confusion, and delay in the marching column.

In my command we were well aware of quite an anxiety among officers and men of the army generally to look their very best, and more, too, on this occasion; for new uniforms, sashes, epaulettes, saddle housings, and other gay trappings almost disguised some of our hardiest veterans, who were not insensible to the new order of spectators before whom they were now to pass their ordeal. I hesitate to admit that in the revulsion from this on the part of the officers and men of my division, there might be a scornful pride more sinful than that of vanity. We knew many a dude in dress who expressed in this way a consciousness of personal worth which rang true in the tests of battle. We could not pretend to be better,—proud of our humility. Perhaps we thought we could not look equal to what we deemed our worth and possibly our reputation; so we resolved to do nothing for show, but to look just what we were, and be judged by what we wore, letting our plainness tell its own story. The men brought themselves up to regulation field inspection; themselves, their dress and accouterments clean and bright, but all of every-day identity. And for officers no useless trappings, rider or horse; plain, open saddle, with folded gray army blanket underneath; light, open bridle with simple curb and snaffle-rein; service uniform—shoulder-strap, belts, scabbards, boots, and spurs of the plainest,—no sashes, no epaulettes; light marching order, just as in the field, but clean and trim. No doubt this might make us somewhat conspicuous, as things were; but homeliness was a character we thought we could maintain, even "before company."

It was a clear, bright morning, such as had so often ushered in quite other scenes than this. At nine o'clock the head of column moved. First Meade—commanding all—our old Fifth Corps commander, knightly in bearing as ever, grave of countenance now, thoughtful perhaps with foreshadowings. With him rode his principal staff: chivalrous "Andy Webb," in earlier days familiar friend, inspector of our corps,—since that, meeting with his superb brigade the death-defying valor of Pickett's charge,—now rightly chief-of-staff of the army; grim old Hunt, chief of artillery, whose words were like his shot, whose thunder-sweeps had shaken hearts and hills from Antietam to Appomattox; Seth Williams, adjutant-general, steadfast as the rocky crests of Maine from which he came, whose level head had balanced the disturbances and straightened the confusions of campaigns and changes of commanders through our whole history. And following these heads of staff, all the gallant retinue well known to us all.

Now move the cavalry: survivors and full-blown flower of the troopers Joe Hooker, in the travailing winter of 1862 and 1863, had redeemed from servitude as scattered orderlies and provost guards at headquarters and loose-governed cities, and transformed into a species of soldier not known since the flood-times of Persia, the Huns of Attila, or hordes of Tamerlane; cavalry whose manœuvres have no place in the tactics of modern Europe; rough-rider, raiders, scouts-in-force, cutting communications, sweeping around armies and leagues of entrenched lines in an enemy's country,—Stoneman and Pleasanton and Wilson, Kilpatrick, Custer, and alas! Dahlgren.

And when the solid front of pitched battle opposes, then terrible in edge and onset, as in the straight-drawn squadron charges at Brandy Station, the clattering sweep at Aldie, the heroic lone-hand in the lead at Gettysburg, holding back the battle till our splendid First Corps could surge forward to meet its crested wave, and John Buford and John Reynolds could shake hands! Through the dark campaign of 1864, everywhere giving account of themselves as *there*. At last in 1865, sweeping over the breastworks at Five Forks down upon the smoking cannon and serried bayonets; thence swirling around Sailor's Creek and High Bridge, and finally at Appomattox by incredible marches circumventing Lee's flying column, and holding at bay Stonewall Jackson's old corps, with Hill's and Anderson's, under Gordon;—alone, this cavalry, until our infantry overtaking the horses, force the flag of truce to the front, and all is over! Fighters, firm, swift, superb,—cavalry—chivalry!

Sheridan is not here. He is down on the Rio Grande,—a surveyor, a draughtsman, getting ready to illustrate Seward's diplomatic message to Napoleon that a French army cannot force an Austrian Emperor on the Mexican Republic. Crook, so familiar to our army, is not here, preferring an "engagement" elsewhere and otherwise; for love, too, bears honors to-day. Soldierly Merritt is at the head, well deserving of his place. Leading the divisions are Custer, Davies, and Devin, names known before and since in the lists of heroes. Following also, others whom we know: Gibbs, Wells, Pennington, Stagg of Michigan, Fitzhugh of New York, Brayton Ives of Connecticut. Dashing Kilpatrick is far away. Grand Gregg we do not see; nor level-headed Smith, nor indomitable "Prin." Cilley, with his 1st Maine

Cavalry; these now sent to complete the peace around Petersburg.

Now rides the provost marshal general, gallant George Macy of the 20th Massachusetts, his right arm symbolized by an empty sleeve pinned across his breast.

Here the 2d Pennsylvania Cavalry, and stout remnants of the 1st Massachusetts, reminding us of the days of Sargent and "Sam" Chamberlain. Here, too, the 3d and 10th U. S. Infantry, experienced in stern duties.

Now, with heads erect and steady eyes, marches the Signal Corps; of those that beckoned us to the salvation of Round Top, and disclosed movements and preparations otherwise concealed in the dense maze and whirl of battle from the Wilderness to the Chickahominy; then from their lofty observatories watching the long ferment on the Appomattox shores. What message do your signals waft us now?

Here come the engineers with their great unwieldy pontoons grotesque to the eye, grand to the thought! Had we not smiled at them—the huge dromedary caravans, struggling along the road, or sliding, leviathan-like, down the slopes of half-sheltered river-coves, launching out to their perilous, importunate calling? Did not the waters of all Virginia's rivers know of their bulk and burden? Had we not seen them—*not smiling*—time and time again, spanning the dark Rappahannock?—as in December, 1862, Sumner and Howard launched them from the exposed bank opposite Fredericksburg into the face of Lee's army—vainly opposing, —bridging the river of death, into the jaws of hell! Had we not a little later, a mile below, crowded over the hurriedly laid, still swaying, boat-bridge, raked and swept by the batteries on Marye's Heights, and rushed up the bloody, slippery slopes to the dead-line stone wall? And on the second midnight after, shall we forget that forlorn recrossing, in murk and rain, on the last pontoon bridge left, and this muffled with earth to dull our stealthy, silent tread, and already half-loosened, and ready to cut free and swing from the touch of that fateful shore? And what of that rear-guard covering the retreat from Chancellorsville in 1863, seeking the bridge-end in utter blackness of darkness and driving storm of rain and rushing river, *not finding it* because the swelling torrent was roaring twenty feet between it and the shore; and when gained by manly resolution or demoniac instinct, already half a ruin, the lashings of chess and rail loosened by rush and pressure of previous passers; crowded plank in heaps and gaps yard wide, amid the yawning, dizzying surges in the pitchy blackness, where only the sagacious horse could smell the distances and leap the chasms, followed by the trusting "brotherhood" of man! "Great arks" indeed they were, these boats, borne above the waters of desolation, and bearing over manhood fit to replenish and repeople the war-whelmed earth!

Last, looming above the broad waters of the James, your thread-like bridge swaying beneath the mighty tread, our horses hardly able to keep their feet, bearing us over to the gloomy tests of Petersburg, the long beginning of the end.

And where are the brave young feet that pressed your well-laid plank at Germanna and Ely's Ford of the Rapidan on that bright morning a summer ago? To what shores led that bridge?

No, we do not smile to-day at the ungainly pontoons! God rest their bodies now! if perchance they have no souls except what have gone into the men who bore them, and whom in turn they bore.

Now rises to its place the tried and tested old Ninth Corps, once of Burnside and Reno, now led by Parke, peer of the best, with Willcox and Griffin of New Hampshire and Curtin leading its divisions,—Potter still absent with cruel wounds, and Hartranft detached on high service elsewhere,—and its brigade commanders, General McLaughlen and Colonels Harriman, Ely, Carruth, Titus, McCalmon, and Matthews. These are the men of the North Carolina expedition, of Roanoke and New Berne, who came up in time of sore need to help our army at Manassas and Chantilly, and again at South Mountain and Antietam. After great service in the west, with us again in the terrible campaign of 1864; then in the restless, long-drawn, see-saw action on the Petersburg lines; through the direful "crater"; at last in the gallant onset on the enemy's flank and the pressing Southside pursuit;—part of us until all was over.

So they are ours, these men of the Ninth Corps, and our proud hearts yearn forward to them as they are whelmed in tumultuous greeting along the thronging avenue. Noble men! As they move out past the head of our waiting column, I look at them with far-running thought. Earnestly remembered by the older regiments of my division; for, sent to support the Ninth Corps at the Burnside Bridge when it was so gallantly carried at the bayonet point by Potter's 51st New York and Hartranft's 51st Pennsylvania, Burnside pushed across the Antietam our single division to replace that whole corps on those all-important heights where he was expecting a heavy attack. How full the intervening years have been! How strained and sifted the ranks! Of those two remembered regiments to-day, there stand: the 51st New York, one hundred and twenty men; the 51st Pennsylvania, forty men!

Here, too, a remnant, the 36th Massachusetts, long ago shipmates with us of the 20th Maine on the transport that bore us forth in 1862 to fields and fortunes far apart, now at last united again. We remember how that splendor of equipment and loftiness of bearing made us feel very green and humble, but we are somehow equalized now! Of them was Major Henry Burrage, now proudly riding, acting asistant adjutant-general of his brigade,—foretokening his place and part in the Loyal Legion of Maine!

Here comes our 31st Maine, brave Daniel White's; consolidated with it now the 32d, those left from its short, sharp experience with Wentworth and John Marshall Brown, at such dear cost leading,—both Bowdoin boys, one the first adjutant of the 20th. Here passes steadily to the front as of yore the 7th Maine Battery, Twitchell, my late college friend, at the head: splendid recessional, for I saw it last in 1864 grimly bastioning the slopes above Rives' Salient, where darkness fell upon my eyes, and I thought to see no more.

Following, in Dwight's Division of the Nineteenth Corps, other brave men, known and dear: a battalion of the 1st Maine Veterans, under Captain George Brown; the brigades of stalwart George Beal and clear-eyed "Jim" Fessenden, my college classmate; the sturdy 15th Maine from its eventful experiences of the Gulf under steadfast-hearted Isaac Dyer, Murray, and Frank Drew; soldierly Nye with the 29th, made veterans on the Red River and Shenandoah; royal Tom Hubbard, with his 30th, once Frank Fessenden's, whom Surgeon Seth Gordon saved; a third of them now of the old 13th,—these, too, of the Red River, Sabine Cross-Roads, and Grand Ecore, and thence to the Virginia valleys; rich in experiences, romantic and Roman!

And now it is the Fifth Corps. The signal sounds. Who is that mounting there? Do you see him? It is Charles Griffin. How lightly he springs to the saddle. How easy he sits, straight and slender, chin advanced, eyes to the front, pictured against the sky! Well we know him. Clear of vision, sharp of speech, true of heart, clean to the center. Around him group the staff, pure-souled Fred Locke at their head.

My bugle calls. Our horses know it. The staff

gather,—Colonel Spear, Major Fowler, Tom Chamberlain, my brave young brother, of the first. The flag of the First Division, the red cross on its battle-stained white, sways aloft; the hand of its young bearer trembling with his trust, more than on storm-swept fields. Now they move—all—ten thousand hearts knitted together. Up the avenue, into that vast arena, bright with color—flowers, garlands, ribbons, flags, and flecked with deeper tones. Windows, balconies, house-tops, high and far, thronged with rich-robed forms, flushed faces, earnest eyes. Now it seems a tumult of waters; we pass like the children of Israel walled by the friendly Red Sea. Around us and above, murmurs, lightnings, and thunders of greeting. The roar of welcome moves forward with our column. Those in the streetways press upon us; it almost needs the provost guard to clear our way.

Now a girlish form, robed white as her spirit, presses close; modest, yet resolute, eyes fixed on her purpose. She reaches up towards me a wreath of rare flowers, close-braided, fit for viking's arm-ring, or victor's crown. How could I take it? Sword at the "carry" and left hand tasked, trying to curb my excited horse, stirred by the vastness, the tumult, the splendor of the scene. He had been thrice shot down under me; he had seen the great surrender. But this unaccustomed vision—he had never seen a woman coming so near before—moved him strangely. Was this the soft death-angel—did he think?—calling us again, as in other days? For as often as she lifted the garland to the level of my hand, he sprang clear from earth—heavenwards, doubtless,—but was not heaven nearer just then? I managed to bring down his fore-feet close beside her, and dropped my sword-point almost to her feet, with a bow so low I could have touched her cheek. Was it the garland's breath or hers that floated to my lips? My horse trembled. I might have solved the mystery, could I have trusted him. But he would not trust me. All that was granted me was the Christian virtue of preferring another's good and passing the dangerous office of receiving this Mizpah token to the gallant young aide behind me. And I must add I did not see him again for some time! All this passed like a flash in act; but it was not quite so brief in effect. From that time my horse was shy of girls—sharp eyes out for soft eyes—I dare say for his master's peace and safety!

All the way up the Avenue a tumult of sound and motion. Around Griffin is a whirlpool, and far behind swells and rolls the generous acclaim. At the rise of ground near the Treasury a backward glance takes in the mighty spectacle: the broad Avenue for more than a mile solid full, and more, from wall to wall, from door to roof, with straining forms and outwelling hearts. In the midst, on-pressing that darker stream, with arms and colors resplendent in the noon-day sun, an army of tested manhood, clothed with power, crowned with glory, marching to its dissolution!

At this turn of the Avenue, our bugle rings out the

signal: "Prepare for Review!" The bands strike the cadenced march; the troops take up the step; the lines straighten; the column rectifies distances; the company fronts take perfect "dress," guide left, towards the side of the reviewing stand ahead, arms at the ceremonial "carry."

All is steadiness, dignity, order now. We are to pass in final review. The culminating point is near; the end for us nearing; a far-borne vision broods upon our eyes; world-wide and years-long thought,—deep, silent, higher than joy!

Still there is some marching more, in this restrained, cadenced order. We approach the region of the public offices and higher residential quarter, welcomed by yet fairer forms and more finely balanced salutations. Ah! women sitting at the balconied windows, with straining eyes and handkerchiefs now waving, then suddenly, at some face seen, or not seen where once belonging, pressed to faces bowed and quivering. Some of you I have seen where the earth itself was trembling, beneath the greetings wherewith man meets man with wrath and wreck—you and those like you, for heaven, too, is wide,—searching under the battle smoke to find a lost face left to be unknown, bending to bind up a broken frame made in God's image, or skillfully, as divinely taught, fashioning the knot to check an artery's out-rushing life, nay, even pressing tender fingers over it till what you deemed better help could come; to catch a dying message, or breathe a passing prayer, or perchance no more than give a cup of water to men now of God's "little ones,"—so done unto his Christ!

You in my soul I see, faithful watcher by my cotside long days and nights together through the delirium of mortal anguish,—steadfast, calm, and sweet as eternal love. We pass now quickly from each other's sight; but I know full well that where beyond these passing scenes you shall be, there will be heaven!

But now we come opposite the reviewing stand. Here are the President, his Cabinet, ambassadors and ministers of foreign lands, generals, governors, judges, high officers of the nation and the states. But we miss the deep, sad eyes of Lincoln coming to review us after each sore trial. Something is lacking to our hearts now,—even in this supreme hour. Already the simple, plain, almost thread-bare forms of the men of my division have come into view, and the President and his whole great company on the stand have risen and passed to the very front edge with gracious and generous recognition. I wheel my horse, lightly touching rein and spur to bring his proud head and battle-scarred neck to share the deep salutation of the sword. Then, riding past, I dismount at the President's invitation, and ascend the stand. Exchanging quick greetings, I join those at the front. All around I hear the murmured exclamations: "This is Porter's old Division!" "This is the Fifth Corps!" "These are straight from Five Forks and Appomattox!" It seemed as if all remained standing while the whole corps passed.

Surely all of them arose as each brigade commander passed, and as some deep-dyed, riven color drooped in salutation; and the throng on the stand did not diminish, although for more than three hours the steady march had held them before ours came to view.

For me, while this division was passing, no other thing could lure my eyes away, whether looking on or through. These were my men, and those who followed were familiar and dear. They belonged to me, and I to them, by bonds birth cannot create nor death sever. More were passing here than the personages on the stand could see. But to me so seeing, what a review, how great, how far, how near! It was as the morning of the resurrection!

The brigades to-day are commanded by General Pearson, General Gregory, and Colonel Edmunds, veterans of the corps. First is the Third Brigade, bearing the spirit and transformed substance of Porter' old division of Yorktown, and Morell's at Gaines' Mill and Malvern Hill. These are of the men I stood with at Antietam and Fredericksburg, and Chancellorsville and Gettysburg. Of that regiment—the 20th Maine—a third were left on the slopes of Round Top, and a third again in the Wilderness, at Spottsylvania, the North Anna, Cold Harbor, and the Chickahominy; to-day mingling in its ranks the remnants of the noble 2d and 1st Sharpshooters. Beside it still, the 118th Pennsylvania, sharing all its experiences from the day when these two young regiments took ordeal together in the floods of waters beneath and of fiery death above in the testing passage of Shepardstown Ford in 1862. More Pennsylvania veterans yet, the storied 83d and 91st, and brilliant 155th Zouave, and the shadow of the stalwart 62d, gone, and 21st Cavalry passed on. With these the 1st and 16th Michigan, ever at the front, the keen-eyed 1st and 2d Sharpshooters and proud relics of the 4th, left from the wheat-field of Gettysburg. Here is the trusted, sorely-tried 32d Massachusetts, with unfaltering spirit and ranks made good from the best substance of the 18th, wakening heart-held visions. These names and numbers tell of the men who had opened all the fiery gateways of Virginia from the York River to the Chickahominy, and from the Rapidan to the Appomattox.

Now Gregory's New York Brigade—the 187th, 188th, and 189th,—young in order of number, but veteran in experience and honor; worthy of the list held yet in living memory, the 12th, 13th, 14th, 17th, 25th, and 44th,—one by one gone before.

One more brigade yet, of this division; of the tested last that shall be first: the splendid 185th New York, and fearless, clear-brained Sniper still at their head; the stalwart fourteen-company regiment, the 198th Pennsylvania, its gallant field officers gone: brave veteran Sickel fallen with shattered arm, and brilliant young Adjutant Maceuen shot dead, both within touch of my hand in the sharp rally on the Quaker Road; and Major Glen, since commanding, cut down on the height of valor, colors in hand, leading a charge I ordered in a moment of supreme need. Captain

John Stanton, lately made major, leads to-day. These also coming into the bloody field of the dark year 1864, but soon ranked with veterans and wreathed with honor: In the last campaign opening with the brilliant victory on the enemy's right flank; of the foremost in the cyclone sweep at Five Forks; and at Appomattox first of the infantry to receive the flag of truce which bespoke the end. Each of these brigades had been severally in my command; and now they were mine all together, as I was theirs. So has passed this First Division,—and with it, part of my soul.

But now comes in sight a form before which the tumult of applause swells in mightier volume. It is Ayres, born soldier, self-commanding, nerve of iron, heart of gold,—a man to build on. What vicissitudes has he not seen since Gettysburg! Of those three splendid brigades which followed the white Maltese cross to the heights of Round Top, compact in spirit and discipline and power, only *two regiments* now hold their place, the 140th and 146th New York,—and of these both colonels killed at the head of their heroes: O'Rorke at Gettysburg and Jenkins in the Wilderness. Where are the regulars, who since 1862 had been ever at our side, —the ten iron-hearted regiments that made that terrible charge down the north spur of Little Round Top into the seething furies at its base, and brought back not one-half of its deathless offering? Like Ayres it was—in spirit and in truth,—when asked at the Warren Court, years after, then reviewing the Five Forks battle, "Where were your regulars then?" to answer with bold lip quivering, "Buried, sir, at Gettysburg!" Whereat there was silence,—and something more. And of what were not then buried, fifteen hundred more were laid low beneath the flaming scythes of the Wilderness, Spottsylvania, and the other bloody fields of that campaign. And the Government, out of pride and pity, sent the shredded fragments of them to the peaceful forts in the islands of New York harbor,—left there to their thoughts of glory.[1]

Their places had been taken by two brigades from the old First Corps, dearly experienced there: the thrice-honored Maryland Brigade, 1st, 4th, 7th, and 8th, in whose latest action I saw two of its brigade commanders shot down in quick succession; and the gallant little Delaware Brigade, with its proud record of loyalty and fidelity, part of the country's best history. Brave Dennison and Gwyn, generals leading these two brigades to-day; both bearing their honors modestly, as their hardly healed wounds manfully

Now the First Brigade: this of New York,—the superb 5th, 140th, and 146th, and the 15th Artillery, their equal in honor. At the head of this, on the fire-swept angle at Five Forks the high-hearted Fred Winthrop fell; then Grimshaw and Ayres himself led on to the first honors of that great day. At its head to-day rides the accomplished

[1] The losses of the regulars must in honor be here recalled:
At Gettysburg, 829, The Wilderness, 295, Spottsylvania, 420; North Anna, 44, Bethesda Church, 165, The Weldon Road, 480; Peebles' Farm, 76; a total of 2309.

General Joe Hayes, scarcely recovered from dangerous wounds. It was a hard place for brigade commanders—the Fifth Corps, in those "all summer" battles—and for colonels too.

So they pass, those that had come to take the place of the regulars; they pass into immortal history. Oh! good people smiling, applauding, tossing flowers, waving handkerchiefs from your lips with vicarious suggestion,—what forms do you see under that white cross, now also going its long way?

But here comes the Third Division, with Crawford, of Fort Sumter fame; high gentleman, punctilious soldier, familiar to us all. Leading his brigades are the fine commanders, dauntless Morrow, of the "Iron Brigade," erect above the scars of Gettysburg, the Wilderness, and Petersburg; resolute Baxter, and bold Dick Coulter,—veterans, marked, too, with wounds. Theirs is the blue cross,—speaking not of the azure heaven, but of the down-pressing battle smoke. And the men who in former days gave fame to that division,—the Pennsylvania Reserves of the Peninsula, Antietam, and Gettysburg, with their strong "*esprit de corps*" and splendor of service,—only the shadow of them now. But it is of sunset gold.

Here draws near a moving spectacle indeed, the last of the dear old First Corps; thrice decimated at Gettysburg in action and passion heroic, martyr-like, sublime; then merged into the Fifth, proudly permitted to bear its old colors, and in the crimson campaign of 1864 fought down to a division; in the last days the ancient spirit shining in the ranks where its scattered regiments are absorbed in other brigades,—shining still to-day! But where are my splendid six regiments of them which made that resolute, forlorn-hope charge from the crest they had carried fitly named "Fort Hell," down past the spewing dragons of "Fort Damnation" into the miry, fiery pit before Rives' Salient of the dark June 18th? Two regiments of them, the 121st Pennsylvania, Colonel Warner, and 142d Pennsylvania, Colonel Warren, alone I see in this passing pageant,—worn, thin, hostages of the mortal. I violate the courtesies of the august occasion. I give them salutation before the face of the reviewing officer—the President himself,—asking no permission, no forgiveness.

Here, led by valiant Small, that 16th Maine, which under heroic Tilden held its appointed station on the fierce first day of Gettysburg, obedient to the laws, like Spartans, for their loyalty and honor's sake; cut through, cut down, swept over, scattered, captured; so that at dreary nightfall the hushed voices of only four officers and thirty-eight men answered the roll-call. With them the 94th New York, which under Colonel Adrian Root shared its fate and glory.

And here are passing now those yet spared from earth and heaven of that "Iron Brigade," of Meredith's, on whose list appear such names as Lucius Fairchild, Henry Morrow, Rufus Dawes, and Samuel Williams, and such regiments as the 19th Indiana, 24th Michigan, and 2d, 6th, and 7th

Wisconsin, which on the first day's front line with Buford and Reynolds, in that one fierce onset at Willoughby's Run, withstood overwhelming odds, with the loss of a thousand, a hundred and fifty-three of highest manliness; that of the 24th Michigan largest of all,—three hundred and sixty-five,—eighty-one out of every hundred of that morning roll-call answering at evening, otherwhere. One passing form to-day holds every eye. Riding calmly at the head of the 7th Wisconsin is Hollon Richardson, who at Five Forks sprang to take on himself the death-blow struck at Warren as he leaped the flaming breastworks in the lurid sunset of his high career.

Pass on, men, in garb and movement to some monotonous; pass on, men, modest and satisfied; those looking on know what you are!

And now, Wainwright, with the artillery of the corps, guns whose voices I should know among a hundred: "D" of the Fifth Regular, ten-pounder guns, which Hazlett lifted to the craggy crest of Little Round Top, its old commander, Weed, supporting; whence having thundered again his law to a delivered people, God called them both to their reward. "L" of the 1st Ohio, perched on the western slope, hurling defiance at deniers. I see not Martin of the 3d Massachusetts, whose iron plowed the gorge between Round Top and the Devil's Den. But "B" of the 4th Regular is here, which stood by me on the heart-bastioned hillock in the whirlwind of the Quaker Road. And here the 5th Massachusetts, which wrought miracles of valor all the way from the Fifth Corps right, across the valley of death at Gettysburg, to the North Anna; where, planted in my very skirmish line, Phillips, erect on the gun-carriage, launched percussion into buildings full of sharpshooters picking off my best men. And where is Bigelow of the 9th Massachusetts, who on the exposed front fell back only with the recoil of his guns before the hordes swarming through the Peach Orchard, giving back shot, shrapnel, canister, rammer, pistol, and saber, until his battery—guns, limbers, horses, men—and he himself were a heap of mingled ruin? Which, also, a year after, with Mink's 1st New York and Hart's 15th, came to support the charge at the ominous Fort Hell; whence Bigelow, with watchful eyes, sent his brave men down through hissing canister, and enfilading shell, and blinding turf and pebbles flying from the up-torn earth, to bring back my useless body from what else were its final front.

Roar on, ye throngs around and far away; there are voices in my ear out-thundering yours!

All along in the passing column I have exchanged glances with earnest, true-hearted surgeons, remembered too well, but never too much loved and honored; with faithful chaplains, hospital attendants, and ambulance men, never to be forgotten, of the few who know something of the unrecorded scenes in the rear of a great battle. I have caught glances also from bright-eyed young staff officers who in the kaleidoscope changes of eventful years had been of my field family. Their look was sometimes confidential, as if slyly reminding me of the salutary discipline of camp, when they were turned out at reveille roll-call to "get acquainted with the men"; and after guard-mounting, the college men of them called up to demonstrate Euclid's "*pons asinorum*" with their scabbards in the sand; and for those who were not men of Bowdoin or Amherst or Yale or Columbia, the test commuted to shivering with pistol shot the musty hard-tack tossed in air, or at race-course gallop, spitting with saber-point the "Turk's head" of a junk of "condemned" pork on the commissary's hitching-post, or picking up a handkerchief from the ground, riding headlong at Tartar speed. Other pranks, of spontaneous and surreptitious discipline, when they thought it necessary to teach a green quartermaster how to ride, by deftly tucking dry pine cones under his saddle-cloth. You are ready to do it again, I see, you demure pretenders, or something the sequence of this skill, more useful to your fellow-man!

Have they all passed,—the Fifth Corps? Or will it ever pass? Am I left alone, or still with you all? You, of the thirteen young colonels, colleagues with me in the courts-martial and army schools of the winter camps of 1862: Vincent, of the 83d Pennsylvania, caught up in the fiery chariot from the heights of Round Top; O'Rorke, of the 140th New York, pressing to that glorious defense, swiftly called from the head of his regiment to serener heights; Jeffords, of the 4th Michigan, thrust through by bayonets as he snatched back his lost colors from the deadly reapers of the wheat-field;

Rice, of the 44th New York, crimsoning the harrowed crests at Spottsylvania with his life-blood,—his intense soul snatched far otherwhere than his last earthly thought—"Turn my face towards the enemy!"; Welch, of the 16th Michigan, first on the ramparts at Peebles' Farm, shouting "On, boys, and over!" and receiving from on high the same order for his own daring spirit; Prescott, of the 32d Massachusetts, who lay touching feet with me after mortal Petersburg of June 18th, under the midnight requiem of the somber pines,—I doomed of all to go, and bidding him stay,—but the weird winds were calling otherwise; Winthrop, of the 12th Regulars, before Five Forks just risen from a guest-seat at my homely luncheon on a log, within a half hour shot dead in the fore-front of the whirling charge. These gone,—and of the rest: Varney, of the 2d Maine, worn down by prison cruelties, and returning, severely wounded in the head on the storm-swept slopes of Fredericksburg, and forced to resign the service; Hayes, of the 18th Massachusetts, cut down in the tangles of the Wilderness; Gwyn, of the 118th Pennsylvania, also sorely wounded there; Herring, of the same regiment, with a leg off at Dabney's Mill; Webb, then of the corps staff, since, highly promoted, shot in his uplifted head, fronting his brigade to the leaden storm of Spottsylvania; Locke, adjutant-general of the corps,—a bullet cutting from his very mouth the order he was giving on the flaming crests of Laurel Hill!

You thirteen—seven, before the year was out—

shot dead at the head of your commands; of the rest, every one desperately wounded in the thick of battle; I last of all, but here to-day,—with you, earthly or ethereal forms.

"*Waes Hael!*"—across the rifts of vision—"Be Whole again, My Thirteen!"

What draws near heralded by tumult of applause, but when well-recognized greeted with mingled murmurs of reverence? It is the old Second Corps—of Sumner and of Hancock,—led now by one no less honored and admired,—Humphreys, the accomplished, heroic soldier, the noble and modest man. He rides a snow-white horse, followed by his well-proved staff, like-mounted, chief of them the brilliant Frank Walker, capable of higher things, and "Joe Smith," chief commissary, with a medal of honor for gallant service beyond duty,—a striking group, not less to the eye in color and composition, than to the mind in character. Above them is borne the corps badge, the clover-leaf,—peaceful token, but a triple mace to foes,—dear to thousands among the insignia of our army, as the shamrock to Ireland or rose and thistle of the British Empire.

Here comes the First Division, that of Richardson and Caldwell and Barlow and Miles; but at its head to-day we see not Miles, for he is just before ordered to Fortress Monroe to guard "Jeff Davis" and his friends,—President "Andy Johnson" declaring he "wanted there a man who would not let his prisoners escape." So Ramsay of New

Jersey is in command on this proud day. Its brigades are led by McDougal, Fraser, Nugent, and Mulholland—whereby you see the shamrock and thistle are not wanting even in our field. These are the men we saw at the sunken road at Antietam, the stone wall at Fredericksburg, the wheat-field at Gettysburg, the bloody angle at Spottsylvania, the swirling fight at Farmville, and in the pressing pursuit along the Appomattox before which Lee was forced to face to the rear and answer Grant's first summons to surrender. We know them well. So it seems do these thousands around.

These pass, or rather do not pass, but abide with us; while crowd upon our full hearts the stalwart columns of the Second Division—the division of the incisive Barlow, once of Sedgwick and Howard and Gibbon. These men bring thoughts of the terrible charge at the Dunker church at Antietam, and that still more terrible up Marye's Heights at Fredericksburg, and the check given to the desperate onset of Pickett and Pettigrew in the consummate hour of Gettysburg. We think, too, of the fiery mazes of the Wilderness, the death-blasts of Spottsylvania, and murderous Cold Harbor; but also of the brilliant fights at Sailor's Creek and Farmville, and all the splendid action to the victorious end. Here is the seasoned remnant of the "Corcoran Legion," the new brigade which, rushing into the terrors of Spottsylvania, halted a moment while its priest stood before the brave, bent heads and called down benediction.

Webb's Brigade of the Wilderness is commanded

to-day by Olmstead; the second, by McIvor—veteran colonels from New York; the third by Colonel Woodall of Delaware. This brigade knows the meaning of that colorless phrase, "the casualties of the service," showing the ever shifting elements which enter into what we call identity. Here are all that is left of French's old division at Antietam, and Hays' at Gettysburg, who was killed in the Wilderness, Carroll's Brigade at Spottsylvania, where he was severely wounded; Smyth's at Cold Harbor, killed at Farmville. Into this brigade Owen's, too, is now merged. They are a museum of history.

Here passes, led by staunch Spaulding, the sterling 19th Maine, once gallant Heath's, conspicuous everywhere, from the death-strewn flank of Pickett's charge, through all the terrible scenes of "Grant's campaign," to its consummation at Appomattox. In its ranks now are the survivors of the old Spartan 4th, out of the "Devil's Den," where Longstreet knew them.

Heads uncover while passes what answers the earthly roll-call of the immortal 5th New Hampshire, famed on the stubborn Third Corps front at Gettysburg, where its high-hearted Colonel Cross fell leading the brigade,—among the foremost in the sad glory of its losses, two hundred and ninety-five men having been killed in its ranks.

What is that passing now, the center of all eyes, —that little band so firmly poised and featured they seem to belong elsewhere? This is what was the 1st Minnesota, sometimes spoken of, for valid reasons, as the 1st Maine; more deeply known as of Gettysburg, where in the desperate counter-charge to stay an overwhelming onset, they left eighty-three men out of every hundred! With ever lessening ranks but place unchanged at the head of its brigade from Bull Run to Appomattox, to-day a modest remnant, Colonel Hausdorf proudly leads on its last march the 1st Minnesota.

What wonder that, as such men pass, the outpoured greetings take on a strangely mingled tone. You could not say from what world they come, or to what world they go. Not without deep throbbings under our breath,—ours who in heart belong to them,—as if answering some far-off drum-beat "assembly" summons.

But now comes on with veteran pride and far-preceding heralding of acclaim, the division which knows something of the transmigration of souls: having lived and moved in different bodies and under different names; knowing, too, the tests of manhood, and the fate of suffering and sacrifice, but knowing most of all the undying spirit which holds fast its loyalty and faces ever forward. This is the division of Mott, himself commanding to-day, although severely wounded at Hatcher's Run on the sixth of April last. These are all that are left of the old commands of Hooker and Kearny, and later, of our noble Berry, of Sickles' Third Corps. They still wear the proud "Kearny patch" —the red diamond. Birney's Division, too, has been consolidated with Mott's, and the brigades are now commanded by the chivalrous De Trobriand

and the sterling soldiers, Pierce of Michigan and McAllister of New Jersey. Their division flag now bears the mingled symbols of the two corps, the Second and Third,—the diamond and the trefoil.

Over them far floats the mirage-like vision of them on the Peninsula, and then at Bristow, Manassas, and Chantilly, and again the solid substance of them at Chancellorsville, and on the stormy front from the Plumb Run gorge to the ghastly Peach Orchard, where the earth shone red with the bright facings of their brave Zouaves thick-strewn amidst the blue, as we looked down from smoking Round Top. Then in the consolidation for the final trial bringing the prestige and spirit and loyalty of their old corps into the Second,—making this the strongest corps in the army,—adding their splendid valor to the fame of this in which they merged their name.

Now come those heavy artillery regiments which the exigencies of the service drew suddenly to unexpected and unfamiliar duty, striking the fight at its hottest in the cauldron of Spottsylvania, and, obeying orders literally, suffered loss beyond all others there: the 1st Massachusetts losing three hundred, and the 1st Maine four hundred and eighty-one officers and men in that single action. This same 1st Maine, afterwards in the rashly-bidden charge at Petersburg, June 18, 1864, added to its immortal roll six hundred and thirty-two lost in that futile assault. Proudly rides Russell Shepherd at their head,—leaving the command of a brigade to lead these men to-day. Deep emotions stir at the presence of such survivors,—cherishing the same devotion and deserving the same honor as those who fell.

Here passes the high-borne, steadfast-hearted 17th Maine from the seething whirlpool of the wheat-field of Gettysburg to the truce-compelling flags of Appomattox. To-day its ranks are honored and spirit strengthened by the accession of the famous old 3d Regiment,—that was Howard's. Some impress remains of firm-hearted Roberts, brave Charley Merrill, keen-edged West, and sturdy William Hobson; but Charley Mattocks is in command in these days,—a man and a soldier, with the unspoiled heart of a boy. Three of these, college mates of mine. What far dreams drift over the spirit, of the days when we questioned what life should be, and answered for ourselves what we would be!

Now passes the artillery, guns all dear to us; but we have seen no more of some, familiar and more dear: Hall's 2d Maine, that was on the cavalry front on the first day of Gettsyburg, grand in retreat as in action, afterwards knowing retreat only in sunset bugle-call; Stevens' 5th Maine, that tore through the turmoil of that tragic day, and gave the Louisiana "Tigers" another cemetery than that they sought on the storied hill; roaring its way through the darkness of 1864, holding all its ancient glory. Most of the rest we knew had gone to the "reserve."

The pageant has passed. The day is over. But we linger, loath to think we shall see them no more together,—these men, these horses, these colors afield. Hastily they have swept to the front as of yore; crossing again once more the long bridge and swaying pontoons, they are on the Virginia shore, waiting, as they before had sought, the day of the great return.

We were to have one great day more. The Sixth Corps had come up from its final service of perfecting the surrender, and on this bright morning of June 8th was to be held in review by honoring thought and admiring eyes. We who had passed our review were now invited spectators of this. But there was something more. Something the best in us would be passed in review to-day.

The military prestige of this corps was great, and its reputation was enhanced by Sheridan's late preference, well-known. The city, too, had its special reasons for regard. The Sixth Corps had come up from its proud place in the battle lines in days of fear and peril, to save Washington. Besides, this corps was part of the great Army of the Potomac.

The President and all the dignitaries were on the reviewing stand as before. Multitudes were filling the streets, and the houses bloomed their welcome from basement to summit. The ordering was much as before. Column of companies; files equalized. Space now permits some features of a regular review. Instead of close order, the column moves at wheeling distance of its subdivisions; all commissioned officers salute; division and brigade commanders after passing the reviewing stand, turn out and join the reviewing officer; the bands also at this point wheel out and continue playing while their brigade is passing. The ambulances, engineers, and artillery follow as before.

The symbol of the flag of this corps is the Greek cross—the "square" cross, of equal arms. Symbol of terrible history in old-world conflicts—Russian and Cossack and Pole; token now of square fighting, square dealing, and loyalty to the flag of the union of freedom and law.

These are survivors of the men in early days with Franklin and Smith and Slocum and Newton. Later, and as we know them best, the men of Sedgwick; but alas, Sedgwick leads no more, except in spirit! Unheeding self he fell smitten by a sharpshooter's bullet, in the midst of his corps. Wright is commanding since, and to-day, his chief-of-staff, judicial Martin McMahon. These are the men of Antietam and the twice wrought marvels of courage at Fredericksburg, and the long tragedy of Grant's campaign of 1864; then in the valley of the Shenandoah with Sheridan in his rallying ride, and in the last campaign storming the works of Petersburg—losing eleven hundred men in fifteen minutes; masters at Sailor's Creek, four days after, taking six thousand prisoners, with Ewell and five of his best generals,—of them the redoubtable Kershaw; in the van in the pursuit of Lee, and with the Second Corps pressing him to a last stand, out of which came the first message of surrender.

First comes the division of Wheaton; at its head, under Penrose, the heroic New Jersey Brigade which at the Wilderness and Spottsylvania lost a thousand one hundred and forty-three officers and men. Next, and out of like experiences, the brigades of Edwards and Hamblen, representing the valor of Massachusetts, Rhode Island, Connecticut, Pennsylvania, and Wisconsin.

Now passes Getty's Division. Leading is Warner's Brigade, from its great record of the Wilderness, Spottsylvania, and Cold Harbor; then the magnificent First Vermont Brigade, under that sterling soldier, General Lewis Grant; as their proud heads pass, we think of the thousand six hundred and forty-five laid low at the Salient of Spottsylvania. Now we think we see the shadow of that "Light Division" with Burnham storming Marye's Heights in the Chancellorsville campaign of 1863. For here, last, is the Third Brigade, once of Neil and Bidwell, with the fame of its brave work all through Grant's campaign, led now by Sumner's 1st Maine Veterans, of which it is enough to say it is made up of the old 5th, and 6th, and 7th Maine,—the hearts of Edwards and Harris and Connor still beating in them. Can history connote or denote anything nobler in manliness and soldiership, than has been made good by these? Commanding is the young general, Tom Hyde, favorite in all the army, prince of staff officers, gallant commander, alert of sense, level of head, sweet of soul.

The infantry column is closed by Ricketts'

Division, its brigades commanded by Trueman Seymour and Warren Keifer, names known before and since. These men too, knowing what was done and suffered—shall we say in vain?—in that month under fire from the Wilderness to Cold Harbor; in these two battles losing out of their firm-held ranks a thousand eight hundred and twenty-five men; knowing also of the valley of the Shenandoah and the weary windings of the Appomattox. Of the heart of the country, these men: Vermont, New York, New Jersey, Ohio, Pennsylvania, Maryland. These twelve regiments were to close that grand procession of muskets, tokens of a nation's mighty deliverance, now to be laid down; tokens also of consummate loyalty and the high manhood that seeks not self but the larger, deeper well-being which explains and justifies personal experience.

Now follows the artillery brigade, under Major Cowan; eight batteries representing all the varieties of that field service, and the contributions of Rhode Island, Vermont, New York, and New Jersey, and the regulars. What story of splendors and of terrors do these grim guns enshrine!

Now, last of all, led by Major van Brocklin, the little phalanx of the 50th New York Engineers, which had been left to help the Sixth Corps, pass once more the turbid rivers of Virginia. Here again, the train of uncouth pontoons, telling of the mastery over the waters as of the land. This last solemn passage now, waking memories of dark going and dark returning, deep slumbering in our souls. Thanks and blessing, homely pontoons! Would to God we had a bridge so sure, to bear us over other dark waters—out of the pain—into the Peace!

Home again, Sixth Corps! Home to your place in our hearts! Encamp beside us once more; as for so long we have made sunshine for each others' eyes, and watched with hushed voices guarding their rest; and wakened to the same thrilling call, guided on each other through maze of darkness to fronts of storm and over walls of flame!

Sit down again, Sixth Corps! with the Fifth and Second, holding dear to thought the soul and symbol of the vanished First and Third. Sit down again together, Army of the Potomac! all that are left of us,—on the banks of the river whose name we bore, into which we have put new meaning of our own. Take strength from one more touch, ere we pass afar from the closeness of old. The old is young to-day; and the young is passed. Survivors of the fittest,—for the fittest, it seems to us, abide in the glory where we saw them last,—take the grasp of hands, and look into the eyes, without words! Who shall tell what is past and what survives? For there are things born but lately in the years, which belong to the eternities.

CHAPTER X

SHERMAN'S ARMY

THE day after the review of our Second and Fifth Corps of the Army of the Potomac was appointed for a review on the same ground of Sherman's famous Army of the West. A feeling of comradeship and admiration rather than anything of jealousy or disposition for invidious comparison took many of us over to witness that grand spectacle. It was well worth a day's devotion to see the men who had fought those tremendous battles of the West and had marched nearly two thousand miles, cutting through the midst of an enemy's country with such demonstration of power that all obstacles fled before them. And our admiration of the brilliant soldier who had the ability to plan and the resolution to execute a movement so masterly in strategy and tactics lent a certain awe to our emotion.

The preparations for the review and the formation of the column were much as they were for the Army of the Potomac. The sky was wonderfully beautiful and the earth gave good greeting under foot. As before, the streets were lined and thronged with people, and the houses and especially the stands in the vicinity of the President's House were even more crowded than the day before. The prestige of this army that had marched from the Great River to the Sea, and thence up half the Atlantic coast, bringing the fame of mighty things done afar, stirred perhaps more the hearts and imaginations of the people than did the familiar spectacle of men whose doings and non-doings had been an every-day talk, and who so often had walked their streets in hurrying ranks or pitiful forlornness and thronged their hospitals, year after year, in service and suffering, unboastful and uncomplaining. But not a craven thought was in our spirits because these that came after us were preferred before us. We rejoiced in the recognition given them and led in the applause.

Down the avenue poured the shining river of steel, gay with colors and rippling with cascades of mounted staff and burnished cannon. At the head proud, stern Sherman, who with thoughtful kindness had brought brave Howard, now ordered to other important duty, to ride by his side in this pageant. Following next is swarthy John Logan, leading the Army of the Tennessee, and Hazen with the Fifteenth Corps. Each division is preceded by its corps of black pioneers, shining like polished ebony, armed with pick and spade, proud of their perfect alignment, keeping step to the music with inborn stress. Significant frontispiece. Almost equally interesting was the corps of foragers, familiarly known as Sherman's "bummers," following each brigade. These were characteristic representatives of the career of that army, and they tried to appear as nearly as possible like what they were in that peculiar kind of service. Their dress, and free and easy bearing, as well as their pack-mules and horses with rope bridles, laden with such stores as they had gathered from the country through which they passed, was a remarkable feature in a military review.

We were told that General Sherman witnessing our review had told his leading commanders that our military appearance and even marching could not be surpassed or even equalled by their own men, and it was resolved that they would not make the attempt to rival us in this regard but would appear as nearly as possible as they looked while "marching through Georgia." But they did both. As was to be expected, their marching was superb, both steady and free, not as if forced for the occasion, but by habit or second nature: distances maintained; lines perfectly "dressed" on the "guide left"; eyes steady to the front.

Further evidence of the liberality of their commanders in yielding something to the spirit of liberty, or at least to the instinct so significantly planted in man to establish relations with the kingdoms or subjects of nature supposed to be below him, appeared in the tokens of personal freedom allowed the men in the midst of their military discipline and the formalities of this occasion. The monotony of these formalities was strangely relieved by what seemed to us Army of the Potomac men hazardous breach of discipline. A comical medley of pets had their part in the parade and the applause: in one of the regiments an eagle borne on a perch beside the colors; in others, a cat, or a coon, favorably mounted for reciprocal inspection, as well as the pack-mules, laden, as was their wont, with stores,—but mostly quite a variation upon those issued by the commissary or quartermaster, symbols of extinguished domestic dynasties, and lost civilizations. In another place, a genre picture of the farmyard: milch-cows, ponies, goats, and figuring proudly in the center Chanticleer, loudly defying his mates, —no longer rivals,—responding lustily from some corresponding elevation, whether allies or aliens. As a climax, with significance which one might ponder, whole families of freed slaves, as servants, trustfully leading their little ones, obedient to fate, silent, without sign of joy; more touching in some ways than the proud passing column; more touching in some deep ways than the spectacle of captive kings led in the triumph of imperial Rome.

So pass in due order of precedence all the corps of that historic army,—the men of Shiloh, of Corinth, of Vicksburg, of Missionary Ridge, of Chattanooga, Chickamauga, and Altoona. We cannot name them familiarly, but we accord them admiration.

And now comes a corps which we of the Army of the Potomac may be pardoned for looking on with peculiar interest. It is the Twentieth Corps, led by Mower, the consolidation of our old Eleventh and Twelfth (Howard's and Slocum's), reduced now to scarcely more than two divisions, those of Williams and Geary. We recognize regiments that had last been with us on the hard-pressed right wing at Gettysburg: the 2d Massachusetts; 5th and 20th Connecticut; 60th, 102d, 107th, 123d, 137th, 149th, 150th New York; the 13th New Jersey; the 11th, 28th, 109th, 147th Pennsylvania; the 5th, 29th, 61st, 66th, 82d Ohio; and the 3d Wisconsin. We also gladly see the 33d Massachusetts, with the gentle and chivalrous Underwood. Leading one of the brigades we recognize the manly Coggswell of Massachusetts. These were the men with Hooker on Lookout Mountain, in "the battle above the clouds," whither also their fame has risen. Not cloyed nor stinted is the greeting we give to these returning men,—for them, as for those that have passed on. Strong is the brotherhood of a common experience,—the kinship of a new birth to the broader life of a regenerated country.

And now the shadows draw around us; for the long summer day is scarcely long enough for the mighty march of these far-marched men. General Sherman has told us he mustered in these armies when last gathered more than fifty-seven thousand men. Well might the passing of so many fill all the hours since the well advanced morning of the start.

The shadows deepen. It has passed,—the splendid pageant; it is gone forever,—the magnificent host that streamed from the mountains to the sea; that flaming bolt which cut the Confederacy in two,—or shall we say that left its deep track upon the earth to mark the dark memories of those years; or to shine forever as a token of saving grace in the galaxy of the midnight sky?

The same high personages were on the reviewing stand with the President as on the day before,—a distinguished and august company. As General Sherman with Howard and Logan after saluting at the head of the column mounted the reviewing stand and exchanged warm greetings with all, Sherman took pains to make it manifest that he refused to take Stanton's offered hand. This was surprising to many, but those of us who while encamped along the Southside Railroad after Lee's surrender had occasion to know about the circumstances attending Sherman's negotiations with Johnston for surrender, could not wonder at it. When Sherman, supposing he was acting in accordance with the policy of the government as he had understood it from Lincoln, made terms for the surrender of Johnston's army, involving matters pertaining to the political status of the Southern people and a policy of reconstruction,—undoubtedly therein exceeding any prerogatives of a military commander,—the President disapproved of them and gave directions for hostilities to be resumed. But in carrying these into effect, Secretary Stanton took an equally unwarrantable course in his orders to Meade and Sheridan, and to Wright (then at Danville), to pay no attention to Sherman's armistice or orders, but to push forward and cut off Johnston's retreat, while in fact Johnston had virtually surrendered already to Sherman. Halleck repeated this with added disrespect; and still more to humiliate Sherman, Stanton gave sanction by his name officially signed to a bulletin published in the New York papers entertaining the suggestion that Sherman might be influenced by pecuniary considerations to let Jeff Davis get out of the country. This was not short of infamous on Stanton's part. Sherman meant so to stigmatize it, and he did, in the face of all on a supreme public occasion. With our experience of discipline, we wondered what the next move of Stanton would be. Sherman might have declined the President's hand; but President Johnson had assured him that he knew nothing about the bulletins, as Stanton had not consulted anybody nor shown them to any member of the Cabinet. Had the President sanctioned them, I doubt not Sherman would have resented the act from whomsoever coming. Sherman was a "hale fellow well met," but a hard fellow when unfairly treated.

For all General Sherman's compliments on the appearance of our army, he was quite sensitive about the comparison of the intrinsic merits of his army and ours. He did not hesitate to affirm that his army was superior to ours in drill and discipline. In precisely these points we could not agree with him. It is true that his troops in passing in review did keep their relative distances well, and their shoulders square and eyes steady to the front, while it may be possible that some of our men may have turned their eyes towards the personages they were honoring,—as surely is the rule of courtesy in civil society, with which these men might be more familiar. But I think the General made too wide an inference from the narrow field of his observed instances. If comparisons are to be instituted, it may be that in marching his troops surpassed ours. That had been a large part of their business; our occupations had been more varied. We had done some running on several occasions, and a good deal of fighting. As to drill and discipline, the direct comparative evidence was scanty. But the probability that the Army of the Potomac would be deficient in these respects is negatived by the presumption from the nature of the case: in the military character of our commanders, and the exigency of the situation, which demanded that the men should be made proficient for their pressing need, and by every possible means drilled, instructed, and inured to the discipline of the field; as also our proximity to the capital and the eyes of exacting critics. Foreign military observers had pronounced our drill and discipline to be of the highest order.

It is possible that General Sherman may have felt the usefulness of bold assertion on this subject of his superiority in drill and discipline. We do not deem the decision a vital matter for our fame; but when invidious comparisons are announced by high authority, we may justly call attention to the evidence. In the qualities which make up human nature our Western compatriots were certainly our equals.

After this review, things were not so pleasant as they might be in our big camps along the river. At first the greetings were such as good-fellowship and novelty of intercourse prompted. But we were soon made aware of a feeling we had not before suspected on the part of many of our comrades of the Western army. We certainly had never had an intimation of it among the many Western men in our own army. There seemed to be a settled dislike to us, latent at least, among Sherman's men. In a certain class their manner was contemptuous and bullying. They threatened to come over and "burst us up," and "clean us out." Some directed their objurgations upon the whole "East,"—the Yankees generally; and more against the Army of the Potomac in particular. "You couldn't fight." —"You are babies and hospital cats."—"We did all the marching and all the fighting."—"We had to send Grant and Sheridan up to teach you how to fight."—"Lee licked you, and was running away to get something to eat, poor fellow."—"You wouldn't have caught him if we hadn't marched two thousand miles to drive him into the trap." On some of these points we might be a little tender; though on the whole we thought the charge a perversion of fact.

But we had some "Bowery Boys" and Fire Zouaves in our army too; and what they wanted was to get at these "Sherman's Bummers" and settle the question in their own Cossack and Tartar fashion. In fact, so serious did the discord grow that the division commanders had to take positive measures for defense,—as thoroughly as before on the flanks of the Petersburg lines. We doubled all camp guards, and detailed special reserves ready for a rush; sleeping ourselves some nights in our boots, with sword and pistol by our sides. This was a serious condition of things. No wonder Sherman asked to move his army to the other side of the river. But the national authorities thought this would savor too much of recognition of a new secession, between the East and West. Such is the strange nature,—the human, likeness of interest holding masses together for the attainment of a great common cause, in which they show both loyalty and amity; but differences on a narrower scale, quickly throw men into an attitude quite antagonistic. It must be said that this hostile feeling towards the East was not a general sentiment among our Western comrades, but only of a certain class accustomed to put their individualistic sentiments into execution more frequently and energetically than their sense of loyalty to the country. For our part, surely, we had no dislike to Western men, but quite the contrary, as very many of them bore close relationship to our New England families; and as to the merits of Sherman's army we did not hesitate to do it justice or give it sincere and generous praise. The taunts thrown at us by men on that side met the retort from similar characters on our side that in their boasted march to the sea they met only fat turkeys and sucking pigs. What little truth there might have been under this satire we were not disposed to inquire, but did our best to rebuke such expressions and cultivate all around a spirit of broad loyalty and common good-will; as to the claim that "Sherman's army did all the fighting," we rested on the testimony of official figures, which showed the losses of Sherman's army from Chattanooga to Atlanta, 31,687 men; Meade's losses for the same period, from the Rapidan to Petersburg, 88,387. Time, however, soon settled these bickerings by separation and return to the duties of a common citizenship.

CHAPTER XI

THE DISBANDMENT

THE last days of our encampment before Washington gave us plenty of work, especially for the officers, making up returns of government property: arms, clothing, tents, supplies of all kinds, for which they were responsible and must give satisfactory account before they could be honorably discharged. For the most part the men were to take their equipments with them, as a matter of courtesy, I suppose, as these belonged to the United States. It was fair that these veterans should be allowed to take to their homes the arms they had honored, and permission was given them to purchase at a nominal value, it would not have been too much if the Government had granted these with such proud associations, to cheer the soldier in his resumed citizenship, rather than consign them to rust and oblivion in government stores. What I think very reprehensible was the practice permitted of selling overcoats at a cheap rate among workmen willing to buy them. This was a degradation of the uniform and of the men, and should never have been permitted. A soldier's overcoat should stand for honor and not for poverty.

The men were kept at such work, whether of drill or other military duty, as the situation allowed. But it will be understood that it was no easy matter to keep things smooth, when so many men were congregated, and the imperative motive for discipline and good order was overpassed. The visitors became embarrassing. It was well and it was pleasant to afford to soldiers and their friends an opportunity to compare the methods of army life and home life. But these "friends" became a very extensive immigration, and some of them disturbed our soldiers with temptations of things that could not be tolerated either in camp or home. It was necessary to send some of these out of camp limits under escort and sometimes to greater distance; and finally to establish rigorous regulations about visitors.

On the other hand, visits of our officers and men to the city soon became a feature of importance. Fair attractions across the river, dinners, parties, receptions, and other social entertainments, broke in upon the monastic habits of even the higher officers. A pleasant evening found most of them on the civil side of the river. Applications for leave of absence swelled to an inundation, and had to be met with restrictions. At last the War Department took notice of it; and one night at about two o'clock an order came from Stanton requiring every commanding officer to sign a receipt, on the order presented; and the result showed that only two generals of our camp were in their quarters.

Now that the approaching close of our long and eventful career brought upon us a mood of reflection, we gave more free thought to many things we had "pondered in our hearts." Our minds were still affected by disturbing impressions as to the peculiar management of tactics in our campaign of the Appomattox. We could not understand why the Army of the Potomac was so broken up and buffeted about. No merely military reasons for this could be conceived by us who certainly were interested parties, and competent witnesses, if not admissible as judges. This latter function was not part of our duty, but to some degree our privilege, and perhaps our right. We would not criticize our orders when received, but were not readily reconciled to measures which contradicted common sense and, as we thought, military economics. Why was the Army of the James marched a long, hard jaunt from its position on the right of the Petersburg lines and put in between the Sixth and Second Corps of the Army of the Potomac? Why not hold that army where it was next to the James River, and let our Sixth and Ninth Corps close in upon its left, and thus bring the Army of the Potomac together, instead of wedging it apart, and breaking up its continuity and identity? And why, in the early operations of the campaign, were matters so managed that the Fifth Corps, which had by hard fighting made an important break on the right of the enemy's defenses, should in the midst of this success be suddenly withdrawn, abandoning all its advantages to go to the support of Sheridan's cavalry, which was not at any strategic front,—instead of having this cavalry support and follow up our infantry advance as the exigencies of the situation, specific field orders, and the main objective of the campaign justified and required? And why, in the pursuit of the broken enemy, were the Fifth and Sixth Corps time and again transposed from extreme right to extreme left, and the converse, now under Meade, now under Sheridan, they hardly knew at any moment which? And why was the Fifth Corps halted six miles short of Appomattox Station, to let the Army of the James pass it to join Sheridan at the front? There was another matter which perplexed our thought, although it brought honor rather than injury to the Fifth Corps. Why did Grant leave the front of Meade and the Army of the Potomac where the principal negotiations with Lee had already begun, make the journey to Sheridan's front where Ord of the Army of the James was in chief command, and arrange for the formal surrender to be carried out at this point? And why were the two remaining corps of the Army of the Potomac dispersed and detailed elsewhere, leaving its commander to exercise the functions of a mere adjunct office? Was this because the sterling Humphreys and Wright could not be made prominent without bringing in Meade, already doomed to the shades? We were left to our own opinions on these unanswered questions,—and we took them home with us.

One question frequently brought to our minds by outside inquirers was whether from our observation and experience we regarded Grant as a great general,—particularly in comparison with Lee. While our opinion could in no degree affect the reputation of either of these generals, it might disclose our own competency as judges. Hence, as these memoirs are supposed to reflect the intellectual as well as the military character of our soldiers, it may be proper to express what I understood to be their sentiment on this question.

But first let us understand the meaning of our principal term. There are two conceptions of great generalship: one regarding practical material effects; the other essential personal qualities. In the former view we regard Attila, Genghis Khan, and Tamerlane as great generals. In the latter conception,—that of intrinsic qualities,—there are two views to be taken. This rank may be accorded to one who has the ability to accomplish great things with moderate means, and against great disadvantages; of this William of Orange is an example. Or, on the other hand, it may be applied to one who can command the situation, gather armies, control resources, and conquer by main force. Examples of this are familiar in history: Alexander, Cæsar, Napoleon.

A current and I think correct definition of great generalship regards not so much the power to command resources, or the conditions of a grand theater of action, as the ability to handle successfully the forces available, be they small or great. And this, it will be seen, involves many qualities not readily thought of as military. Among these is economy in the expenditure of force. Another is foresight, the ability to count the cost beforehand and to discriminate between probabilities and possibilities,—prudence might be the word for this, did it not border on hesitation, which has wrecked some reputations, if it has made others. There is also astuteness, the ability to judge characters and the probable action of an adversary in given conditions. And we may add humanity, regard for the well-being of the men employed in military operations, which might come also under the head of economics.

Having thus considered the qualities involved in the term generalship, we will take up our opinion of the title to it on the part of the two opposing generals.

Grant was a strategist; he was not an economist. He saw what was to be done, and he set himself to do it, without being much controlled by consideration of cost or probabilities. His mechanical calculations often failed to hold good,—flank movements were often belated, and so anticipated and neutralized by the enemy's vigilance and celerity; direct front attacks often proved direful miscalculation and murderous waste. Great cost of human life involved in a proposed plan was not taken into the reckoning beforehand; though regretted afterwards, it was not given weight in laying plans following.

Though he studied lines of operations, foresight was not a characteristic of his; the resolve to do overbore all negations, and obliterated the limits of the possible. He so bent his energies on the main object ahead that he did not consider the effect of subordinate movements. He never seized the moment to turn disaster into victory. He seemed to rely on sheer force, rather than skillful manœuvre. Grant kept his own counsel, almost to the extent of stolidity. He was rather critical in his estimates of subordinates; but did not study sufficiently the abilities and temperaments of his antagonists; so he was sometimes outgeneraled—we do not like to say outwitted—by them. We would rather say he was checkmated by his own moves. He was tender-hearted, but did not admit that sentiment into his military calculations. We could see why he wanted Sheridan and not Meade for his executive officer.

But for all this, and perhaps because of it, Grant was necessary to bring that war to a close, whether by triumph of force or exhaustion of resources. His positive qualities, his power to wield force to the bitter end, must entitle him to rank high as a commanding general. His concentration of energies, inflexible purpose, unselfishness, patience, imperturbable long-suffering, his masterly reticence, ignoring either advice or criticism, his magnanimity in all relations, but more than all his infinite trust in the final triumph of his cause, set him apart and alone above all others. With these attributes we could not call him less than great.

Then looking at the question on another side, the great scale of action and its incalculable results, we shall find this judgment abundantly corroborated. He had a great problem before him, involving issues which the wrestlings of nations and of ages had left unsolved,—the confirmation of a new world in its service to mankind and the purposes of God. Grant was a chosen minister of the Divine will, and in a manner was the responsible agent for the execution of this vast design. He doubtless felt this.

And what was revealed from on high he realized in fact. What other men could not do, he did. And to one who did this, to one who led these mighty hosts to mighty ends, we must accord the rank of great, whether as general or as man. This is the verdict of those who were witnesses,—servants and sufferers,—and it is our proud remembrance.

Our estimate of General Lee was that he exemplified remarkable ability as a commander. In military sagacity and astuteness we recognized his superiority. In singleness of purpose, and patient persistence, like our own great commander, he was remarkable. In his constant care for his men, and especially in conduct after disaster, he won our respect and in some ways our sympathy. We regarded him as a master in military economy, making best use with least waste of material. And in defensive operations we looked upon him as a skilful tactician, taking best advantage of a situation.

In offensive operations, however, involving strategic considerations, he seemed to us not to reach the ideal of generalship. His two positive operations in Maryland and Pennsylvania, culminating in the Antietam and Gettysburg campaigns, must be accounted at best as failures, detracting, we must say, from the highest conception of military ability.

At Antietam, where he made us the attacking party, he showed his tactical skill in subjecting us to terrible losses; at Gettysburg, where he chose to take the offensive, he showed much less of that skill; and the result in each instance reflects on his strategic ability, in not taking into account the probabilities in such an enterprise. However, in the main, considering the great responsibilities with which he was charged and the great difficulties which he had to meet and did meet so successfully and for so long a time, we cannot consider him as ranking less than great among generals, and of the best of them.

As to personal qualities, Lee's utter unselfishness, in fact his whole moral constitution, appeared to us singularly fine. In his high characteristics as a man he compelled admiration among those who knew him,—even as we did,—and he will command it for all the future.

We do not consider these statements of characteristics as complete or conclusive. Whatever may be the general or permanent estimate as to the place of these great commanders, we simply record this testimony from our own point of view.

A consideration which had great influence on the habits of thought which go to confirm character, was the cause in which each side was engaged. On both sides we had been fighting for what we respectively held to be the nature of our political life as a people. On the Confederate side they were fighting for existing institutions, having historic warrant, and, as they claimed, constitutional warrant also. As the war had to be carried on in the territory whence the challenge came, there was opportunity to make the gist of their cause very clear and expressible in quite concrete terms. They could say, for instance, that they were fighting for their homes.

On our side the same general principles were affirmed; but their application was not limited to the existing status or institutions; rather to guiding and germinant ideals: the expressed intent and purpose of our fathers in establishing the government of one great people, and the inborn right of every human being to make the best of himself, and the duty of all to help him to this. That is indeed a high ideal.

It was night around us; but overhead were the stars. Things were in a chaos of transition; but the forward look was clear. If in these later days they have not yet been fully realized, these principles have been clearly reaffirmed, and our consecration has been made more binding by the priceless cost of the vindication.

This vast concourse of citizen soldiers was now about to be broken up, its individual constituents scattered widely over the land, to resume their part in the wholesome and helpful activities of social life. Going forth from their homes at the call of a supreme duty, should they return home better or worse men than they went? It had been a careful and congenial effort of those charged with the care of the men in the field, not only to provide for their personal material comfort and well-being as far as possible under the circumstances, but also to encourage the keeping up and even the growth of the nobler qualities of character. The narrow and rude life of the field in warfare, so far from the saving and salutary influences of home, does not tend to promote the highest personal elements of character. Not that this life necessarily leads to vice; but no doubt it gives place to negligence of the better social instincts, and thus tends to narrow and harden the better sensibilities. Hence the great care that should be taken that our young men who sacrifice so much for the country's well-being shall suffer no detriment to their manly worth. Such care was manifest in the army life within our knowledge,—both in our army and Lee's, and presumably in others.

Then as to the reactionary effect of warfare on the participants,—in the first place we cannot accept General Sherman's synonym as a complete connotation or definition of war. Fighting and destruction are terrible; but are sometimes agencies of heavenly rather than hellish powers. In the privations and sufferings endured as well as in the strenuous action of battle, some of the highest qualities of manhood are called forth,—courage, self-command, sacrifice of self for the sake of something held higher,—wherein we take it chivalry finds its value; and on another side fortitude, patience, warmth of comradeship, and in the darkest hours tenderness of caring for the wounded and stricken—exhaustless and unceasing as that of gentlest womanhood which allies us to the highest personality. Such things belong to something far different from the place or sphere assigned in the remark of the eminent exemplar of the aphorism. He was doubtless speaking of war in its immediate and proximate effects as destruction. He did not mean to imply that its participants are demons As to that, we may say war is for the participants a test of character; it makes bad men worse and good men better.

After a while we were not looked upon with such wondering interest as at first. Nay,—we began to be feared as likely to be in the way of those who had a preemption right to civil favors. Now our camps were thinning; our army was melting away. We too, in this fading camp, had opportunity to observe many things. Most manifest and largely shown it was that not a few about the capital were sorry the war was over; for this took the "soft snaps" away from them, and the soft spots out from under them. These persons soon pretended to be sole judges and champions of loyalty. There was a certain Demetrius once who made silver shrines for Diana, and did not like Paul because his teaching disturbed this sinecure. He skillfully therefore turned the issue upon religious loyalty. "Not only is this, our craft, in danger to be set at nought," he cries, "but also the temple of the great goddess Diana would be despised, and her magnificence destroyed, whom all Asia and the world worshipeth." And they all cried, "Great is Diana of the Ephesians." There were some loud-mouthed "patriots" about the capital whose zeal was rooted in the opportunity given by the country's distress for their own personal greed, and whose part in the service had been to get government contracts, and furnish cheap meats and musty and wormy hardtack and shoddy clothing to our worn, suffering soldiers, and even defective arms elsewhere rejected, to fail them in the desperate moment of the country's defense. There were concerns there and in some of the loyal States who made it their business to furnish even "bogus" men,—men never born, and christened only by them in lists of fictitious names, sold to recruiting agents for towns trying to fill their quota of men for the depleted army in the darkest moment of the country's need,—and appropriate to themselves the high bounties paid by towns to "avoid the draft." Under the loud professions of such as these, it was easy to see the real regret and disgust they felt when the country had won its deliverance and the war was over, and their opportunity gone, —until they could get a chance at new commissions and agencies in the whirlpool of reconstruction then setting in.

Disturbed at the thought that some deserving

soldiers might be found by the Government for places of trust and honor, these patriots began to detract and undermine, by suggestions of "disloyalty,"—an ambiguous phrase, meaning to them not blind following of some party chief and boss.

The story that could be written of these things—will not be written. Even the proofs have disappeared in the free opportunities for this so easily obtained. It was well known to some of us that the records at the War Department had been rummaged and that documents important for truth and dangerous for pretenders had been withdrawn and doubtless destroyed. It came to our knowledge that even Treasury vouchers had been tampered with and the rascality undetected.

The Government was kind: it meant to be just. But in its great burden of responsibilities it could not consider minor matters. The country had been saved; other interests must adjust themselves as best they could.

I feel that I must not omit to mention here a species of injustice which affected us within strictly military aspects. I refer to the inconsiderate or reckless bestowal of brevets. This was very unjust to merit as well as injurious as policy. We had seen considerable lack of equity in this matter before the close of the war in the unevenness of scale on which different commanders secured brevets for their subordinates. One result of this was the relative injustice among those holding similar commands in different corps. Warm-hearted generals like Sheridan would be generous in their recommendation. Others of a severer temperament would move more slowly. Clear-seeing Humphreys, just and zealous for truth, protested against this inequality and tried to resist it, by recommending only for distinguished merit. But the key-note had been set; and to grant brevets for merit only would work practical injustice considering that others had been so promoted on other grounds. I have to confess that in some vexation of spirit I resolved to keep up with the best in recommending this honor for the officers of my division at the close of the war. But in the meantime the Government at Washington was adopting this sweeping policy. Everybody was breveted one grade who asked for it,—one general order embracing very many ranking at one and the same date, which being arbitrarily fixed at a time previous to the heavy fighting of the last campaign, antedated the commissions of several who had won that honor as a special distinction in battle. The meaning of the brevet is honorable distinction; this leveled all distinction. It destroyed the value of the brevet as recognition of past service or incentive for the future. There were those who had won their brevets while the life blood ran from their veins, at the deadly front, only to find themselves now equaled, parodied, outranked even, by their own subordinates and men who had scarcely seen the field at all.

I may remark that being included in that general list referred to, although I had not asked for it or in any manner suggested it, I declined this brevet, but in the first battle of the last campaign receiving the brevet of Major-General for special service reported by my corps commander, I did not officially accept the latter until we reached Washington, and the army was about to be mustered out. So this brevet was not officially recognized by the Government in the final orders for the disbandment of the army and my assignment to another corps. In truth I did not feel it now as a token of honor or an object of desire The Government, however, thereupon sent me the later commission, which purported to be something worth receiving with responsive regard.

Only the "Congressional Medal of Honor" had been held sacred,—not to be bought or sold, or recklessly conferred. It was held to be the highest honor,—recognition of some act of conspicuous personal gallantry beyond what military duty required. Knowing what has happened with the cross of the "Legion of Honor" in France, and how sacred the "Victoria Cross" is held in England, we trust that no self-seeking plea nor political pressure shall avail to belittle the estimation of this sole-remaining seal of honor whose very meaning and worth is that it notes conduct in which manhood rises above self. May this award ever be for him who has won it, at the peril of life, in storm of battle, but let us not behold the sublime spectacle of vicarious suffering travestied by the imposition of vicarious honors.

To resume the narrative, on the first day of July, while encamped before Washington, we received an order, which, though expected, moved us most deeply. The first paragraph was this:

"HEADQUARTERS, ARMY OF THE POTOMAC,
"June 28, 1865.

"By virtue of special orders, No. 339, current series, from the Adjutant General's office, this army, as an organization, ceases to exist."

What wonder that a strange thrill went through our hearts.

Ceases to exist! Are you sure of that? We had lately seen the bodily form of our army, or what remained of it, pass in majesty before the eyes of men; while part of it was left planted on the slopes of the Antietam, on the heights of Gettysburg, in the Wilderness, on the far-spread fields and lonely roadsides of all Virginia,—waiting the Resurrection.

The splendor of devotion, glowing like a bright spirit over those dark waters and misty plains, assures us of something that cannot die! The sacrifice of the mothers who sent such sons was of the immortal. All this must have been felt by those who gave the order. The War Department and the President may cease to give the army orders, may disperse its visible elements, but cannot extinguish them. They will come together again under higher bidding, and will know their place and name. This army will live, and live on, so long as soul shall answer soul, so long as that flag watches with its stars over fields of mighty memory, so long as in its red lines a regenerated people reads the charter of its birthright, and in its field of white God's covenant with man.

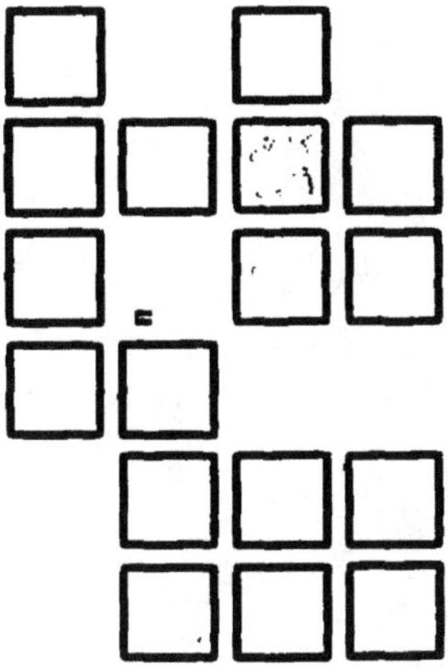

CPSIA information can be obtained
at www.ICGtesting.com
Printed in the USA
LVHW052219281220
675217LV00041B/699

9 781363 756858